GEM ELIXERS AND VIBRATIONAL HEALING, VOL. II

BY GURUDAS

CHANNELED THROUGH

KEVIN RYERSON AND JOHN FOX

CASSANDRA PRESS
BOULDER, CO. 80306

CASSANDRA PRESS
P.O. BOX 2044
BOULDER,CO. 80306

Printed in the United States of America.

First printing 1986

ISBN 0-961-58751-2

The use of the material described in this text is not meant to replace the services of a physician who should always be consulted for any condition requiring his or her aid.

"That which is looked upon by one generation as the apex of human knowledge is often considered an absurdity by the next, and that which is regarded as a supersitition in one century, may form the basis of science for the following one."

Paracelsus

Other books by Gurudas

Flower Essences and Vibrational Healing
(Formerly Flower Essences)
Gem Elixirs and Vibrational Healing, Vol. I
Numerous other books are in various stages of preparation.

The author wishes to thank Bonnie Schwab and Rebecca Browning for their assisting in reviewing the astrological information that appears in this text. Acknowledgement is also due to Gabriel Cousens, M.D., Lauri Adato and to John and Alena Rae.

Front cover photograph by Tim Murphy
Front cover art by Gary Ray

Both are copyright 1986 Gurudas. All rights reserved.

TABLE OF CONTENTS

PREFACE

Much of the material presented in this book has been trance channeled through Kevin Ryerson, a professional psychic and trance channel with over twelve years experience in the field of parapsychology. Since the age of five, Ryerson has experienced psychic phenomena such as seeing future events in his dreams. During his teenage years he studied the Edgar Cayce material, which stimulated his spiritual and psychic unfoldment. After further experiences with his psychic and clairvoyant abilities, he developed his own trance state at the age of twenty-one. He received his formal training in this field through the University of Life in Phoenix, Arizonia. This school, which was established by Dr. Richard Ireland in 1960, trains people in psychic development. Many have learned of Ryerson and his main guide John through the recent best seller, *Out On A Limb* by Shirley MacLaine.

Important segments of this text were also provided by the master Hilarion through John Fox, a channel in California. Fox has become increasingly respected for his ability to accurately research a wide variety of technical subjects. He began his channeling career four years ago as a conscious channel. In recent years, he has expanded his gift to include trance channeling, because that often makes it easier to present technical information. Like Ryerson, Fox's main interest is to do research channeling that will present new scientific technologies and concepts. Fox now conducts group readings with numerous people in California. I will be working more with him in the future.

Hilarion focalizes the fifth ray, which consists of technical and scientific information. Some may be aware that Hilarion has recently been the source of an entire series of channeled books from the Marcus press in Toronto. Hilarion has provided inspirational guidance and technical advice to many people for thousands of years.

While almost finishing a master's degree in political science and being in law school for a year, I have also for some years been involved in various spiritual practices. This interest stimulated three trips to India in the early 1970's. Since 1976 I have worked with gem elixirs, homeopathic remedies, and flower essences, first as a student and then from 1978 until 1982, in my own private practice. This work also included giving advice relating to herbs, nutrition, and bath therapies. Since 1978, moreover, I have taught classes on different natural healing topics.

In the summer of 1979, I learned of a psychic surgeon from the Philippines, and with my keen interest in this form of healing, I visited him. In the middle of the session, several of my guides appeared, and they stated that my healing research would improve if I worked with a good trance channel. A few days later, a friend returned from San Diego describing Kevin Ryerson's work, and I was interested. I borrowed several tapes of Ryerson's public talks in trance and after listening to John's voice, one of Ryerson's guides, and hearing the information that was being discussed, I felt there might be a deep connection here. After a period of meditation, I called Ryerson and in October 1979 he visited San Francisco. From that period, we have done numerous research readings.

The nature of channeled teaching is such that to produce much information many questions must be asked. If one were to just sit back and listen, a fair amount of information would be presented, but it usually would not match what can be given if the inquirer comes prepared with many questions and a good background and training in the field of inquiry.

Fortunately, I have an inquiring mind, an academic background that demands objective information, a natural gift for asking questions to beget specific information, and a fair degree of training in several holistic health modalities. Channeled teaching is a slow time consuming process in which a certain amount of information is discussed, which I gradually assimilate. Then I return to discuss new information and to sometimes ask additional questions to expand on previously discussed material. The main focalizer for Ryerson's work is John. To many

The main focalizer for Ryerson's work is John. To many who work with Ryerson, John appears to be John the Apostle, the disciple of Jesus and author of the Book of Revelations. In the Bible, John 21:20-23, Jesus asked John to stay behind in service.[1] For the last 2,000 years John has inspired many people, including Leonardo da Vinci, on inspirational and trance channeling levels. John, who is the most universal of Ryerson's guides, has full access to all the information and wisdom from Atlantis, Lemuria, and regions beyond this planet. (Atlantis and Lemuria were two ancient land masses and civilizations. Lemuria covered much of the Pacific Ocean, while its colony Atlantis covered much of the Atlantic Ocean.) Carl Jung would call this the collective consciousness of the planet.[2] With this ability Ryerson, in trance, discusses highly technical issues on any subject including advanced concepts in physics, building specific machines, complex medical questions, or philosophical and spiritual truths. Fox has the capacity to do similar work with Hilarion.

One reason why John and Hilarion are allowed to render so much technical information in such detail is because many people are now ready and willing to receive this new material. As a society, we have reached a state of conscious and technological development so that, while some of the information these masters share may seem radical at times, many people now have the capacity to assimilate and apply it. Partly because of these facts, it is now time for channeled data to manifest from the fifth ray, which carries detailed and technically specific information. In the past, most channeled material came from the second ray, which is more a frequency of love and spirituality.[3] (The seven rays are seven primary energies that influence everyone.)

Except for the information provided by Fox and Hilarion in the last year, the research presented in this book was obtained in my private readings with Ryerson. Most of that research took place from July 1981 until September 1982. In various sections of the book, the actual questions with the verbatim responses are included so that the reader will comprehend how the information was obtained. The indented words are comments that I have added to clarify, unify, and expand certain concepts. In my readings with Fox, Hilarion answered all of the questions. During the readings with Ryerson, almost all the material was directly presented by John. Occasionally, another guide, a physician from India, presented some information. Assisting John and Hilarion in this work are a number of other guides, many of them historically respected spiritual and healing masters. While some of these individuals are also my personal guides, some of them contributed to this work because of their background and expertise in the use of gemstones for healing and conscious growth.

1 F.C. Eiselen, Edwin Lewis, and D.G.Dower, eds., *The Abington Bible Commentary* (Garden City,NY: Doubleday & Co., 1979),p. 1092.
2 Carl Jung, *Man And His Symbols* (Garden City,NY: Doubleday and Co.,1969).
3 Hilarion, *Symbols* (Toronto:Marcus Books,1979),p.25-26.

INTRODUCTION

This book represents a further attempt to restore the mineral kingdom to its rightful place in the healing arts and in conscious growth. For too long gemstones have been relegated to the role of magic and superstition. It is again time for people to appreciate the great treasures stored in the mineral kingdom.

The book begins with a chapter on quartz crystals. Many now appreciate the profound importance of quartz crystals for the continued conscious evolution of the human race. New information on wearing gemstones as amulets and talismans is then provided. Indeed, there is great value in the folklore of minerals. The relationship of gemstones to various astrological configurations is the topic of the next chapter. There is a Lemurian system of using a mandala pattern with gemstones to represent future astrological alignments to project one's consciousness into the future to transform it. Nostradamus used this ancient technology. Various gem elixir combinations are also presented to better attune to astrological configurations. Techniques are also offered to enhance spiritual and psychic development with gems.

Several chapters are presented focusing on using gem elixirs with various healing modalities. There is a detailed discussion on the relationship between gem elixirs, flower essences, and homeopathic remedies. Some information is also provided on the use of herbs, incense, and essential oils in this work. This material includes information on how these vibrational remedies work differently in people, how they can interfere with each other if taken at or near the same time, and how gem elixirs affect the miasms. Most experienced homeopathic practitioners consider the miasms to be the root cause, or primary factor, in all chronic diseases. While the miasms were discussed in my first book, *Flower Essences and Vibrational Healing*, much new material on this complex subject, as well as on the real causes of all disease, is presented in this book. It is time for people in the holistic health movement to understand the tremendous impact that the miasms have on our health and well-being. Gem elixirs, as well as flower essences and homeopathic remedies, can have a major impact on weakening and discharging the miasms from our system.

A section on bath therapies using gem elixirs is also included, and there is an examination of how gemstones were used in agriculture and animal husbandry in ancient Atlantis and Lemuria. These interesting techniques can still be used today. Fascinating new information is revealed on using gemstones during pregnancy and the birthing process. Information on merging gem therapy with color and sound healing is also included. Natural quartz crystal music is now available because an instrument originally invented by Benjamin Franklin using natural quartz crystals has recently been restructured.

There is an outline of the relationship of gemstones to the still developing concepts of new physics, with an expanded explanation of how the seven rays greatly influence our lives. Next is a chapter outlining the use of gemstones in the ancient architectural designs of Atlantis and Lemuria. This understanding emanated from an attunement to the earth as a living being.

Each year scientists discover new minerals. In the next few years, five currently unisolated elements will begin to appear in new minerals, plants, and in the atmosphere. These elements will have a profound effect on manifesting the New Age consciousness. There is also a brief discussion on the return of the Teacher of Righteousness and the possibility that he will soon step forward to expand the Christ consciousness on this planet.

In the final chapter, the social implications of this work are examined. Gemstone technologies will increasingly influence the spiritual transformation of our society. Gemstones will become increasingly popular in the coming years, partly because new diagnostic equipment will soon make it easier to test and prove the clinical validity of minerals in various medical modalities.

In my previous two books, I presented an appendix on the nature of channeling. That material has not been repeated here partly because it is felt that most people reading this text will have already read the previous two books. People who do not understand the role of channeling in this age and in one's personal life would benefit from reading that material. The information on channeling provided in *Gem Elixirs and Vibrational Healing, Vol. I,* is an updated and expanded version on what was published in the previous book on flower essences.

As recently discussed in Volume I of this series, originally I was going to release one text on gem therapy with an advanced book in ten or twenty years, but when this material was completed, there was so much information I decided to release it in two volumes. The first volume deals with more practical issues in gem therapy, while the second volume is more esoteric and focuses more on the theoretical aspects of using gemstones. I also focus on how gem elixirs can be applied in many different modalities in the second volume. Each volume complements the other. In several years, I will also release a short book on using quartz crystals. There was too much information available on quartz crystals to include all that material in this text.

The information presented in this book is not meant to be the final word. It is my sincere wish that this book stimulate greater awareness, understanding, and clinical research of these remedies. In the coming years, much new information on gemstones will be revealed by various sources. This is especially true with quartz crystal technologies.

The objective observer will agree that a good deal of valuable new information has been provided in this text concerning the clinical use of gem elixirs. The spiritual guides providing the information for this text have decided that not all the information on gem therapy is to be provided here. Part of our work and responsibility in this learning process is to expand, on our own, our understanding of how these healing agents can be utilized in mind, body, and spirit.

After working with this channeled information for six years and being able to test and prove many different preparations in the clinical setting of my own private practice and that of several associates, including various doctors, I am confident that the test of time will prove the accuracy of the information presented in this text. I now receive many reports of people using and confirming the symptoms for the many new flower essences and gem elixirs as described in my first two books, *Flower Essences and Vibrational Healing* and *Gem Elixirs and Vibrational Healing, Vol. l.* There is a long tradition in many societies of using minerals in different healing modalities and various spiritual practices, and I am now working with various practitioners to expand our understanding of how to use these minerals. In time, I will complete a book of case studies and double blind studies demonstrating how these gem elixirs and flower essences have been used.

This book is presented in the tradition of the empirical school of thought. Two main traditions have dominated Western medical history. While practitioners did not necessarily clearly follow one of these schools, this philosophical schism has generally been present in Western medicine?

The rationalists see the human body as a material or mechanical vehicle, and seeks to understand the causes and treatment of disease in an analytical fashion. They put labels on the disease process and tend to treat diseases, not people.

In the empirical tradition, reliance is placed more on experience, observation, and the individuality of each person. There is general recognition of each person as a spiritual being with a life force connecting him or her to the spiritual realms or forces of the soul. In this belief system, there is more openness to working with intuition and to testing the validity of channeled teachings. In these days, increasing numbers of people are accepting channeled teachings as a reliable source of information. This trend will certainly continue in the coming years.

1 Manly Hall, *The Inner Lives of Minerals, Plants, and Animals*, (L.A: Philosophical Research Society,Inc.,1973), p.8-9.
2 Harris Coulter, *Divided Legacy: A History of the Schism in Medical Thought*, Volume III, (Washington,D.C: Wehawken Book Co.,1973).
Sandra LaForest and Virginia MacIvor, *Vibrations: Healing Through Color, Homeopathy, and Radionics*, (York Beach,Me: Samuel Weiser,Inc.,1979),p.28-31.

CHAPTER I

QUARTZ CRYSTAL TECHNOLOGIES

Today a great many people are being drawn to the inner clarity and illumination offered by quartz crystals. In time many people will discover that quartz is a doorway to the entire mineral kingdom. Indeed, the dental profession is already using liquidified quartz. Ultimately, quartz will be used in many areas of medicine.

Q Discuss the basic principles involved in using quartz crystals?

"Gemstones and crystalline structures are forces unto themselves. They have properties contained within themselves independent of any other forces. Moreover, they represent crystallizations in direct relationship to the consciousness that has become man and woman on this planet. Indeed, thy very adaptation and sympathetic resonancy with crystals come in the accord that they have been used to shape the very evolution of thy consciousness upon this plane. And crystals as embedded in their natural state upon the planet are an expression of the planet as a living entity. These are, in part, a focus of the meridian points upon the planet as a whole.

"As a living expression of consciousness you find thyself in a dimension that is the accord of a biological dimension. So in turn, as a biological life form, you have adapted to natural evolution upon the planet through a physiological process but have been drawn up by the evolution of crystalline structures. Crystalline structures are but the accord of perhaps being the purest crystal structure and the finest stabilized merger of various mineral states and aspects of the basic elemental table. These forces represent windows to the levels of the ethereal planes. The resonating properties of crystals, which come through the principles of natural physics, are now becoming the threshold or breakthrough, not only in the accord of physical sciences, but also to the point where there will be the merger of physical sciences and consciousness. You are now looking for those forces which unify the forces of thy universe itself. Upon subatomic levels, in the behavioral patterns, there is same, or that which ye term as the unified field theory. When consciousness and thy physical sciences merge, you will find that the portals to this understanding shall be those structures which ye term crystals. Crystals are as windows or portals to the levels of the ethers, which indeed represent the higher dimensions in both consciousness and even in the activities of thy physics.

"Quartz is perhaps the master gemstone. In its functions quartz is interlinked with at least three of the critical chakras, which are the solar plexus, heart, and pituitary chakras that can interlink with the crown chakra. Quartz has properties for healing and thought form amplification, and it may be used both to broadcast and to store information of a broad universal accord. It is currently used in thy society as an industrial gem, and it has significant potential as a power source. Note its abundance. Moreover, it can be used in measurable psychic experimentation.

"Quartz has been used in practically all cultures, has long been noted for its healing properties, and is a critical point of focus for meditation. Yet in all these activities it has remained not unlike the spirit itself. It has remained not so much rare, such as in diamonds and other precious stones, but has remained in abundance, always seemingly available in many areas. Historically, quartz was one of the first substances to be used to confirm the practicality and the concept of invisible or ethereal energy, when this stone was used in the first broadcast of radiowaves. Thus, thy technology has even confirmed that there is significance to the properties of quartz crystal. It has been used thoughout many cultures, even into the modern 20th century. Its properties make it the central focus for studying the spiritual and technological properties of gemstones.

"Quartz as such a focus finds its origin as far back as the Lemurian civilization. Then it was a cornerstone for enhancing thought form amplification. So great is the degree of thought form amplification with quartz that if there was the placement of quartz and then a concentration placed through it with a mild electromagnetic or low-voltage field of brainwaves, it could be discovered that there is an active field about quartz that is measurable by sensitive intruments. There could be constructed a device with the use and properties of quartz to make possible broadcasting based only on the technologies of brain waves. Or, if quartz crystals were placed in seed beds of plants and then one meditated upon those seeds and plants, this would significantly increase the growth of those plants by 5 to 8 percent. There would need to be proper meditation by individuals benevolent to agriculture. There could also be the transference of creative visualization by meditation. The significant properties of quartz are that it has the ability of thought form amplification and the ability to store thoughts or to continue the resonancy of the dominant factor of thought forms. However, the uniqueness of the properties of quartz are that it can easily be cleansed in salt, salt water, or in crushed quartz. The simplicity of such cleansing techniques makes quartz available to the general practitioner and to individuals who desire to experiment within the current technologies of thy society.

"Its use as an amplifier of the seats of consciousness throughout the body physical makes it a significant tool for diagnosis for those who use its energies on the body physical. This may be a lens, a simple plate, or even just the basic crystal itself, placed upon the approximate area of the physical location of an organ. Clairvoyance or percussion would increase the diagnostic insight by approximately 15 to 27 percent. This is because of the energy emitted by the body physical. Quartz has also often been used for its properties of thought form amplification as a pendulum in many societies.

"Quartz can furthermore be used to increase the effectiveness of other therapies. If acupuncture points were stimulated by stainless steel needles with approximately 35 percent of the shaft coated with quartz crystal, there would be an enhancement of the treatment's effectiveness by approximately 10 to 18 percent. This is because there would be the enhancement of the life force stimulated by the vitality of the needle, and there would be a drawing off of the negative energy causing blockages at that point. These needles would then have to be cleansed.

"Quartz can also be used to enhance muscle testing. Quartz enhances the property of sending forth thought forms, and the mild influence that these have upon the auric fields and their reintegration into the muscular tissues. Moreover, wearing quartz crystals offers protection against all forms of radiation because it helps people adapt to such factors. It is often wise to place quartz on a flat copper surface for further amplification. Each of these practices brings forth balance concerning sojourns into the area of quartz crystals."

Q Explain how people can better attune to and harmonize with quartz?

"Place any quartz beneath a blue light to the point where the light penetrates and illuminates the quartz. The quartz should be on a flat surface in a skeletal pyramid structure. Then the individual should meditate on the quartz for fifteen to twenty minutes. This allows the personal vibration of that quartz to attune to the personal needs of the individual. Blue is a balancing aspect that allows for the full activation of any quartz structure. It also stimulates personal attunement for most individuals. Emerald also carries such properties. This is one technique for a person to attune to quartz.

"Because quartz spans so many levels and spectrums of the chakras, perhaps more than any other stone, simple placement of a quartz before the individual and then meditation upon each of the main chakras would attune the individual to this stone as well as to the properties of the main chakras. It is also wise to place quartz about the household or to wear it. Using a double terminated quartz further sensitizes people to the natural resonancies of quartz."

In past years John has described several techniques to explore with quartz crystals. In a darkened room, early in the morning or at night, place a quartz in front of you with a candle lighted behind it. The quartz should be at the same height as your eyes. Stare into the quartz and picture the light traveling first into your eyes and throughout specific areas of your body. This is a powerful technique to project the energy of quartz crystals into the body. This also stimulates the pituitary and pineal glands and chakras, thus bringing further illumination in the meditative state. During this technique it is also wise to project certain positive thoughts that you would like to experience into the quartz. They will reverbate back into you in a more illuminated form.

A second powerful technique is for two people to sit facing each other in a darkened room. Have a quartz between the two people again at the level of the eyes. Have lighted candles below the quartz and stare into each others eyes though the illuminated quartz. This is a way for two people to develop a deeper understanding and attunement with each other. People working together on projects such as writing a book or couples striving for a deeper attunement would benefit from this technique. People doing this would become more sensitive to each other.

Couples could also attune to the seven main chakras while doing this technique. When couples do not do this technique, it usually takes around nine years for a natural flow to develop between the chakras. When couples do this technique, directly working to harmonize the flow of the chakras, it generally takes around one year for a deep alignment to develop. What occurs is that couples develop a true understanding of the inner nature of each other. False images fall away. Sometimes information released during these meditations can force couples to face difficult issues that would not have surfaced for many years. If people are ready to face such issues, there can be a deep cleansing and harmonizing. Couples should do this exercise twice a week for half an hour during each session. After doing this meditation for three or four months, many people would come to appreciate the value of this practice. Then, if not sooner, it would be wise to attempt to do this practice every day for fifteen to twenty minutes.

Both these practices were often used in Atlantis. Generally, put the crystal you are staring into under sea salt once a month for up to one day as a cleansing. There is no set time for doing these techniques. This depends on the unique needs of each individual. Initially, you might feel lightheaded or uncomfortable for a while. This is because toxicity is passing out of the body. This period will usually soon pass. Some may want to chant a mantra while doing these practices. I sometimes play quartz crystal music or the Tibetan bells. Peruvian flute music is also quite powerful.

Another good technique is to put a quartz on top of your TV. It draws in the radiation that the TV emits. Once every three months put the crystal in sea salt for at least one day to draw off the radiation. But when doing this pick up the crystal with a cloth. Otherwise some of the radiation on an energy level would enter your body.

Q In recent years several crystal skulls have been found.[1] The industrial knowledge to construct such skulls does not presently exist. Please discuss the historical background of these skulls and how they can be consciously used today.

"These skulls were used in latter Lemuria and early Atlantis to divide the androgynous bodies that then existed into the male and female forms that ye now exist in. Originally, there were seven fully shaped humanoid crystals, not just crystal skulls. Each crystallized human form existed as a central thought form to aid in dividing the sexes in each of the seven races. The entire body, including the many organs, was formed out of quartz. This was a highly sophisticated form of genetic engineering. At the present time, two of the races are submerged in the genetic pool of humanity. In the coming years members of these races will again surface, especially in India, California, and Australia. Some may be aware of the existence of a blue-skinned race from India. Even today there remains a belief that Krishna had blue skin.

"The crystal skull was also used for apportation, or the ability to be transported through the spheres, by those who were highly skilled in meditation. In the days of Lemuria and Atlantis, there was a fairly constant flow of communication and transportation through the spheres to races in other constellations. Indeed, the fully formed crystalline shape was used as a vehicle to project information back to one of the home planets in the constellation Sirius."

Q Why is one of the crystal skulls that have been discovered pink while the others are clear?

"Different types of thought forms and various levels of consciousness went into the formation of these crystal skulls and bodies.

"The skulls are being discovered today because you now have the technology and level of consciousness that may make it possible to release and use the information stored in these crystals properly. These crystal skulls are storehouses of information that can be isolated using telepathy and holographic thought forms. To unlock the information stored in these skulls, it would be wise to meditate and chant OM continuously until a mantra develops which could be the key to unlock that information."

Q Edgar Cayce said Atlantean fire crystals would be discovered in these years. How were these crystals used?

"Their basic purpose was to generate power for the Atlantean technologies. Ultimately, the misuse of these technologies upset the natural balance in the atmosphere and in the center of the earth."

Q Why do some quartz crystals have an internal phantom pyramid?

"This occurred because the quartz merely stopped growing for a brief moment in time. It later continued to grow and left a shadow at that spot. The pyramidal shape is part of the natural flow of energy inside the quartz."

Several years ago I visited Israel and Egypt partly to meditate in the King's chamber in the great pyramid by Giza and by the inner chamber of King Solomon's temple in Jerusalem where the religious scrolls were kept. In each place I meditated while holding a clear and smoky or black quartz. Different stones were used in each place. While in the great pyramid I chanted the Lords Prayer in Coptic as John had suggested. The great pyramid is a giant computer holding many keys to the history and heritage of the human race. These meditations enabled much of the wisdom from each sanctuary to pass into these four quartz pieces. Hilarion provided some information on how gem elixirs of these stones can be used.

Q Explain how gem elixirs of these four quartz gems can be used?

"Elixirs of these four pieces are unique in that they can only be used by individuals who have a personal alignment with you Gurudas. People using these elixirs must have some common past life karma or soul connection or bond with you if the healing and spiritual properties stored in these elixirs are to be released when these stones are prepared as gem elixirs."

Q I have never before been told this. Does this apply at all to any of the other hundreds of vibrational preparations that I sell?

"No."

Q Why are there such unique properties in these stones?

"This is because the nature of these stones is in a healing process with the owner and that owner happens to be you Gurudas. It is also the nature of these stones to amplify the vibrations of people that they are around."

Q How would people who have a personal alignment with me use these four elixirs?

"These elixirs can be used by healers to accelerate their own willingness to heal others and to learn from the process. In doing this such people will draw to themselves people who have lessons to experience that they also need to learn. For instance, if a healer is using one of these elixirs, the healer is likely to treat someone soon with a disease or problem that the healer also needs to learn from. These elixirs help healers to work on themselves and to increase their diagnostic skills to then work better in treating other people."

Q Can such healers use these elixirs to treat people or should they only be used on themselves?

"These elixirs would work as clear and dark quartz normally do if they were given to clients. So these elixirs can be given to clients, but do not expect them to be far superior to elixirs of the clear and dark quartz that would normally be given."

Q John noted that much of the wisdom and teachings from the temple of Solomon and the great pyramid at Giza went into these stones during my meditations there. Can people using these elixirs tap into those teachings?

"Much of this wisdom has been transferred to the elixirs, but not many individuals are ready to receive such information. People would not know how to use it and would not be ready to bring it into their lives. Perhaps by 1992 or so some of these properties may be more easily transferred to people's consciousness, but during the present period it is unlikely that these elixirs will have much effect in this regard."

Q Can anyone go to the temple of Solomon and the pyramid at Giza, as well as to other key areas on the planet, and meditate with clear and dark quartz to attune such gems to the healing and spiritual properties stored in such holy areas?

"Yes, there are many such areas about the planet. Part of the process is that individuals feel an alignment with the area in which they wish to meditation with these quartz. It also depends, of course, on the willingness of individuals to experience this. Such things can be accomplished by most people. There must be a true inner desire to manifest this and a willingness to accept what comes from this process. The resonance of the persons inner being with the crystal lattice in an interlocking pattern is that which holds the information and knowledge within an individual. If at a later time a person is not still willing to learn from such an inner process and alignment with the teaching of the planetary focal point and the crystal lattices, then the resonance and actual information and awakening stored in the quartz will gradually be reduced."

The material in this chapter represents a very small degree of the available information on quartz crystal technologies. I was originally going to have a much larger chapter on quartz in this text but have decided instead to release a book just on quartz crytals in several years. So much new information is available on the mineral kingdom that it will take an entire series of books so that data can be released gradually.

"Seek to be at peace with those things which ye receive from spirit, for they are to further thy Father's works, and indeed, ye are that work. Seek to encompass the whole of these things which are as represented by crystals. Crystals are as isolated spectrums of thy own thoughts, representing and corresponding to the seats of consciousness within the body physical that ye would represent. You are as a threefold being of mind, body, and spirit, and crystals help to amplify these various aspects of the self. But you would also find that ye are as a greater spirit which is indeed the soul, which is unique unto the Father. In aligning the self use crystals to amplify thy consciousness, which has the knowledge that indeed ye are as spirit. But always align thyself with the higher forces you meet as the Father-Mother-God, in which resides all of thee. Always seek ye first this kingdom which is the true creator as stored within thee. Then in this ye would perhaps become as living crystals, resonating unto all frequencies of love and mind as comes forth from the Father-Mother-God who resides in thee now. Walk in this thy Father's light."

1 Richard Garvin, *The Crystal Skull* (New York: Pocket Books, 1974).

CHAPTER II

TALISMANS, AMULETS, AND GEMSTONES

There is much folklore on using gemstones as good luck charms and to ward off evil influences. Use of the ring in the marriage ceremony is one of the more common ways gemstones are used as talismans in our society. Other talismans include bells, bracelets, earrings, necklaces, signets or seals, and various religious symbols such as the cross.[1] As many have sensed, the folklore of gemstones contains much valuable information because so much of it is accurate. In the past, in many societies gemstones were commonly used as talismans and for healing and spiritual practices. In the coming years, this tradition will again become quite common in many parts of the world. The current explosion of interest in quartz crystals is an early indication of this trend.

Q Please discuss the historical use of gemstones as talismans?

"A talisman in this unique work upon minerals is either the carving of gemstones into a specific shape with significant symbols on it, or various combinations of minerals whose combined properties have certain vibrational influences. Talismans in their own right may as find themselves as ancient as the Egyptian scarab within known history, even dating back further in known history to be as used amongst Neanderthal man and other recorded anthropological lineages of man.

"Primarily, talismans are the shaping of a gemstone to a specific and isolated usage. There is first the study of a gemstone and the isolation of desired properties to be heightened. This does not necessarily nullify the other beneficial influences of the stone but seeks to heighten one specific isolated aspect. This may be done by carving specific symbols which act as the focus for mandalas upon the mineral. Or minerals may be arranged into patterns as with a mandala, but this would be done more so along the principles of talismans. A mandala pattern activates all the properties inherent in minerals, while talismans activate specific parts of a gemstone's properties. This activates talents within individuals that are superstitously known as "good luck." This increases the capacity of the individual to function better within society by activating positive attitudes and hidden talents from past lives. This contributes to one's fortune by perhaps advancing them in one location occupationally. This should not be directly linked to spiritual forces, but should more so be thought of as enhancing isolated spiritual properties that have been interwoven into the tapestry that is the personality.

"A further property to understand with talismans is that they should not be looked upon as objects of worship. They should be looked upon as objects to focus concentration upon to keep the mind always in its purest element within the higher forces. A talisman should never be carried or used as anything but as an object of focus for the general awareness that may enhance natural properties that could be obtained through other forces such as meditation, prayer, and fasting. A talisman should not be looked upon as bypassing any of these other practices but only as enhancing such disciplines. Talismans work better when they are present as but a point of focus for applied meditation, not unlike the principles of the mandala.

"Talismans also work independent of the individual's thoughts, and their effects are cumulative when they are continuously worn by the individual. The purpose and pattern of the mandala, which is specifically combined with meditation, may be as more immediately enhanced as a focus of concentration. The talisman's effects are carried with the individual for the cumulative effect and only come into full force when the individual is fully aware of both these spiritual and psychospiritual principles. For instance, when the Egyptian scarab is carved with lapis lazuli and worn close to the throat chakra, it naturally enhances the individuals speaking and articulation abilities. It does not give one power of voice over other individuals but does clear any blockages in the throat chakra. The alleviation of these tensions and stresses to have clearer expression of communication with others naturally adds to the individual's lifespan. Scarab is historically considered to be a stone of immortality or longevity. The individual's vitality is increased by the focus of thought and the isolation of scarab as it enhances these properties. This allows the individual to develop the type of articulation specifically beneficial to his or her health.

"Talismans are as carved specifically into a shape that is a portion of the collective unconscious. Therefore, even though the symbol itself is impersonal, it becomes personal when combined with the consciousness of the individual. Ancient symbols are reflective, as are all alphabets, of these sciences and still carry some of these principles. Chants function exactly upon the principles of mantras, and are not ancient verbose murmurings or magics, but activate internal organs vibrationally. Talismans are not associated with discarnate entities. They merely activate natural properties already inherent in the individual. Again, the influences are cumulative. Thus the carrying of the talisman, not for protection but for a heightened sense of well-being, heightens the faculties already within the psychospiritual dynamics of the individual.

"Much information on talismans and amulets is preserved in thy known historical perspectives. However, they are a remnant and a rudimentary technology that remains from the more advanced technologies of the Lemurian time period. The mandala was and is the master source of that technology. All other talismans are a primitive breakdown from that technology.

"Amongst the Arabs there came as a primitive merger from remnants of Egyptian understanding of talismans. These Egyptian technologies in many ways came forth from Atlantian alchemy. This Egyptian influence spread throughout Nubia to Babylon and the Greeks. It was the sweeping Arabic influence throughout Africa to Spain, and then cultural exchanges with Europe, that allowed talismans to become linked to Christian metaphysics in Europe.[2] Some Egyptian, Arab, and Hebrew influences merged to eventually become that which became known as the kaballah. Some of this knowledge was preserved amongst those religions at Stonehenge, with its pure status preserved in India. It reached a heightened art form in Tibet and is preserved in some degrees of purity in China. The Olnecs, Mayans, and Aztecs also achieved advanced understanding of these technologies."

Q Do you agree with the belief that the word amulet came from the Arabic word "camulet?"
    "Yes."

Q Speak on the impact of different shapes of gemstones?

"Certain geometrical shapes allow for vibrational principles to be stabilized and indeed to be enhanced, especially with the softer stones. It is wise to use some minerals as they are usually found in nature to have an enhancement of that stones properties. For example, use a pearl that is perfectly round. It would be wise for the student to study the references to shapes of spherical, cubical, and pyramidal forms and then study the properties of mantras and select those that would be desired to be placed upon the talisman for either enhancing or focusing its properties. It is not the desire of the channel speaking to as give forth the total constructs of various talismans. This would be unwise and could even lead the manuscript into superstitious elements."

Q How are talismans influenced by words or letters added to them?

"These are symbols drawn from the collective unconscious, and they become personal when integrated with the personal aspect of the personality. The focusing of thoughts with a universal symbol triggers psychospiritual integration. The actual words or letters can also have another impact if they are understood within the structure of a known language."

Q It is claimed that wearing numbers greatly enhances the metals they are on. Speak on this.

"Psychological information is released. Again, you are tapping into the collective unconscious, translated both genetically and telepathically."

Q Is it also true, as some claim, that you should not wear inverted crosses or pyramids?

"Inversion of these symbols brings about forces that may cause damage psychological in nature. Inversion of symbols which are personal in their own right would translate into being personal to individuals."

Q Do you mean like when people get attached to quartz?

"Yes, these forces are personal to the individual as is given in religious significance and may atrophy the energy. These forces, especially pyramids, if not properly aligned with the forces they seek attunement with, would naturally atrophy the energy, although it does not necessarily have direct negative energy. These are personal to the individual, usually to their own psychological state."

Q Speak on the traditional belief that certain stones such as the Hope diamond are cursed.[3]

"Such stones become the focus of intense negative thought form amplification. There are certain individuals with negative karmic patterns. When they come into contact with such stones as the Hope diamond, their own consciousness and rudimentary thought form amplification abilities trigger negative events. It becomes almost a self-fulfilling prophecy on psychological, conscious, and karmic levels. This may proceed into activities that seem like curses, or violent or negative acts. It is also due to the peculiar psychological makeup of the individual who is being afflicted."

Q Are such people vibrationally drawn to such stones so that the pattern can continue for many years?

"Correct. They would naturally be drawn to such forces, possibly from past lives and associated with similar faculties in the gemstones, even to the point, in some instances, of them being the originator of some of the forces of the superstitions associated with certain stones."

Q Is it true that certain gemstones commonly misused in the past, can be affected in their use today?

"While a general misuse of specific gemstones in the past does affect the group consciousness, this would only be valid for the small number of individuals who misused these stones in the past. This negative energy pattern is not stored in the gemstones, more so it is stored in the consciousness of those who activate same. If such an individual attempted to use such a gemstone, there would be a weakness of the personality from the natural cleansing properties of the stone. Negative qualities attributed to certain stones can be relieved by a cleansing of consciousness. Always remember it is the consciousness, not the stone itself, that focuses these negative properties.[4] It takes the critical aspect of karma and consciousness to activate these negative properties. The vast populace should not be concerned with these affairs."

Q Previously, you mentioned that it is best to get passion flower essence in Hawaii because that plant was formed by the Lemurian priesthood and Hawaii was a key part of Lemuria.[5] Does this concept also apply to various gemstones? Is it best to obtain them from certain areas partly because of their past beneficial use in that region?

"This we find to be accurate."

Q Speak on the belief that a stone does not protect its owner if it is purchased or gotten illegally.

"This is accurate in the sense that the clarity of consciousness cannot possibly function in the context of balance in such circumstances. This principle is also somewhat applicable even if the individual is not aware of this situation. The stone as a thought form amplifier and storer of information may record some of these negative impressions. It is generally wise to cleanse a stone when you initially obtain it. This concept does not quite approach levels of superstition but was incorporated into the cultural aspect or collective consciousness of certain societies in the past.

"Furthermore, stones do not offer an element of protection. They have the ability to amplify the awareness and greater clarity of individuals. They enhance the capacity of awareness rather than seek to as bring a special property to the individual. It is not as though there are individual manipulative properties in gemstones independent of the individual's consciousness. Individuals must learn to be in harmony with the greater degrees of awareness that gemstones generate."

Q Is it true that gemstones lose their powers if handled, or even looked at, by impure people?

"In extreme cases this could be true, but this concept has often been used as a prejudice more than as a fact."

Q Comment on the view that autosuggestion explains much of the lure of gemstones?

"There is some accuracy here in the sense that in the past hypnotic principles were used to enhance the properties of many gemstones. But to suggest that all or most of the properties attributed to gemstones is due to autosuggestion would be incorrect."

Q Please comment on the belief that certain gemstones such as amethyst and turquoise change luster to warn a person of danger.

"This is true of opal as well and of many other gemstones. But again it is that such stones are affected by the amplified consciousness of the individual."

We on a soul level through the higher self are able to attune to future positive and negative events. For instance, Edgar Cayce mentioned that he once did not get onto an elevator because he suddenly realized no one on the elevator had an aura. Seconds later that elevator crashed and everyone was killed. Those individuals understood that they would soon die. The transition had already begun. Gemstones have the sensitivity and consciousness to attune to these patterns emanating from the higher self. Thus they can warn us of future dangers. Cloudy stones also can become clearer when owned by someone of a higher consciousness.

Q Is this the same pattern regarding the belief that certain gemstones change color because of toxic environmental factors?

"Correct."

Q Please comment on the belief that certain gemstones give off a vibration that is injurious to people.

"Sometimes a gemstone can cause an imbalance by overstimulating internal organs. All the internal organs of the body physical are of such a nature as to be wholly integrated. When, for example, there is a closing off or damage to the heart tissue and an atrophying of blood flows to the lungs, there could be the application of a single gemstone to healing the lungs due to a shortness of breath. The heart could seek to balance itself without proper enhancement, which could strain the heart tissue due to the integration of these two organs and their singular function in sustaining life."

Q Some gemstones emit a negative force field that might become too absorptive and perhaps cause injury. Is this true, for instance, with uranium?

"In part. No activity within the bands of nature would be as considered negative so much as transformational. It is possible that all fields, even those which are considered of a positive element, may indeed cause overstimulation, but to use the concept of negative field, unless referring, of course, to aspects of positive and negative electrical flows, would be incorrect."

An interesting relevant topic is the wearing of radioactive jewelry. This is mainly a health problem when naturally radioactive or artificially irradiated jewelry is worn for many years. There are indications that long term wearing of radioactive jewelry can cause cancer. But this does not seem to be a major problem because very little jewelry is irradiated in the gem trade. Traditionally, consumer products most readily available that were irradiated have been watches and clocks with luminous dials.[6]

Q Is it easier for a person's thoughts to impregnate a gemstone that is softer in structure?

"There is no particular pattern here. All gemstones have the property of thought form amplification mostly because of their crystalline structure. Some, however, are better binders of thought forms, such as herkimer diamond. It is simplistic to say that either hard or soft stones would as dictate such activities. There are many complex factors here. For instance, the strongest emotions one experiences are often those which one considers 'negative.' These residues are often easier to detect. The weight of a stone would not be relevant in such cases."

Q Is it correct to say that softer stones more easier absorb outside vibrations than harder stones?

"This would be more accurate."

Q Speak on the belief that astrological configurations influence the shape and wearing of various talismans.

"It is true that a gemstone's properties may be enhanced if it is carved during certain favorable astrological accords such as certain planetary and stellar positions. Gemstones have a close attunement to these influences. Wearing gemstones carved under such influences can amplify the gemstone's properties. But it is not critical to do this. At times, in the past, this concept has created areas of superstition."

Q Please comment on the belief that a gemstone used in healing and spiritual work should be at least one or two carats.

"This is not critical, although some displaying rudimentary degress of consciousness would feel more comfortable with a larger stone. The actual size of a gemstone is of little consequence, except with certain stones that deal mostly with emotional qualities and with gemstones that directly integrate with the physiological forces in the body physical. For instance, malachite, pearl, turquoise, lapis lazuli, and other soft stones can be applied through the skin's tissue. However, since gemstone therapy functions under vibrational principles, the stone's size is not critical. If the amplification techniques we recommend are followed, size is of even less importance."

Q Is it true that a gemstone lighter in weight or lighter in gravity would be slightly enhanced if it weighed more?

"There is some truth to this, but it is a minor principle."

Q Please explain the principles involved in wearing gemstones on the body?

"Potent areas on which to wear gemstones include the throat, heart, wrist, naval, ear lobes, index fingers, medulla oblongata, base of the spine, directly behind the knees, center of the brow, under the tongue,and sensitive areas close to the nostrils. It is also wise to place the stone along meridian points to which the stone is attuned. For instance, ruby could be placed along the heart meridian. These areas have high concentrations of neurological tissue.

"If a gemstone is placed close to or inside the nostrils or under the tongue, it should always be cleansed in alcohol for hygienic purposes. The tongue is a critical reflex point. Placing a gemstone or gem elixir just beneath the tongue activates certain homeopathic properties. And saliva acts as a physiological stimulant. When the gem is held under the tongue, the meridians and midbrain are especially stimulated, with the pineal gland acting like a quartz crystal.

"While specific parts of the body are identified as places to wear gemstones when the individual gem elixirs are discussed, it is also not the desire of the channel speaking to break the body physical down into units with gemstones to be placed in each region. The student should study the properties of the chakras, Chinese five element theory, and the individual psychospiritual areas of the body physical to better understand and apply these concepts."

Q Will you now speak on placing gemstones along the vertebrae?

"Gemstones have a particular point of resonancy when placed along the spinal column and meridians. Surgical tape can be used to apply a gem to these areas. Place a gemstone along either side of the spinal column close to a specific vertebra that stimulates healing in accordance to the internal organ matching the placement of the gemstone. To illustrate, place emerald along the vertebra point that stimulates the heart because emerald has a close attunement to the heart. This stimulates healing by translating the gemstone's resonancy into the neurological tissues which go directly to the internal organ. A one or two carat stone would be best to place along the spine. It is also wise to place gemstones along the vertebrae because the magnetic fluidium within the spinal fluid aids in attuning the resonancy of the gemstone to the internal organs."

Q Does Western medicine fully understand the existence and activities of the magnetic fluidium?

"Only in part."

Q Is the ethereal fluidium important when a gemstone is placed along the spinal column to activate certain internal organs?

"It plays only a minor role in this process.

"It is also true that bone tissue is highly responsive to vibration and that as much as 69 to 79 percent of sounds heard on the audible level are as translated through the bone structure. Thus bone structure should be considered an inductive element within the body physical. The bone structure itself is as a point of resonancy continuously balancing and translating information from more subtle levels into the neurological tissue, and this is part of the interpretative perceptual reality of the individual. Therefore, the individual vertebra within the spinal column with their high concentration of neurological tissues, along with the activities of the medulla oblongata and coccyx, become highly active, sensitive resonators. Thus the gemstones, in carrying their resonancies in either close conjunction with or in balance with the individual vertebra, have specific empathy in the construct of each vertebra. When an internal organ is found to correspond with the neurological tissues as they extend from the spinal column, a certain vertebra then could be as isolated as the specific point of resonancy with the gemstone. These properties then bring forth logistics in resonancy, so that which is considered the gemstone's vibration is then amplified through the individual sympathetic vertebra into the neurological tissues, and the subtlety of it is amplified between the medulla oblongata and coccyx. The gemstone then reaches continuous resonancy until it actually takes on a degree of consciousness. This then makes the body physical sympathetic to the vibration of the gemstone as a continuous pulsation of energy throughout the major priorities of the sympathetic nervous system, eventually extending even to the activities of the endocrine system. This brings the physical body entirely into alignment with the resonancy of the gemstone.

"It is also wise to place quartz crystals by the medulla oblongata and coccyx when gemstones are being placed along the spine. This further amplifies and stabilizes the gemstones' properties to benefit the internal organs."

Q Speak on wearing or holding gemstones for meditation and various other spiritual practices.

"One suggestion is to sit in a lotus or semi-lotus position with the hands turned upward holding a quartz crystal in the center of each hand. As discussed in traditional palmistry literature, certain gemstones could be placed on the hand to activate parts of the body to stimulate various spiritual practices. Or gemstones could then be placed on the forehead or along the spine. It is best to do this technique in the morning for at least twenty minutes, although benefits would be derived if the exercise were conducted for only seven minutes. Westerners unaccustomed to sitting in the lotus position could sit in a chair. Vigorously rub the surface of the skin you want to place the gemstone on. This brings blood to that region and stimulates the nervous system so that the impulse from the gemstone moves more quickly into the body through the nervous system. If possible, use your own saliva to hold the gemstone on the body. If this does not work, then use surgical tape."

Q Is it best to not wear a stone by particular parts of the body?

"There is no particular rule governing this question, unless the properties of the gemstone were atrophied by placing the stone on that part of the body. There are certain natural points in the body physical that do not enhance the gemstone's properties. In fact these points may even atrophy the gemstone's properties. There are various points in the body on which this could occur, but it is unique to each gemstone. For instance, it would be unwise to wear diamond by the chest. Many people have deep karmic patterns in that area that would be bought to the surface much too quickly if a diamond were worn on the chest. In addition, the energy pattern of the stone would feed back on itself. The subtle bodies would form what is called a vortex in that part of the body. The effect would be fairly rapid, with a certain discomfort experienced. However, not everyone would have this sensation if wearing a gem on the wrong part of the body.

"When the energy patterns of diamond are negative, the presence of that gem so near the heart chakra will energize those energy patterns. The bridging or uniting nature of this chakra will connect these patterns to the mental body, changing one's self-image. This new pattern, now enhanced by diamond, may disturb the heart chakra by creating new images of oneself. This new self-image, enhanced by diamond, will bring more old patterns to the surface, so that a kind of biofeedback is created.

"The student should also understand that wearing certain jewelry for too long slows down the life force and can be detrimental. Toxic metals not to wear include lead, aluminum, and iron, unless iron is in a pure state of stainless steel. Tin should not be worn unless intermixed with bronze. Wearing a stone for too long can also amplify negative personality traits."

Q Speak on wearing gemstones to stimulate the various chakras.

"Gemstones can be used in relationship to the chakras to alter and balance the psychospiritual forces of the individual. The cleansing of the psychospiritual and spiritual structures within the individual eventually merges into but one area of concentration. That is for the spiritualization of the personality through the body physical or the concept of the body-mind coming into the totality of focus. It is generally best to place the gemstones along the spinal column to stimulate the main chakras.

"A system of study suggested by the channel speaking is to examine the patterns of the individual chakras because these would be the main power points for gemstones to be applied to the body physical for an even distribution of their energy. There is a concentration of intelligent energy and thought form within the chakras. Study each of these areas in the body physical and you will find them the most sensitive to either the storing of tensions or the release of tensions within the body. For instance, the abdominal chakra is highly sensitive to stress that could as even lead to ulcerous conditions. The abdomen allows the individual to deal with the full emotional spectrum, with levels of sensitivity, and with personal initiatives in the area of self-esteem. The abdomen is also concerned with the parental image known as the mother. Pearl or moonstone, if applied to the abdomen or related meridian point, could bring not only levels of illumination concerning areas of the mother and emotional sensitivity but also clarity regarding financial affairs. The kidneys are associated with hidden fears. The lungs are associated with sibling rivalries between brothers and sisters, the ability of the individual to communicate from many emotional levels, and the ability to express the emotional states held within the self. This, of course, enters the subject of esoteric anatomy, which is a major topic."[7]

Q Is it best to set gemstones in certain metals for the wearing of jewelry?

"Yes, here we isolate gold, silver, copper, and platinum. Each of these are the primary elements for the setting of minerals, because these in particular allow for the natural enhancement of any stones that are worn. These particular enhancers manifest greater balance and understanding of the stones' properties. And these metals, as natural enhancers, both amplify or decrease the influence of the worn stones depending on the personal metabolism of the individual. All of these metals are found to be as natural and high in conductivity and resistant to most quickening forms of oxidation, except copper. The oxidation process with copper may actually enhance another stone's properties by the taking in of oxygen and by mildly increasing the electrical field. These metals stabilize the influence of other stones due to their high degree of conductive properties. Silver and platinum are more feminine, while copper and gold are more masculine. There is only a minor enhancement if men only wear gold and copper and women only wear silver and platinum.

"Wearing these metals also allows for psychological information and principles of the collective consciousness to be translated genetically and telepathically to the individual. There are certain metals which are used in healing that have their properties passed on by telepathy through the collective unconscious to which each person is connected through their genetic makeup of direct ancestry. Therefore, certain metals and various stones stimulate healing on psychological levels from the collective unconscious by direct ancestry. For instance, gold is attributed to having certain healing properties. The ancestral memories of using gold are passed on through each succeeding generation as part of the collective unconscious, and those conditions may as lay dormant within the subject until activated by the direct memory process or by the presence of the metallic substance itself. In other words, actually wearing gold may stimulate past life recall of when the healing properties of gold were used by the individual.

"In certain cases, if the gemstone is used for its nutrient properties, such as with pearl when touching the skin, then it is best that the gemstone come into direct contact with the skin. It is also usually best that a gemstone come into direct contact with the skin when it is desired to have the stone attune directly to certain acupuncture or acupressure points. Whether or not a stone is placed inside a metal, care must be taken as to where it is placed on the body to attain a more perfect balance. Meditation will help many in this regard.

"Some minerals, such as garnet, especially when worn with others, are best to cut rather then to remain in their natural state. Use traditional gems cut by gemmologists to enhance their qualities. The cutting and polishing of certain stones makes for better points of concentration for general usage by many individuals. In addition, there are some stones when worn as talismans that would be best to cut to remove their impurities. It is also sometimes wise to cut gems if they are being shaped into specific enhancing forms such as the pyramid, or if various facets are being applied to the stone. For instance, if a stone is being used to stabilize someone, an eight-sided shape would be beneficial. However, those who are detached from the physical beauty of stones generally benefit more from an uncut stone. Gemstones rarely work differently if they are cut or uncut when worn on the body. It is just that their properites may be enhanced, especially depending on the psychological attitudes of the individual."

Q Elsewhere you said that there would be a discourse on wearing platinum. Please present that now.

"Platinum when worn upon the body physical has activities of broad medical use. This is mostly because it has an impact on the endocrine system, and its activities contain forces that are desirable to specifically enter through the skin's tissue. Platinum, even on the physical level, is beneficial in the healing of neurological tissues, muscular tissue, and again, the endocrine system. These forces come about because the activities of platinum increase the capacity of neurological synapses within the body physical. Platinum, when worn close to the medulla oblongata, base of the spine, center of the forehead, or to the solar plexus, is quickly incorporated into the body on two levels, because of the high concentration of neurological stimulus in these areas. First, the physical molecular structure of platinum is literally ingested through the skin's surface and is then quickly displaced throughout the body physical, especially influencing the endocine system. This balances the body physical as a whole. Moreover, the ethereal and electrical properties of platinum, because of its ability to become slightly magnetized, resonate with the mild electromagnetic field of the neurological tissues. Therefore, quantities of those ingested portions of its molecular structure are as immediately sympathetically aligned with the neurological tissues. Platinum is beneficial in a manner similar to magnetic healing."

Q How often should one cleanse a gemstone worn on the body?

"Generally, a simple cleansing of the gemstone every two months is sufficient. Individuals involved in deep meditation or mantric practices should usually cleanse the gemstones more often. Sensitive individuals may not want to wear certain gems, especially the powerful ones, by key meridian or spinal points for more than a few days or even for more than a few minutes. If someone feels a state of disharmony or an uncomfortable feeling from wearing jewelry, then there may be a state of overamplification. Cleansing the jewelry may solve the problem. In other cases, the jewelry should not be worn by the individual.

"It is generally wise to use a mineral in its raw state with no impurities. That which is considered of gem quality is of a purer content. Then the properties are enhanced.

Especially when a gemstone is to be worn, cutting and polishing the stone may be wise in some cases. These basic principles are applicable to all gemstones, but they are not so relevant when using gemstones as gem elixirs. For instance, while it is often better to wear a garnet that is cut, its properties as a gem elixir are further amplified when a rough specimen of garnet is obtained."

Q From a point of consciousness, what is the difference between precious and semiprecious gemstones? The precious stones have more commercial value.

"From a point of consciousness, there is no difference, except that people often are instinctually drawn to promote or become strongly attracted to those things which enhance consciousness. This is an important reason why so many have been traditionally drawn to gold. It is only when there is the material focus that you have terms such as precious and semiprecious."

While it is generally easier to benefit from the properties of a mineral through ingesting a gem elixir, wearing jewelry is also wise. Some may want to make their own talismans or amulets[8] or obtain them in various stores. Quartz crystal talismans have now become quite common.

1 Alice Beard and Frances Rogers, *5000 Years of Jewelry* (N.Y: J.B. Lippincott Co.,1947).
George F. Kunz, *The Magic Of Jewels and Charms* (Philadelphia: J.B. Lippincott Co.,1915), p. 241-376.
Beth B Sutherland, *The Romance of Seals and Engraved Gems* (N.Y: The Macmillan Co.,1965).
2 Cyril Aldred, *Jewels of the Pharaohs* (N.Y: Ballantine Books,1978).
E.A. Wallis Budge, *Amulets and Superstitions* (N.Y: Dover Publications,Inc.).
Yvonne Hackenbrouch, *Renaissance Jewelery* (London: Sotheby Parke Bernet Publications,1979).
William Pavitt, *The Book of Talismans, Amulets and Zodiacal Gems* (N. Hollywood,Ca: Wilshire Book Co.,1974).
3 Isidore Kozminsky, *The Magic and Science of Jewels and Stones* (N. Y: G.P. Putnam's Sons,1922),p. 212-216.
4 H.P. Blavatsky, *Isis Unveiled* (Wheaton, IL: The Theosophical Publishing House,1972),p.462.
5 Gurudas, *Flower Essences and Vibrational Healing* (Albuquerque,N.M: Brotherhood of Life,Inc,1983),p.174-175.
6 *Radioactive Jewelry* (Brodheadsville,Pa: Biohazard Press, 1984).
"Is Your Jewelry Radioactive," *Science Digest,* (Oct., 1983), p.30.
7 Hilarion, *Body Signs* (Toronto: Marcus Books,1982).
8 Israel Regardie, *How To Make and Use Talismans* (Wellingborough, Northamptonshire, England: The Aquarian Press,1982).

CHAPTER III

ASTROLOGY AND GEM ELIXIRS

In this chapter, there is a review of how gemstones relate to and can be used in conjuction with various planets and constellations, or zodiac signs. The zodiac is a stellar configuration constructed thousands of years ago to represent twelve of the many constellations in the sky. The use of birthstones expresses the ancient belief that certain stones bring us luck and protection. The information presented in this text on using astrology with various gemstones is basic information that anyone can apply. One does not need to be an astrologer to understand this material.

Q Please present a full discourse on how the planets and constellations affect us, including information on how their radiation affects us and how radical emotional imbalances may result. Elsewhere you said that you would include some information about the effects of Orion, Sirius, and the Pleiades because they are the three constellations that influence us the most.

"Distant stellar bodies such as the constellations[1] of Orion, Sirius, and the Pleiades have an influence on people not so much due to the potency of the forces released from these regions, but because of the heightened sensitivity which should be accredited to the human instrument. The human instrument has continuously adapted to the environment over many millions of years of evolution, similar to patterns stated by Darwin. The evolutionary impact of the influence of constellations is cumulative. The misunderstood heightened sensitivity of the human instrument may be displayed through various activities confirmed by thy scientists, to such degrees of sensitivity so as to detect the thoughts of another individual, even at great distances. This ye term telepathy. Therefore, students should not think that there is a great potency of force in stellar influences; it is more so that one should learn the true levels of sensitivity in the body physical. Then one can better study the properties of Orion, Sirius, and the Pleiades to better understand their unique influences. All astrological bodies influence the human instrument.

"The study of the stars by the ancients was not so much that there were attributed to the stars symbols according to the shape of the stars, but was more so that direct meditation upon these stellar influences drew up from the collective unconscious of the ancients the direct meaning and impact that they had. This developed through the skillful observation and continuous studying of events that transpired over many thousands of years. This brought forth balance and understanding in the development of the science that is now known as astrology.

"One way astrological bodies influence people is upon psychological levels. Study of and continuous focus upon the stars by the ancients led to the cornerstone of forces which have become universal symbols in the Jungian system of thought. These universal symbols have become the very focus of the principles that are known as the collective unconscious. These particular forces slowly began to make up the very foundation of men's and women's unconscious governing functions. As these universal symbols found their seat in the subconscious mind, they could as draw forth visions from the subconscious and drift to levels of the conscious state to become integrated with the personality. They tend to become the functional portion of the personality. These forces have even been noted by Freud when he sought in various mythos to explain human behavior and the interactivity with each individual upon these mythos as concepts related to the activities of functional human thought.

"These stellar influences, even if this discourse is upon rudimentary psychological levels, have a tremendous influence upon the psyche of men and women as a whole. To clarify even further, for thousands of years there has been the study, at a simple psychological level, of the stellar bodies. People have long been fascinated by these objects; they have been arranged in complex images throughout all the great civilizations. Often identical meanings have been reached regarding the various stellar bodies. This suggests a universality concerning the nature of interpretating the stellar patterns. These complex symbols have always related directly to the destiny of men and women and even of nations. This is true even if these universal symbols were only used as a focal point for celestial suggestion or power of suggestion as a point of visualization for men and women in their psyche. This in turn is a powerful influence. As a point of focus, study, and fascination, these stellar bodies have a major psychological impact on people. Order is brought to this psychological impact by giving meaning, depth, and above all the suggestion of direct influence through the symbols and the associated human behavioral patterns associated with these symbols. This then passes on to the activities of men and women in general. These symbols have almost a post-hypnotic quality that is preserved in the traditions of a culture and then is passed on through the collective unconscious, stored deep within the genetic memory and other levels. This is a prototypical model for individuals to use in approaching the concept of the reality that stellar influences may have upon people.

"The entire night sky is as an immense mandala influencing individuals through their personal associations with these astrological symbols. There is the continuous exposure of thy planet to particles of light and energy from these various stellar forces. There is no portion of life on earth that is not constantly exposed to these stellar influences, even if it is not upon levels of radiation that the eye may detect. There are continuous and slight adaptions within the physiology of species over many millions of years of evolution. Life is always in a state of delicate balance upon the planet in its own right. Life on earth has adapted to living in an environment in which organisms must survive background radiation and voltages of the earth's electromagnetic field and other forces. These are indeed part of the evolutionary force. There has been the activity of adapting cumulatively to these stellar forces, not as through gravitational influence, but more so as steady cumulative forces of continuous exposure for millions of years of evolution, contributing to that very evolution. Indeed, the constant rotation and position of the planet itself, as it moves at various angular perspectives to these stellar forces, exposes individual life forms to interactivities with those stellar forms. These influences have been amplified through psychological association, when as drawn up into the consciousness by the methodologies suggested earlier in this discourse.

"Astrological influences upon metabolism and evolution, and therefore upon consciousness, is cumulative and as arises in the consciousness through increased study and awareness of these fields. The stellar influence of constellations extends over many years. These are, however, amplified, although bent in shape, when the gravity of a planetary sphere closer to the earth can then focus its influence. Then there is the passing of a planet through the constellation's field of influence. This indeed activates focus, even as all light spent by gravity on a planet passes through these stellar influences, disrupting or bending those influences. These forces are then felt within the individual, imprinting both the planetary influence and the activities of the stellar field.

"It is suggested for students to begin studying traditional astrology to understand stellar influences in their own right and how this relates to better understanding human behavioral patterns. The constellations Orion, the Pleiades, and Sirius indeed have unique properties of influencing the earth because from these particular stars there came forth individuals from other planes and spheres who had sojourns to this planet ages ago when there were cultural exchanges between Lemuria, Atlantis, and those who traveled between the spheres. This refers to those ye would now term as alien life forms or extraterrestrials. These individuals have always sought to bring forth balance and structure, and have actually contributed much to the genetic matter in the gene pool of human consciousness in these days. So in many ways there is a sympathetic resonancy between these particular constellations and those of this race.[2]

"These astrological forces interlink with gemstone principles because, in their positioning and exposure to planets, gemstones absorb and store resonancies,[3] even as various metals have the capacity to conduct or resist electrical influences. Gemstones, in their early days of formation, were as much better able to store certain frequencies or resonancies. These forces are cumulative. Therefore, the various gemstones associated with different zodiacal signs find their resonance with the ability to isolate and store direct stellar influences by either allowing other influences to pass through or even amplifying or eliminating them. Thus, there can indeed be the isolation of specific gemstones in relationship to zodiac signs and other forces.

"If there is the direct linkage of various therapies to stellar influences, therapies could be developed based strictly upon an angular diagnosis of an individual's position at birth relative to the position of the stellar influences. There could then be an entire therapy developed for cleansing the individual of karmic influences and many of those related forces. This comes about by matching the behavioral physiological patterns associated with stellar influences as is now done in medical astrology. Then, work with the individual gemstones to either balance or purge the individual of particular influences. For example, if Mars passes through Cancer at birth, particularly if it squares Uranus, this could lead to a bleeding ulcer. Diamond is the key gemstone to use in treating this condition. A combination of diamond and silver or diamond and moonstone would restore balance here. Each gemstone has its own particular and unique makeup totally independent of stellar influences. But if a gemstone is found to be matched or ruled by certain stellar influences, it would indeed store the principles and influences of that stellar body. Mars is associated with diamond through its broadcast of energy. Cancer rules the activities of the abdominal walls, and Uranus rules the activities of the circulatory system. Right angles of these positions can indeed stimulate disruption, even to physiological levels. These are but suggestions for students to pursue in their own studies. These points may be as expanded upon at a later point in time.

"All minerals exist in harmonics with planetary motions. If certain gemstones are used in accordance with certain astrological movements, there is some enhancement of the stones' properties. For instance, moonstone and pearl are amplified during a lunar eclipse, since the qualities associated with these stones are in accordance with the qualities of energy expressed by the moon. Similarly, the use of ruby and emerald are amplified during a solar eclipse."

Q You said the soul's forces are not linked to the different planets and constellations in their influence on us, but it surrenders portions of its consciousness to the biological personality. Please expand on this statement?

"It is that the soul's force is not beneath thought, it is thought. Therefore, the soul's forces are not so much linked to the planets but find a focus for their activities within the activities of the body physical because of the ability of planets and other forces to have a focus within the body physical. This is not the force of the soul; it is the surrender of the soul to the natural disciplines of the physical universe into which it has penetrated. Until it can totally become conscious of the self and its higher nature, the soul falls under these disciplines."

Q Discuss the general principles involved in using gemstones as birthstones?

"There can exist a personal alignment with the forces that are associated with the time periods of the various months. This can be as a personal point of focus, when individuals can gain some knowledge of gemstones' properties and of their enhancement in areas of an individual's spiritual awareness. Due to the popularity of birthstones,[4] they can be a principle point of focus for desirable impacts of meditation, stimulating the psychology of individuals in the sense of their association with the context of their birth sign. These activities bring forth balance and perspective for individuals desiring to have a greater understanding of the principles applied to gemstones. In their capacity for aligning with popular meditative accords, gemstones have greater activity in the seasons that are attributed to them or within the time periods ascribed to them. They indeed actually make up a calender of physiological activity contained within the body physical."

Q You said birthstones were activated at different times of the year and in different parts of the body. Please expand upon this?

"This can be isolated according to the zodiacal makeup of characters. Or the student may find hints of such activities within the months of the year associated with the four seasons. Elements of the body physical are hinted at in astrological studies such as in medical astrology. Use the twelve birthstones and the twelve zodiac stones."

Q Is it true that a function of birthstones is to maintain the stability of your vibration?
    "Correct."

Q What is the origin of the belief in birthstones?

"Most originate with Babylonian and Chaldean systems of thought, dating back, of course, to the days of Lemuria. It involves a long-term coordination of stones and their forces with individuals of certain personality structures and the observation of astrological transitory periods."

Q What are the birthstones for each month?

"Spessartine garnet represents January, amethyst is for February, red jasper is for March, white diamond is for April, emerald represents May, light pearl is for June, ruby is for July, moonstone represents August, cherry or light opal is for September, aquamarine is for October, topaz represents November, and bloodstone is for December."

Q Can there be other birthstones for these months?

"Yes, but popular stones are now presented for easy access and experimentation on the part of individuals."

Q Would it be wise to take a combination of these twelve gemstones?

"Yes. There are people who are not yet ready for the more powerful aspects of gem therapy, for awakening on a deep spiritual level or to understand their link with the cosmos. These people have many things to accomplish in the world before they are ready for these things. Such individuals will often benefit from a combination of this birthstone elixir because they will not only recognize the additional energy that they receive from such an elixir, but they will also be more open to the more spiritual properties of gemstones.

"Birthstones are what you might call an underlying shared planetary idea. Birthstones relate to earthly activities in a more mundane sense. Thus, taking this birthstone combination eases stress, and this elixir can be of great value when people are working together in a physical task to accomplish certain goals relevant to the raising of consciousness. The individual becomes capable of accomplishing more than would usually be the case. People working together on a research project that required much physical labor would greatly benefit from this combination. Gradually, the work along with the elixir would lead to inspiration. All tasks on the earth, if they are to benefit an individual, lead to a level of greater understanding about oneself and one's environment. A spiritualization of more mundane tasks is eventually experienced in the taking of the birthstone combination. The birthstone elixir would also gradually stimulate an alignment with the earth and cosmos and with the consciousness of many individuals."

Q Review each sign of the zodiac and the relevant gemstones?

"With each sign there will be a brief review of the impact of the gemstone on specific organs, spiritual qualities, mental forces, and interpersonal relations. Only one will be listed with each constellation or zodiac sign. Others could be given, but there is a desire to keep things simple. This is a training procedure for more advanced work to be given in the future. The gemstones that are listed here are the most valuable because they have the broadest general application.

"When a particular month has a birthstone different from the zodiac stone, there is a careful selection of the two gemstones so that they intermix to bring about a singular point of focus. When this occurs the two gemstones should usually be combined into one preparation. Both tend to have similar properties. It is desired to have an overlapping system, combining the astrological influences with the actualization processes expressed in birthstones."

In this system, as presented by John, the zodiac sign for each month is pushed forward by one month from what is usually done in western astrology. For instance, for August the constellation is Virgo not Leo as would traditionally be the case. John briefly spoke about this.

"The primary element is always at the beginning, when there exists the most potent force as with seeds that sprout the life force. For example, Virgo finds its initiation in the latter degree of the month of August, which is generally thought of as Leo's month. This initiates the cycle of astrological zoning. There is much material regarding this system in the work of Cyril Fagan.[5] He describes a system called sidereal astrology based on the houses, the planets, the position of fixed stars, and the way the ancients viewed the zodiac. A fixed star is usually at a reference point 15 degrees different from that usually used in most systems of astrology. Astrologers would greatly benefit in many ways by actually meditating on the stars. At night, go outside and gaze at a specific star and meditate on its properties. You could also ingest a gem elixir prepared from the properties of fixed stars. Fixed stars influence people more than is generally realized.[6]

"Sidereal astrology allows people greater accuracy when choosing the way they see the planetary motions throughout their lives. Sometimes this accuracy conflicts with popular astrology. And sometimes the planets and zodiac signs are moved back. There is still quite a bit of overlap and similarity in the larger, slower moving planets. However, what will be seen is that individuals must make their own choices about such a system. Some individuals will not find harmony, no matter how hard they try, with such a sidereal system. These people will have to revert to a topical system. Choose a certain point that is a very powerful crisis or crux point in the person's life, casting the chart with as much accuracy as possible using this system in which the signs are set back. The chart is progressed to that crux point in the person's life. The person then looks for attunement and balance with that point, as if to say 'yes, the action of my Mars moving at that time into my Aries did allow a complete shift in my understanding.' Therefore, individuals can use such a chart and make their own choices. However, in general, this is a more advanced system that has now been given.

"We will begin with July. The birthstone and zodiac stone for this constellation, which is Leo, is ruby. Ruby has an attunement with the heart chakra, the internal organ of the heart, the thymus, and the spinal column. It integrates the activities of the father parental image, the biological father, or those with whom ye hold images of as the father. One's leadership potential is activated, and one stays centered in one's principles and ideals. A sense of joy, self-esteem, flexibility, negotiation skills, and an ability to resolve things is stimulated. Individuals may develop self-esteem, but if one does not learn the principles of divine love and the principles associated with the heart chakra, there may be a fall from grace.

"Virgo is the focus for August. The birthstone for August is moonstone, and sapphire represents Virgo. There is an improvement in the function of the intestinal tract, adrenals, pancreas, nervous system, and lower spinal column. Mental qualities unnecessary to the self are eliminated. One develops an ability to discriminate, enhanced powers of analysis, increased negotiation skills, and a keener observation of the emotionalism to which the individual clings. The emotions are calmed so that one can speak with clarity. A sense of priority develops for proper spiritual growth. For instance, the conscious mind is calmed so that one can meditate with grace, and unnecessary tensions are eliminated from the body physical. Moonstone amplifies the properties of sapphire, although sapphire does not amplify moonstone.

"For September, or Libra, the birthstone and zodiac stone is light or cherry opal. The kidneys are strengthened, hidden fears and paranoia are alleviated, especially in interpersonal relations, and there is an increased capacity for astral projection. There is an alleviation of general anxiety. Fears can be confronted while meditating to release them properly. There is also some impact on the lungs. One acquires increased negotiation skills in marriage or partnerships in general. Increased balance in the mental state to contact the higher self also results. Better decision making and greater ease in seeing another person's point of view develop. If opal is used with chlorophyll, there is also a major beneficial impact on the body physical. Take two tablespoons of concentrated chlorophyll in eight ounces of distilled water twice daily throughout the period of taking opal.

"Red coral is the point of focus for October, or Scorpio, and aquamarine is the birthstone for that month. The ovaries, uterus, cervix, vaginal walls, fallopian tubes, and other important portions of the female anatomy are augmented. In the male, the testicles, prostrate, penis, and other parts of the male anatomy are aided. The coccyx and sacrum are balanced, and there is a sense of emotional regeneration, especially after depression. Higher wisdom may manifest to bring about greater integration with the personality. There is a release of tension and emotional complexes caused by stored anger, particularly arising from childhood problems. Grief, especially associated with the loss of life, is eased. One learns to accept one's own mortality so that the fear of death lessens. Sexual identity improves, and problems in interpersonal relationships are eased. There is a greater balance in all aspects of tantric practice. Astral projection abilities improve, and the kundalini energy is released.

"For November, or Sagittarius, the birthstone and zodiac stone is topaz. Topaz augments the muscular tissue, releasing stored tensions. Circulation increases to the muscles, and there is improved assimilation of protein. Athletes develop a better mental attitude; there is increased competence and ability to perform physical feats. People are stimulated to pursue higher philosophies and teachings, often in an academic environment. There is a desire to develop increased clarification of one's personal philosophy. The life's philosophy are the principles and ethics by which people conduct themselves as individual members of society. People may feel a need to be alone to pursue higher goals. There is an alleviation of tension or anxiety associated with aloneness.

"Jet is the stone for December, or Capricorn, and the birthstone is bloodstone. Here we find the following focus: the entire skeletal structure and skin tissue are aided. Career pursuits and life goals are clarified. Spiritual and mental discipline develop. More structured meditation may develop during periods of self-examination and contemplation. In a period of retreat one may focus on giving more of the self selflessly.

"Use spessartine garnet for January, or Aquarius, as well as for that month's birthstone. Circulatory flows increase, especially the plasma and capillary action in the area of the skin, lungs, and ductless gland system. The lymphatics are also cleansed. This stone activates the spiritual revolutionary for it crystallizes insight. Sri Aurobindo exemplifies this pattern. The individual learns to surrender to events over which he has no control, but which also benefit and completely revolutionize him. This would be an ideal time to negotiate new friendships, especially to achieve new goals.

"In February the birthstone is amethyst, and the zodiac stone for Pisces is jade. These stones penetrate to and strengthen all levels of the endocrine system, and there is improved circulation in the lower anatomy, particularly in the area of the base of the feet. Confusion eases, the dream state is stimulated, and a deceitful nature is lessened, especially when it involves a compulsion such as kleptomania. These two gem elixirs alleviate depression and drug addiction through increased self-understanding as a spiritual being. In interpersonal relationships, these gemstones alleviate tension, bitterness, and grudges.

"For March the birthstone is red jasper; the stone for the zodiac sign for Aries is white diamond. Here we find a strengthening of the pineal, pituitary, sinus membranes, most functions of the brain's cranial structure, and the inner workings and sensitivity of the inner ears. With these two elixirs, people develop the ability to focus on the self as a portion of God. Mental vitality develops as confusion and impulsiveness are lessened.

"White diamond is the birthstone for April, and the zodiac stone for Taurus is lapis lazuli. These stones enhance the thyroid, esophagus, and bronchials. There is true expression of the self from the real spiritual self and from the personality. Personal expression improves, for without proper personal expression the individual would only internalize. Therefore, these elixirs in combination prevent the inversion of the self or the introvert-like nature. The emotions are balanced, the throat chakra opens, and rudimentary negotiating skills develop as one learns to speak for the rights of the self in a clear context without overextending the self.

"For May the birthstone is emerald, and the gemstone for Gemini is malachite. With the intermixing of the forces of emerald and malachite we find that the entire nervous system and lungs are stimulated. Emerald is classically associated with the heart, and the heart is critical to the element of drawing in the breath and its related capillary activities. Shortness of breath is often asociated with cardiovascular difficulties. The autonomic nervous system is stimulated to allow the mind to extend to these areas. There is a balancing of the mental forces to allow an examination of spiritual qualities. Anxiety and stress associated with neurological diseases are also treatable with these elixirs.

"The birthstone for June is light pearl, which is also the gemstone for Cancer. Enhancement of the pancreas, bladder, gall bladder, abdomen, diaphragm, and spleen result from using pearl. There is a gradual transformation of emotional difficulties into greater sensitivity to others' needs and to explore more thoroughly the realms and functions of the spiritual self. The third chakra is also activated, and balance is restored with the mother.

"Exposure to the various elements of gemstones can stimulate the enhancement of health within any individual. Study the properties and qualities assigned to each stone according to popular astrological interpretations. Health may also be promoted within the physical form by isolating each singular property associated with each gemstone and its astrological symbolism. There could then be isolated the physical properties attributed to each stone. Medical astrology has isolated the relationship of many gemstones to various parts of the body.[7] Isolating this information will give the student insight into how these elixirs work.

"For individuals to take these gemstones as elixirs, the following procedures are suggested: proceed through each month in twenty-eight day cycles, even if the month is slightly longer. There will be a slight overlapping of months and periods of time. Begin with the birthstone and zodiacal astrological stone that is synonymous with your birth. Each day when the sun is at its high point for the day, usually around noon, take seven drops of the elixir or elixirs in sixteen ounces of distilled water. If more than one elixir is involved, it is usually best to combine them."

Q Why is it best to take these elixirs around noon when previously you said it is best to take vibrational remedies in the morning up to noon?

"This is tabulated with the sun's forces because it is wise to begin with the dominant zodiacal accord and to be in sympathy with the sun's vibration. When the sun reaches its zenith, it is at a neutral point concerning the yin-yang principles. This influence extends to the gem elixir then ingested. This is what is most desired. When the sun is at its zenith in the life force in the early portions of the day, gemstone properties are enhanced, but in a somewhat neutralized fashion. This neutralization is wise because, if the gemstone's activity is too potent, there is more likelihood of an aggravation similar to the homeopathic principle.

"Each day in the morning, before taking the gem elixirs around noon, meditate seeking to attune one's consciousness to the specific area of the body physical associated with the monthly astrological configuration. One suggested procedure is to picture white light or illumination in the direct area of the physical anatomy you are attuning to. The meditation should last from three to twenty-one minutes, depending on the skills of the individual. This meditation, which can be the same each month if desired, enhances the spiritual and mental attributes described above for each gemstone.

"It is beneficial to wear as a ring or amulet gemstones used each month, preferably set in silver as a general enhancer. There is no critical point on the body physical where these stones should be worn, but the daily visualization is enhanced if the gemstones are placed in front of you on a white linen. Then the ethereal properties are activated by meditation into the individual's pure consciousness, are enhanced and integrated through the elixir's force, and are reactivated by repeating the meditation each evening. Doing this daily for one year will bring the individual into complete focus.

"Through the process of meditation and visualization as the individual proceeds through the year, there would be an attunement with each portion of the body physical, again over patterns of twenty-eight days in a series of meditations. The meditations in the system should be repeated in association with each area of actualization. Most of the spiritual properties that may be activated are related to the fact that each stone has a point of focus within the chakras. Thus, there is indeed the promotion of unity in mind, body, and spirit, based upon the physiological principles of the stones and their properties being activated through meditation.

"This suggested one-year program can be equally used with the birthstones and zodiac or astrological stones. There are no further complexities to this system. This is meant to be an introduction to physical and mental health and spiritual well-being. The student may then add more complexity to the process by experimentation and a further review of this volume.

"If this program was followed for one year, individuals could experience a total actualization of the self by the application of these simple and popular stones. The individual could also bring forth talents by focusing upon the self in the desired areas of improvement to bring forth maturing in areas of talent, interpersonal relationships, and other activities described in self-actualization processes."

Q Explain the relationship between birthstones and zodiac stones and why people would take one group versus the other?

"Two separate systems exist for those who desire complete clarity in the context of astrological accords. Birthstones are more popular and are presented in a simple fashion. The birthstone has more to do with the current incarnation and the affairs of everyday life, while the zodiac stones are more associated with spiritual activities and the soul's reasons for incarnating. The zodiac or astrological gemstones are more complex and can be aligned with the movement of planets and constellations and the formation of mandalas."

Q How do people better attune to different birthstones and astrological stones?

"This is associated with the person's relationship to the stone as it matches either the month of their birth or the period of time when the sun or the solar force transits their particular day of birth. This will become apparant to individuals as they increase their knowledge of astrological functions. At times, the twelve birthstones are identical with the twelve zodiac stones. At other times, the zodiac stones, which are a more refined and potent system, are different from the birthstones. Other minor points could have been discussed regarding when the birthstones and zodiac stones differ but these stones are sufficiently compatible so that this was not felt to be necessary."

Q Why do some birthstones differ from some zodiac stones even though they have a relationship and most months have a single focus?

"The influence of the zodiac energy is cumulative. A planet's movement, or association in its most sympathetic resonancy with a particular zodiac sign, focuses the cumulative energy of the constellation within gemstones. That is, it is not two separate energies. It is one energy that is cumulative from the formation of the gemstone and is focused by the more dominant closer force of the planet itself. When the birthstone and zodiac stone for a given month differ, they have rulership similarities. When two different gemstones are presented for the birthstone and zodiac sign, it is best that the elixirs be ingested in combination to unify the energy."

Q Why are different gemstones indicated to represent the signs of the zodiac?

"Planets have simple harmonics with the accords and activities of individual stones as are isolated by their astrological rulerships. The planets, which move closer to the earth, have greater exposure to the earth's forces at different angles. Thus, the planets adapt their forces to the stones in a particular fashion because of their closer movements to the native planetary position of the earth. Therefore, these influences are felt more strongly in the stones.

"Zodiac signs which are different points of divergency also develop a sympathetic resonancy within the stones. Constellations develop over many millions of years of exposure to various forces and energies. Therefore, it is possible to have two systems of harmonics, one which is cumulative on the part of the constellations, and one which is almost an adaptation to the cumulative energy of the constellations by the planets through their various movements, adjustments, and influences on the native position of the earth itself."

Because each planet is attuned to a zodiac sign, traditional astrology has determined that each planet rules a specific zodiac sign. For instance, the radiant quality of the Sun rules the constellation of Leo, which emits a similar quality to the Leo archetype. John below assigns specific gemstones to the planets and their rulership over the constellations in the zodiac.

Q List the sun, planets, the zodiac signs that they rule, and the gemstones associated with the sun and each planet?

"The Sun rules Leo and is aligned with emerald, ruby, and red onyx. The Moon rules Cancer and is aligned with moonstone, light pearl, and green tourmaline. Green tourmaline enhances psychic faculties. The earth influences Capricorn, Taurus, and Virgo. Tiger's eye should be used here because of its grounding quality. The emotional and mental forces need to take root to reach stages of fruition. Mercury rules Virgo and Gemini. The Mercury and Virgo attunement is enhanced with moonstone, sapphire, and star sapphire, while alexandrite and aquamarine can be used with Mercury and Gemini. Venus has a dual rulership over Libra and Taurus. The alignment with Libra stimulates an alignment with light or cherry opal, lapis lazuli, and any tourmaline. The attunement of Venus to Taurus is enhanced by lapis lazuli, sapphire, and any tourmaline. Mars rules Aries and is attuned to carnelian agate, bloodstone, and white diamond. Mars also rules Scorpio and the gemstones carnelian agate, ruby, and topaz are applicable. Adding topaz to this combination would be too powerful for some. Jupiter rules Sagittarius, and the gemstones amethyst and malachite may be used. Saturn rules Capricorn, and jet, black onyx, and white onyx apply. Uranus rules Aquarius, and spessartine or rhodolite garnet and blue sapphire apply. Neptune rules Pisces, with an alignment to jade, any tourmaline, and turquoise. Pluto rules Scorpio with an attunement to carnelian agate, ruby, and topaz. It is often best for people to take one or two of these gemstones, instead of the three together. This is not because of healing crises, but because Pluto has a very deep effect on people that is not always immediately felt or understood. Taking one of these stones would make it easier to understand and assimilate the deep changes taking place from the effects of Pluto. The planet Vulcan rules Virgo and is aligned to amethyst, moonstone, sapphire, and star sapphire. Some would find taking moonstone in this combination to be too powerful."

Q Briefly speak about the properties of Vulcan?

"Vulcan is near the orbit of Mercury. Its existence has already been verified through its infrared visibility. It now exists on the physical plane. It is an easy symbol to remember because it acts largely on the unconscious. It especially works to bring to the surface aspects that are hidden within the individual. There are differences between Vulcan and the Moon. Vulcan relates to issues that are long-standing within the individual. When spiritualization of one's consciousness takes place so there is increased understanding, Vulcan enhances a connection to superconsciousness. It stimulates access to information and sources of knowing beyond the usual methods with which one might be acquainted.

"The moon primarily governs those aspects of the personality which motivate you in your current incarnation. These forces are often stored in the unconscious so that there can sometimes be confusion in tapping them. However, the forces associated with Vulcan relate to past life teachings, with messages and lessons from the soul. Because the Moon and Vulcan are both associated with the unconscious, there can be a mixing of their influences. The astrological symbols associated with the Moon and Vulcan help separate these forces."

Q Why is Chiron not included in this system, since you included it elsewhere in this manuscript when describing the mandala system? With the mandala pattern you also said to use Chiron instead of Vulcan.

"We do not recommend that Chiron be employed here because the mandala system involves an entirely different set of precepts. And there is no ephemeris for Vulcan, so it would be difficult to include it in the mandala system."

Q Except in three instances, the gemstones associated with different zodiac signs are exactly the same when the planet's rulership over zodiac signs are presented in attunement with specific gemstones. I refer to the relationship of May and Gemini to malachite, October and Scorpio to red coral, and November and Sagittarius to topaz. In these three instances, could these gemstones also be used in conjunction with the planet's rulership over the the zodiac sign?
"Yes, some may want to add these stones for increased alignment."

Q When some planets have a joint rulership, do the listed gemstones apply to both zodiac signs?
"No, unless these are specifically listed as such.
"When more than one gemstone is given in noting the planets that rule various zodiac signs, it is usually best to take these gem elixirs combined together, especially when the individual is involved in spiritual practices. However, certain people may find the effects too powerful, so some should take only one of the indicated gemstones. When gem elixirs are taken in conjunction with astrological configurations, greater care should be exercised, because there is a slightly greater chance of an aggravation or healing crisis."

The implication of this information is remarkable because each month, planet, and zodiac sign offers an opportunity, through the use of meditation and the appropriate gemstones, not only to provide enhanced balance and understanding of higher spiritual principles but also to foster greater physical and mental health. Thus, after a complete annual cycle, all aspects of the individual will have been activated to their highest potential at the time.

The specific birthstones and gemstones listed in this section for greater attunement to various planets and zodiac signs have been presented because these stones offer the best opportunity for increased alignment to the stellar bodies for most people today. However, those interested in examining other stones suggested in past cultures for use in conjunction with astrology should examine *The Curious Lore of Precious Stones* by Kunz.[8]

We are citizens of the cosmos and are constantly influenced by the vibrations of numerous planets and stars. Understanding astrology is one way to better appreciate how our lives are affected by these stellar bodies. Some may want to use the gem elixir meteorite or the flower essence shooting star to sensitize themselves to better understand this connection.

1 Corinne Heline, *The Twelve Labors of Hercules* (L.A: New Age Press,1974).
2 Ann Ree Colton and Jonathan Murro, *Galaxy Gate II: The Angel Kingdom* (Glendale,Ca: Ann Ree Colton Foundation, 1984),p.29-30, 287-292.
Alice Bailey, *The Consciousness of the Atom* (N.Y: Lucis Publishing Co.,1974), p.155-157.
Wm. Eisen, *The English Cabalah,* Vol. I (Marina del Rey,Ca: DeVorss and Co.,1980),p430-434.
Robert Temple, *The Sirius Mystery* (London: Future Publications Ltd.,1976).
3 Alice Bailey, *Esoteric Psychology,* Vol. I (N.Y: Lucis Publishing Co., 1979), p.245-246.
_____,*Esoteric Psychology,* Vol. II (N.Y: Lucis Publishing Co.,1975), p.721.

4 George Kunz, *Natal Stones* (N.Y: Tiffany and Co., 1909).

5 Cyril Fagan, *Astrological Origins* (St Paul,Mn: Llewellyn Publications, 1971).
_____ and Roy Firebrace, *A Primer of Sidereal Astrology* (Isabella,Mo: Little John Publishing Co., n.d.).

6 Vivian Robson, *Fixed Stars and Constellations In Astrology* (Wellingborough, Northamptonshire,England: The Aquarian Press, 1979).

7 Alice Bailey, *Esoteric Astrology* (N.Y: Lucis Publishing Co.,1979).
Max Heindel, *The Message of the Stars* (Oceanside,Ca: Rosicrucian Fellowship, 1980).

8 George Kunz, *The Curious Lore of Precious Stones* (N.Y: Dover Publications, 1971), p.307-337.

GEMSTONES AND THEIR EQUIVALENT ASTROLOGICAL RELATIONSHIPS

PLANET	SIGN IT RULES	ASSOCIATED GEMSTONES
Sun	Leo	Emerald, red onyx, ruby
Moon	Cancer	Moonstone, light pearl, green tourmaline
Earth	Capricorn	Tiger's eye
Earth	Taurus	Tiger's eye
Earth	Virgo	Tiger's eye
Mercury	Virgo	Moonstone, sapphire, star sapphire
Mercury	Gemini	Alexandrite and aquamarine
Venus	Libra	Light or cherry opal, lapis lazuli, tourmaline
Venus	Taurus	Lapis lazuli, sapphire, tourmaline
Mars	Aries	Agate(carnelian), bloodstone, white diamond
Mars	Scorpio	Agate(carnelian), ruby, topaz
Jupiter	Sagittarius	Amethyst and malachite
Saturn	Capricorn	Jet, black onyx, white onyx
Uranus	Aquarius	Rhodolite or spessartine garnet, blue sapphire
Neptune	Pisces	Jade, tourmaline, turquoise
Pluto	Scorpio	Agate(carnelian), ruby, topaz
Vulcan	Virgo	Amethyst, moonstone, sapphire, star sapphire

GEM ELIXIR COMBINATIONS

A Carbon steel, chromium, copper, gold, magnesium, manganese, molybdenum, palladium, platinum, silver, tin, zinc

B Amethyst, aquamarine, bloodstone, diamond, garnet (rhodolite), herkimer diamond, jade, light pearl, ruby, light blue sapphire, topaz, and ulexite

C Agate-picture, coral, emerald, garnet(spessartine), yellow jasper, lapis lazuli, moonstone, dark opal, light opal, clear quartz, star sapphire, turquoise

D Red coral, diamond, garnet(rhodolite), jade, jet, lapis lazuli, malachite, light opal, light pearl, ruby, sapphire, topaz

E Amethyst, aquamarine, bloodstone, diamond, emerald, garnet(spessartine), red jasper, moonstone, light opal, light pearl, ruby, topaz

F Moonstone and sapphire

G Aquamarine and red coral

H Bloodstone and jet

I Amethyst and jade

J White diamond and red jasper

K White diamond and lapis lazuli

L Emerald and malachite

34

CHAPTER IV

USE OF GEM ELIXIRS TO ENHANCE
SPIRITUAL AND PSYCHIC ABILITIES

Gemstones have long been used to stimulate psychic abilities and to enhance spiritual growth. The use of minerals in the Israeli breastplate as spoken of in the Bible perhaps best exemplifies this custom.[1] The choicest gems have traditionally been used to embellish temples, churches, and other sacred places. Religious symbols have often been carved onto minerals. Various religions have consistently included gemstones in describing the heavenly abodes. The gemstones listed in the New Jerusalem from the Book of Revelations expresses this custom.[2] Many different minerals open one to the spiritual realms. There is also some fascinating material in the Steiner teachings on our spiritual connection with the mineral kingdom.[3]

Q Will you now review the general principles involved in meditating while using gem elixirs and any type of gem therapy?

"It is wise for individuals to understand that whenever vibrational remedies are used, they are greatly enhanced through meditation, especially when combined with creative visualization. These practices may double the effectiveness of gem therapies. Meditation, when incorporated as a procedure, stimulates and aligns the mind, body, and spirit, not just allowing the elixirs to do this. It then becomes a conscious act. This incorporates the individual more fully into the healing process, therefore removing many of the existing tensions. This in general allows for a quickening of the pace and effectiveness of vibrational remedies. By calming and stilling the mind and by allowing the integration and intervention of the spirit, this increases the ability of the individual to practice creative visualization. This also advances the concept to wherein creative visualization becomes well documented in thy society. This also creates more confidence within the self to use vibrational remedies. Of course all these properties work independently of each other, but conscious work in these areas advances the individual to wherein all the properties of meditation and vibrational remedies function as a single unit.

"As for specific strategies in using various spiritual practices with gemstones, many of the techniques previously offered with flower essences are equally applicable with gem elixirs. Mantras, chanting, and creative visualization often stimulate specific areas within the body physical. Visualization of the stone's color can be a critical enhancement of meditating with a stone to activate its primary principles within the self. The mantras that correspond with individual stones could be as deciphered by associating the stone with its astrological properties and their corresponding notes or pitches.

"All gemstones may be used as focuses of meditation for amplifying their abilities to stimulate healing within the body physical. The primary beneficial result of isolating the healing properties of specific gemstones is that this allows individuals to have knowledge of themselves as fully integrated beings in mind, body, and spirit. To understand these capacities within the self amplifies the individual's ability to eventually experience all healing within the self, for this is not based upon systems of magic. Magic is only that which is unknown to man and seems to be as beyond the concepts of conscious knowledge.

"One suggested technique using gemstones with meditation involves the following: put a gemstone in front of you in a device such as a copper pyramid. Then sit in a chair or in the lotus position in front of the gemstone and concentrate on attuning to its thought amplification abilities. To enhance its properties further, place the gem on a spinning device.[4] This creates an electromagnetic field. To bring the properties of the gemstone into a particular part of your body or to send them to another person, mentally picture the mineral's properties traveling to that area. It is also wise to face north when meditating with gemstones. This aligns individuals with the earth's natural magnetic forces."

Q Previously, you stated that many minerals have information stored in them by people in past civilizations. Explain how you can tell exactly what information is stored in different minerals and how to retrieve that information?

"The primary suggested meditation to retrieve information stored in minerals is to learn which chakra each stone corresponds to. Then meditate upon the stone, perhaps in the presence of quartz. This sensitizes the individual to the forces of the stone and its properties. This practice balances the stone to interplay with the forces of the chakras. Isolating certain musical properties in association with each of the specific chakras brings about balance to such a degree that individuals can experience complete resonance with the stone. Pitches for activating the stone could as come through manipulation of the vocal chord for the specific pitch and quality of that stone. Intone each octave vocally with the OM that corresponds to each stone according to its chakric implications. For instance, in the lower part of the eight-note scale we find the lower notes. Thus, the lower pitch of OM is associated with Aries, and we find the application of diamond. By starting at Aries, which is the first sign in the zodiac, you are also starting with the deeper pitches of OM. Each sign has a specific pitch associated with it. The further up the musical scale you go, the further you go around the zodiac. Higher pitches activate different minerals, chakras, and astrological signs. This is a simple way to link music with the chakras, gemstones, and astrological signs. Individuals can also use mandala patterns to retrieve information from gemstones."

Q Is there any further information to add regarding how the breastplate mentioned in the Bible was and can be used for healing and spiritual growth?

"The stones in the breastplate have an alignment with the body of information we have presented with the birthstones and the twelve celestial or zodiacal stones. The breastplate is aligned with and attuned to the individual's forces to have a clearer communication with the higher celestial forces, which were considered agencies or representatives of the natural forces extending from God.

"In a manner given through the Mosaic laws, the priest wore the breastplate to enter communion with God and the holy of holies. This is not unlike the new covenant and body of knowledge as given in the Book of Revelations, where individuals can use gemstones to be as in harmony with the natural forces and orders, which are God's representatives. This is not necessarily to experience a total revelation of God, but to better understand the nature of God."

Q How should one work with various gemstones to increase this communion?

"Gemstones symbolize the crystallized aspects found in nature. People should use certain gem elixirs and then, in a meditative state, see that which transpires within themselves in their communion with the isolated vibration or natural force in nature that each stone manifests."

Q Is there a specific process for selecting the different stones?

"Initially, select one stone that is most aligned with the natural element of the individual's birth chart. Isolate the stone's properties through meditation or from the various bodies of knowledge available elsewhere, such as in this text. One suggested technique is to start with the gemstone which most closely resembles the person's sun sign, as would be revealed through astrological charts. Then proceed from that point around the rest of the zodiac. Use one stone each month and change it each month as you proceed through the zodiac. To be even more accurate, you could isolate the degree throughout the course of the year when there is the shift. For instance, if your sun sign is located at four degrees Taurus, isolate the date when the sun enters four degrees Gemini. At that exact point, you would stop using the gemstone or gem elixir in conjunction with Taurus and shift to the stone used with Gemini. Some could start with the stone associated with the first house, but the birthstone is best for most. After going through the zodiac in this fashion, some might want to pick several gemstones in which there was a special attunement and take them as a combination for a while."

Q Explain how to use gemstones to develop one's psychic abilities?

"Forms of psychic phenomena are but extensions of recall of what the soul already knows. In this sense, alignment of the gemstones to the chakras has as a byproduct clairvoyant insight. Then, concentrating on gemstones that stimulate the mental body stimulates various psychic accords such as clairvoyance and psychometry. By drawing this information into the mental body or into the intellectual process, it then becomes a genuine psychic experience. This gives one the ability of analysis in correlating the memories that are disassociated from the normal waking, functioning state but are as memories extended outside the self when drawn upon from the universal mind. Meditation and creative visualization with gemstones also stimulate psychic capacities."

Q Will you speak about gemstones representing different nations? You said this also referred to the prophecies of nations.

"First, it is necessary to identify correctly the point of the nation's creation. This could be researched by considering the astrological configurations of individual nations. These configurations present much knowledge about each nation. Nations are also represented by individual gemstones and metals. These may be detailed by learning which minerals are mined and supplied by various nations. These forces could be incorporated into the mandalic principles, spoken of elsewhere, to stimulate specific vibrations for those particular people. Or, a mandala pattern may be created for individuals responsible for the guidance of specific nations. All these may be as inclusive in making the mosaic of future activities for individuals and nations."

Q Does each nation tend to be represented by one or several gems?
"Nations are represented by several gems."

Q How do these principles relate to the prophecy of nations?
"These relate to the prophecies of nations based on principles of behavioral patterns described in the elements of geometrical forms, geological structures, and various underlying cities. For instance, previously it was noted that huge quartz deposits exist under Boulder, Colorado. It is simple to observe behavioral patterns that are generated by psychological knowledge of the existence of minerals and metals beneath a particular location. This generates immediate social dynamics based on economic, social, and psychological forces. There are also ethereal forces from geological structures and gemstone deposits beneath various locations. Therefore, these things affect the behavioral patterns of surrounding citizens and the resulting social forces. Since these are the sources of prophecy and consciousness, this in turn affects the destiny and future portent of nations. If there can be the isolation of underlying geological patterns, these can be incorporated into the principles of the mandalas. This becomes a source for the potential understanding of behavioral patterns and a foundation for perceiving future events in various nations."

Q Please review the historical use of gemstones in predicting the future and the principles involved in doing this?
"Quartz has been the central element in the use of minerals to predict the future. Quartz is a powerful point of focus and amplification in all forms of meditation. These principles of amplification are for thought amplification and for projection into the future and then the cyclical return of the individual to the present through penetration of the space-time flow factor. This information is presented partly to provide teachings for those who desire to develop their prognostic ability.
"Quartz crystal has been used throughout all cultures including Atlantis, Lemuria, Egypt, Europe, Asia, and native American societies, all in the context of prognostication, mostly through the force of thought-form amplication and specific thought-form meditation upon specific time flow frequencies. Quartz stimulates the ability to penetrate thought forms beyond the normal time flow in an orderly fashion to retrieve certain information. For instance, prognostication is to amplify the thought process beyond the speed of light but still maintain the personalized magnetic imprint of one's own electromagnetic field. When there is penetration beyond the speed of light, there is an empathetic frequency with the time flow meditated upon, be it in months, years, or centuries. The amplitude of that empathetic vibration acts as a scan and then actually integrates with the life force and the current reigning consciousness in that time period. But since this happens faster than the speed of light, it then returns cyclically, traveling through time periods that would be considered as the past, and consciousness is refocused in the current context of one's own personal time flow. This brings forth balance and objectivity within individuals."

Q What other minerals were historically used to develop psychic abilities?
"The stones used in the breastplate of Israel and the priesthood amplify prognostic abilities. The gemstones mentioned in the Book of Revelations are as a key to certain aspects of a self-actualized personality as would be found in the New Jerusalem. There are many other stones used in this accord. It is the desire of the channel speaking to

focus on the potentials of this technology, rather than upon known history. In Lemuria they actually created a model of what a specific time period might become like to influence the future."

Q Please discuss this technology?
"This technology was used not only in Lemuria but also in Atlantis, India, and Babylonia, by the Aztecs, Toltecs, Olnecs, Incans, Mayans, and amongst the Zoroastrians. There is today much archeological confirmation that these societies had much interest and knowledge of astronomy. The Mayans were especially adept in this technology.[5]

"First, construction is based upon mandalic patterns not unlike the zodiac signs. Individuals should initially draw a circle marking off the different degrees for the zodiac. It looks somewhat like a horoscope. With mathematical calculations you create a future time-space continuum using planetary positions to make a mandala of gemstones and metals.

"Specific metallic structures are used to represent each sign in the zodiac. Each zodiac sign represents thirty degrees. The sign Aries has a special affinity to iron or carbon steel, Taurus to copper, Gemini to molybdenum, Cancer to silver, Leo to gold, Virgo to magnesium, Libra to palladium, Scorpio to manganese, Sagittarius to tin, Capricorn to zinc, Aquarius to chromium, and Pisces to platinum. The metals used need to be at least 95 percent pure. You end up with twelve brackets for the twelve signs.

"Then each planet and house are represented by a specific gem substance. The first house is represented by coral. A combination of several different colored corals is best, although red coral is most superior if only one colored coral is used. The second house is representated by lapis lazuli, the third house by picture agate, the fourth house by moonstone, and the fifth house by yellow jasper. The sixth house is associated with star sapphire, the seventh house with emerald, the eighth house with dark opal, the ninth house with turquoise, the tenth house with clear quartz, the eleventh house with garnet spessartine, and the twelfth house by light opal.

"For the gemstones that represent the planets in this system, the Sun is represented by ruby, which is an important karmic indicator that affects people in many ways. The Moon is represented by light pearl, Mercury by aquamarine, Venus by light blue sapphire, Mars by bloodstone, and Vesta by topaz. Vesta is an asteroid that is considered to be a planet in this mandala system. Jupiter is represented by amethyst, Saturn by garnet rhodolite, and Chiron by white diamond. Many astrologers are aware of this fairly large asteroid. It has an eccentric orbit about the sun. This asteroid, considered to be a planet in this mandala system, will be increasingly recognized as an important symbol in the future. Uranus is represented by ulexite, Neptune by jade, and Pluto by herkimer diamond. The earth could be used in an alternative system, but this would be a system largely heliocentric in nature, and the Sun would then disappear as an important planet.

"Each sign is represented by a metal and each planet and house is represented by a gem for a total of thirty-six distinct symbols. Where possible the gems and metals should be self-contained, not looking like pieces of another stone. It is also best that the stones each be approximately the same size."

Q How does Vesta influence us?

"The asteroid belt, where Vesta is located, partly indicates how you are influenced by this asteroid. It is the leading reminder and remnant of Maldec, the destroyed plant that has become the asteroid belt. Vesta was the core of that planet, so it now expresses the spiritual significance of that civilization. It draws together both sides of a person that are normally out of reach of one another. We refer here to the unconscious and the influence of the higher spiritual realms. Angels often work on both levels simultaneously. Vesta also overshadows the learning process on both these levels. The other aspect of Vesta will eventually be revealed to mankind, as there is the gradual uniting of the will and spirit that was not accomplished on Maldec. These factors bring into a more physical and tangible form forces from the highest spiritual realms and the deepest unconscious."

Q How does Chiron affect us?

"It is associated with Christ consciousness, as it manifests in the human form, and with various spiritual activities in which people may be involved. It affects the endocrine system and the blood chemistry in a manner that enables the kundalini to move through the body from the root chakra to the crown chakra and beyond. However, this is not the normal balance of the endocrine system. Chiron governs the process of biochemistry that is associated with enlightenment. The etheric heart is also balanced because of the uniting of Christ consciousness with these energies. It is a matter of learning to love your enemies. Chiron also governs, on an esoteric level, the hands and the ability to develop therapeutic touch."

Q If someone feels very drawn to use other minerals or metals to represent a sign, planet, or house, would it be wise to use the other stone?

"Yes, within certain limits. Especially in the natal or birth chart, there is a great deal of flexibility and misunderstanding regarding what is called the ascendant or rising sign. Astrologers usually assign the ascendant to when the first breath was taken, but this does not always fit the character of the person. Thus, with some people, there is a need for the soul's entry time to be adjusted up to two hours before or after the first breath to more accurately assess the rising sign. This could mean that an entirely different sign is used as the ascendant. For instance, if the chart is cast two hours before or after the first breath, the house cusps will be different and the planets will most likely fall into different houses. When an ascendant is adjusted for a sign, before or after the sign of the physical birth, each of the remaining house cusps will also show a shift forward or backward in sign. For example, a Capricorn rising would have Aquarius on the second house cusp, working all the way around in normal sequence to Sagittarius behind it on the cusp of the twelfth house. If the ascendant is adjusted to Aquarius, Pisces will now rule the cusp of the second house, Capricorn will move back to the cusp of the twelfth house, and all the other signs will fall in place accordingly. This is discussed in *Astrology Plus* by Hilarion.[6] But there is less flexibility or impact in this regard concerning the relationship to the more fixed points within the zodiac, particularly the relationship of the Sun and Moon and the slower moving planets such as Jupiter and Saturn. However, there will be exceptions, and if someone feels especially drawn to use another stone, we suggest that they meditate on it for seven days before making the replacement. In addition, some may be drawn to use certain flower essences instead of gem elixirs."

Q How can astrologers tell when to adjust the actual birth time?

"It would be fairly simple to use a divining tool like a pendulum to ask for each person. There are many individuals whose actual birth time or first breath time does not correspond to the soul entry time. However, only in a few rare cases will this make a significant difference, with the ascendant being assigned to a different sign. This is very obvious because of the way the ascendant is calculated. The various intervals that are used to determine the ascendant are what make the difference. For instance, if an individual's birth time falls on a cusp, it is quite possible that there will be a change in the rising sign. The ascendant, if it is erected correctly, can make quite a difference in understanding a person's life."

Q Can you make a general statement as to why the birth time would be moved up or back?

"It is an interesting matter. Sometimes you will note that individuals need to learn of the birth process. They need to know it deeply. Such a need is likely to mean that the soul's commitment to the birth time is moved forward. There are other souls who, perhaps by their sensitivity or need not to attune too closely to their parents, especially to their mothers, would choose to make an entry time after the actual birth. This will usually only be seen and understood by the person later in life.

"There are some people who have no interest in how astrology affects their lives. These people are the ones most likely to pick an entirely different time for their soul entry as distinct from the first breath. There are others who have a great deal to learn from this because their outward personality, as reflected by the ascendant, does not fit. If the correct ascendant is assigned, such souls will learn more about themselves. Sometimes, when the soul entry time is adjusted, the new time affects some aspect of the chart where the spirit is called in. Primarily, this will only affect the ascendant because that is what moves the most rapidly.

"To return to the mandala construction, a quartz sheet is placed over the top of the mandala for amplification and visualization of the design through the mandala pattern. The quartz also amplifies the auric properties which have an affinity to the specific time period that is being attuned to, according to each angle or planetary aspect. The quartz sheet should be about six feet across and at least a quarter-inch thick. The bottom of the mandala should be made of a material that is in harmony with each person. Generally, use copper, silver, or gold. A thin sheet of copper is probably the most practical. Some people could use rice paper that does not contain any chemicals. Certain calligraphers could obtain such paper, especially from Japan. The thicknesses of the bottom of the mandala and of the quartz sheet are not an important issue. Jewelers can construct these mandalas small enough so that they can be worn as a pendant. When that is done, the mandala and quartz sheet should be three inches across. The quartz sheet should be as thick as one millimeter or so. It is also wise to have a layer of a silica-based substance, such as crushed quartz, sand, or even glass, placed just above the thin metal sheet on the bottom of the mandala. Use silica glue to bind the crushed material to the bottom of the mandala. However, it is best to use water-based silica glue, not the type that contains acetone or acetic acid. Residues of these chemicals may remain in the silicon, which could be harmful to the user. The crushed material provides some insulation and amplification. This can be done in a fashion similar to the sand paintings of the Navaho, Hopi, and Pueblo Indians."

Q If people find the quartz sheet too expensive, would it be wise to place quartz crystal clusters about the mandala?

"No, this would not sufficiently amplify the properties of the gemstones and metals. Instead, purchase small quartz crystal sheets and glue them together with silica glue and tighten the bond by using quartz tubing. Small quartz sheets or lenses would not be too expensive.

"It is also possible to use a quartz sheet that is smaller than the mandala. However, the quartz sheet should be at least half the diameter of the mandala for the quartz to sufficiently amplify the properties of the gems and metals in the mandala. For instance, if the diameter of the mandala is twenty-four inches, obtain a quartz sheet that is twelve inches in diameter and place it over the center of the mandala. It would also be wise to add a few drops of gem and metal elixirs, even if the physical stones are on the mandala. Allow the elixirs to dry. This further enhances the amplification properties of the quartz sheet, but the elixirs added to the mandala should only be placed on the area of the mandala that is covered by the quartz sheet. When using a quartz sheet that is smaller than the mandala, placing the sheet away from the mandala further amplifies the properties of the quartz. People can experiment to decide how far the quartz sheet should be placed above the mandala. Initially, start by placing the quartz sheet above the mandala at one-half the diameter of the mandala. To illustrate, if the mandala diameter is twelve inches, place the quartz sheet six inches away from the mandala.

"The twelve metals that represent the twelve zodiac signs could also be crushed and spread out over each thirty degree section of the zodiac. However, do not mix the crushed silica with each metal. Or a metallic foil could be used for each bracket to create a more attractive and pure appearance. Crushed metal along with metallic foil could also be used. People can choose what is most practical. It is not too difficult to crush these metals, but magnesium could catch fire when crushed, so that metal should be purchased already crushed. Thus, you have at the bottom a copper, silver, or gold sheet, then the crushed silica material, then possibly metallic foil or crushed metal in each bracket, although most will not use the metallic foil. Next, use a mandala pattern divided into twelve brackets to show the houses, and then spread out the twenty-four gems for the houses and planets with the quartz sheet above that. If metallic foil or crushed metal are not used, add the twelve metals to the mandala. It is not necessary to add the metallic foil or crushed metal as well as the individual metals to this system."

Q Is it best to use only physical gems and metals in constructing this mandala or can gem elixirs be used?

"We have been considering this question for the last thousand years or so. There are some aspects of this that are important to recognize. The colors of the metals are an important factor here, as are the colors, shapes, and textures of the gemstones used. If the mandala is constructed with crushed metals, then gem elixirs could be used to represent the gemstones. However, of the three levels in this system, the substances used for each level must be the actual stones or elixirs. For instance, the stones that represent the houses must all be elixirs or physical stones.

"There is some benefit to a mandala system that is made entirely of elixirs because they are less expensive and easier to work with. The difficulty is that the high presence of water or intervening substances that are chosen to stand for the gems and metals would not convey sufficient meditative qualities to the person working with the mandala. Therefore, as a minimum, it is best that at least one of the three levels be represented by the actual stones. This would be sufficient. People can use only stones on which ever level they feel attuned to.

"If gem elixirs are used, they must be in small glass or quartz vials or tubes, perhaps dish-shaped, small enough to hold just a few drops of the elixir. The vibration of that which contains the gem elixir will influence how the gem elixir works in the mandala. Thus, the gem elixir should not be contained in anything synthetic. The top of the vial or tube should also be made of glass or quartz. If this is too hard to obtain, it would be wise to obtain two different small glass or quartz tubes. Put the gem elixir into one of the vials or tubes, and place it into the other. Seal the connection with silica glue and then apply heat to close the outer two ends of the vial or tubing. It may be possible to obtain glass or quartz that is only open on one end. Although it would not be wise to use a vial with a synthetic closure, if this is done, glue the side of the vial onto the mandala with silica glue.

"An alternative technique would be to use paper that is a color that matches the color of a metal after it is crushed or after it is filed from a larger piece of metal. The colored paper that matches the color of the metal can be used to replace the metal. Then place a number of drops from the metal elixir on each paper. For instance, the colored paper that represents gold should receive some drops of the gold elixir. The number of drops to place on each piece of paper will vary, depending on the size of the mandala.

"If one is wearing a small mandala on one's wrist, it is always preferable to wear the actual stones. Small bottles of gem elixirs would be impractical. As a possible substitute, paper which had gem elixirs placed on it that was allowed to evaporate could be substituted for up to two of the three levels. But at least one level must contain the actual stones. Of course, rice paper which has little or no added chemical is the best paper to use."

Laboratory supply houses have easy access to crushed quartz at an inexpensive price. Sand is, of course, available in many areas. Sheets of copper, silver, or gold are readily available from many industrial sources. Numerous rock shops have hundreds of minerals for sale. The metals can be obtained from jewelry suppliers as well as from laboratory supply houses. People can check the yellow pages in their local phone book for these items. Several helpful addresses have been provided at the end of this chapter.

"Generally, the planets closest to the earth should be closer to the center of the mandala. These planets have a more direct effect on people. The planets further away from the earth should be further from the center of the mandala. These planets have a more spiritual effect on people. These principles are understood in astrology.

"Adjustment of aspects in the chart or mandala using an ephemeris enables individuals to project to an exact point, from a few months to many hundreds of years into the future. In many respects, this duplicates the mass and time-space continuum of that particular state in the past or future. This mandala can be used by nations and large cohesive groups, as well as just for individuals."

As an example of this technology, if one adjusted the gemstones for France's mandala to attune to the Saturn-Uranus conjunction in Libra in 1805, one could perceive that nation being under the influence of someone like Napoleon. This same planetary pair conjuncts in the sign of Sagittarius in 1988. According to Dane Rudhyar, this suggests a period of religious and social upheaval.[7] Adjusting the mandala gemstones to attune to such configurations allows one to experience their energy patterns, to understand and perhaps change future events.

"Thus, not only can this mandala pattern be used for prognostication, to see into the past and future, it can also be used to create unique mandala patterns for individuals to stimulate healing. Appropriate gemstones can be placed at positions in the zodiac mandala that represent future planetary aspects or transits to the natal chart. The gems are then enhanced by the quartz sheet to stimulate healing. The mandala prepares the individual's consciousness for difficult healing crises developing in the future. For instance, if Saturn was approaching a square to your natal Mars, attune to the lessons relevant to that pattern to understand it before the event happens. Then it is often possible for that period to be experienced with much less difficulty. One could also arrange the aspects of the mandala so that, rather than Saturn approaching a square to Mars gradually, the mandala would be constructed to create an exact square between Mars and Saturn. By meditating on this pattern you would speed up the healing crisis by attuning to the positive aspects of Mars and Saturn. Certain natural remedies could then be taken to release the imbalanced pattern. This also enables individuals to perceive the karmic aspects of a disease. Saturn square Mars would usually indicate a blockage of one's self-expression or desires, possibly creating rage and anger. Gem elixirs, flower essences, or homeopathic remedies could be taken to promote a release of this negativity to adapt more harmoniously to the situation."

Q When this mandala is used to see into the past or future, or for physical or spiritual enhancement, is it arranged differently?

"Until people become used to working with this mandala system, it is generally best to work with the natal mandala. If someone is facing a difficult crisis, an astrologer may recognize that there is an attunement to a particular transit. Then it might be wise to construct a transit mandala.

"In each case, the mandala should be arranged in a pattern so that the planets, houses, and signs represent the actual transiting influences and stimulate the individual's consciousness accordingly. In the future, some astrologers may want to construct solar return chart mandalas, as well.

"But generally, it is best to leave the chart or mandala as it is and to meditate on the difficult lessons that may exist in the future, to experience an inner understanding and clarification. There is much to be learned by leaving the gems and metals in their actual future positions.

"As an example let us say that at a period two thousand years ago, you want to learn what the world would be experiencing on July 28, 1951. To do this, you would set the gemstone representing Pluto at approximately nineteen degrees of Leo. The gem representing the Sun would be placed at four degrees of Leo. This pattern would continue throughout the mandala. Thus each gem and metal would be placed at the approximate degree that they would fall upon that day.

"There are exceptions to the general pattern of not moving the stones on the mandala. If individuals feel a particular attunement with one specific sign, planet, or stone, than the mandala can be adjusted to enhance the healing and learning process. For instance, Jupiter may not be part of a learning process in a future difficult aspect, but an individual who feels a deep affinity with Jupiter could temporarily bring the influence of that planet into an area of the chart where there is a block and a lesson to learn. It is not only that the gem representing Jupiter is aiding the cleansing; the person is also using an astrological body to which he feels attuned, to resolve the problem faster. After a while, when the person has meditated on the problem and certain realizations develop, the stone representing Jupiter can be put back into its original place on the mandala.

"The aspects can also be used as an expression of correction. For instance, if someone had a Leo Sun in a ninety degree or square aspect to a Scorpio Moon, you could place the appropriate stones in a more harmonious aspect than the square. A ruby would be placed at the degree of Leo to represent the Sun, and a light pearl would be placed at a 120 degree or trine position, in Aries or Sagittarius, to represent the Moon. Or a pearl could be placed in any favorable aspect to the ruby. For instance, pearl could be moved to another position in the chart so that it was trine to the exact degree in Aries, or preferably Sagittarius. The individual would then have an appropriate alignment to meditate on the configuration to improve the outcome. Students of astrology can easily spot potential problems and adjust the aspects to improve the outcome of future events."

Q How many years would each aspect adjustment represent in the chart?

"This is highly variable, but often the chart should be worked with for a one-year cycle. The one-year cycle always relates to the solar or sun return. That signifies a significant change as the person's karma is allowed to move gradually in its own cycles. Being aligned with the solar return greatly benefits most people. This same principle can be applied with the transits of all the planets through the houses. There will be some difficulty as the planets make their progression through what is called the gem cusp, by which an individual will be making an important transition with some of the slow-moving planets. With Neptune, possibly Uranus, and certainly with Pluto, the person will feel certain changes extending over quite a period of time. They may even notice a period of nonalignment with some of the gems and metals as the slow changes take place.

"During this time period, which may last as long as a month in the case of Pluto, the individual may feel a need for a temporary alignment with some specific mineral or flower essence. This is to be determined by examining the person's chart to see if any other planets are also making transits at that time. There will then be an indication of what gem elixir or flower essence to give to the individual. This related planetary occurrence may be more familiar and helpful to the user of this system than the slower and more difficult house changes of the outer planets. This is because the outer planets make fewer house changes in one's lifetime, since they move so slowly, while the inner planets move more quickly, giving us many opportunities to experience them. For instance, if Mars is making its transit from the seventh to eighth house at the same time Pluto is moving from perhaps the eleventh to twelfth house, then choose the appropriate stones and place them according to the planets in their precise positions. In addition, to ease the Pluto transition, gem elixirs attuned to Mars, such as bloodstone, could be taken. And in general flower essences can be ingested for better attunement to various astrological movements. The difficulty with this system is that there are few hard and fast rules. The length of time one is influenced by various astrological movements will always vary. But usually, the solar return will reveal a great deal of this information and will be quite sufficient for most individuals as they understand and use this mandala chart."

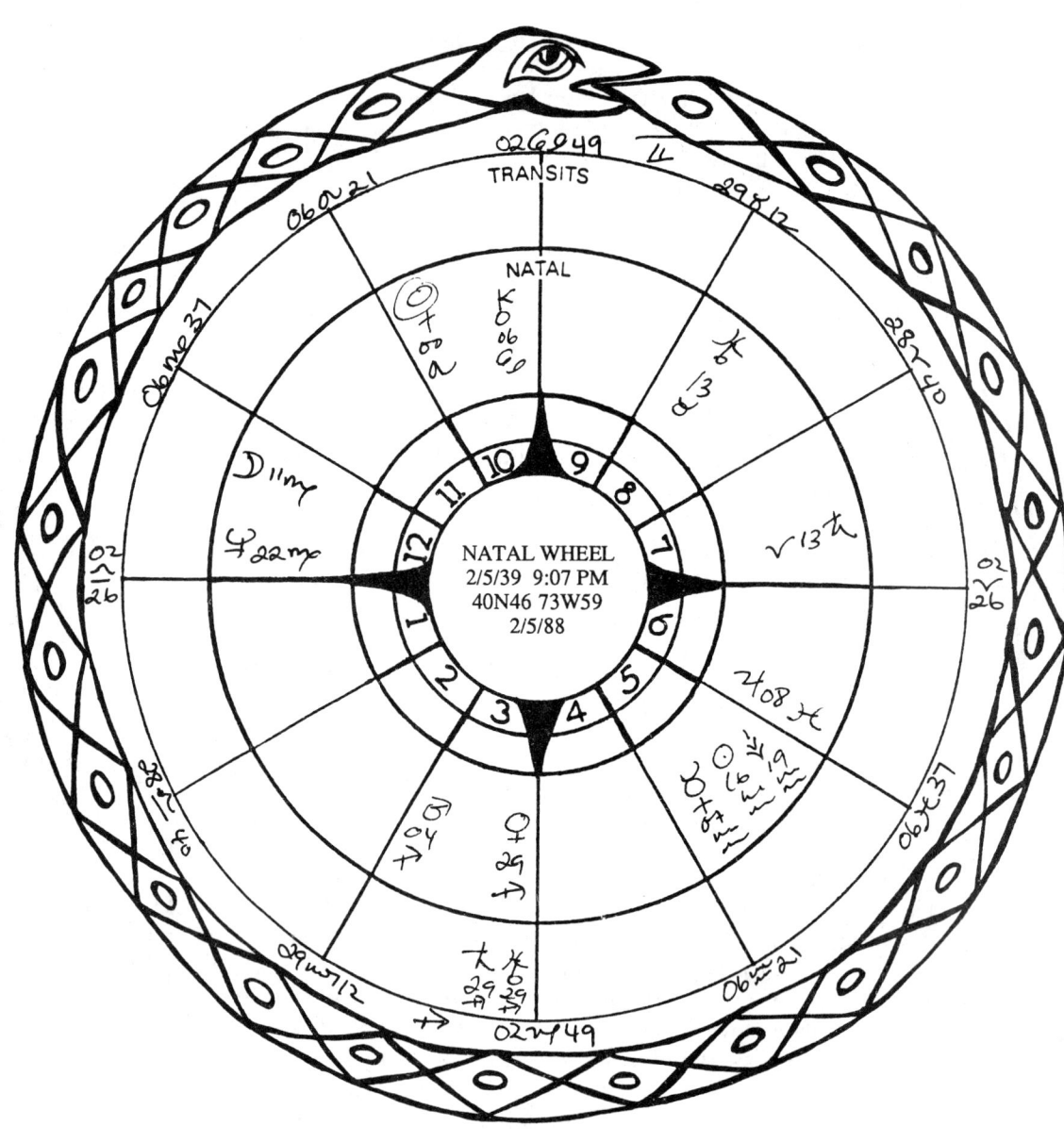

PLANET

⊙	SUN
☽	MOON
☿	MERCURY
♀	VENUS
♂	MARS
⚶	VESTA
♃	JUPITER
♄	SATURN
⚷	CHIRON
♅	URANUS
♆	NEPTUNE
♇	PLUTO

SIGN

♈	ARIES
♉	TAURUS
♊	GEMINI
♋	CANCER
♌	LEO
♍	VIRGO
♎	LIBRA
♏	SCORPIO
♐	SAGITTARIUS
♑	CAPRICORN
♒	AQUARIUS
♓	PISCES

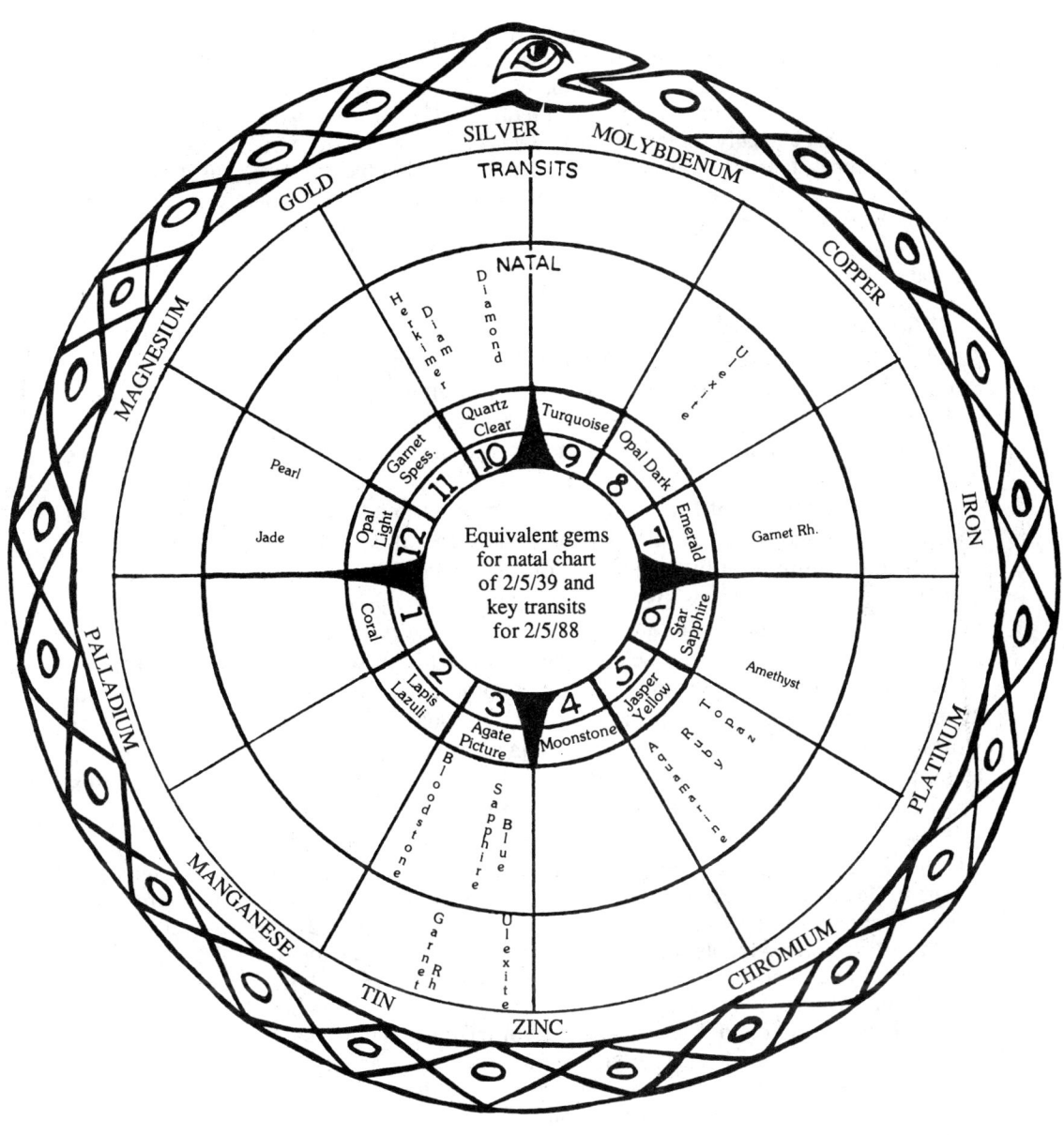

The wheel diagram contains the following labels:

Outer ring (metals): SILVER, MOLYBDENUM, GOLD, COPPER, MAGNESIUM, IRON, PALLADIUM, PLATINUM, MANGANESE, CHROMIUM, TIN, ZINC

TRANSITS
NATAL

Equivalent gems
for natal chart
of 2/5/39 and
key transits
for 2/5/88

Gems: Herkimer Diam, Diamond, Uranite (C-rxe-U), Quartz Clear, Turquoise, Opal Dark, Garnet Spess., Emerald, Pearl, Garnet Rh., Jade, Opal Light, Coral, Star Sapphire, Amethyst, Lapis Lazuli, Agate Picture, Moonstone, Jasper Yellow, Topaz, Sapphire Blue, Bloodstone, Garnet Rh, Ulexite

House numbers: 1 2 3 4 5 6 7 8 9 10 11 12

PLANET		SIGN	
⊙	SUN	♈	ARIES
☽	MOON	♉	TAURUS
☿	MERCURY	♊	GEMINI
♀	VENUS	♋	CANCER
♂	MARS	♌	LEO
⚶	VESTA	♍	VIRGO
♃	JUPITER	♎	LIBRA
♄	SATURN	♏	SCORPIO
⚷	CHIRON	♐	SAGITTARIUS
♅	URANUS	♑	CAPRICORN
♆	NEPTUNE	♒	AQUARIUS
♇	PLUTO	♓	PISCES

ASPECTS

	⊙	☽	☿	♀	♂	♃	♄	♅	♆	♇	ASC	MC	
⊙													⊙
	☽												☽
		☿											☿
			♀										♀
				♂									♂
					♃								♃
						♄							♄
							♅						♅
								♆					♆
									♇				♇
										ASC			ASC
											MC		MC

The solar return refers to the return of the Sun to its position at birth, which usually occurs within a day or two of a person's birthday each year. The Sun moves through each 30 degree zodiac sign every month. Within approximately twenty-four hours on either side of one's birth date, the Sun will return to its exact natal position. A new chart can then be cast annually for that moment. Generally, it will show a new rising sign, and the remaining planets will also take new positions within the zodiac. Thus, the yearly solar return chart will show the evolution of one's essential expression represented by the Sun in relation to the other qualities of one's nature, symbolized by the remaining planets, and will indicate the physical, emotional, and spiritual dynamics of the year ahead.

"With this technology it is also possible for individuals to alter their life patterns by seeing into the future. This mandala does not change the future, it changes the consciousness that creates the future. This mandala design enhances one's consciousness and personality structure and should be used with meditation and other spiritual practices. Individuals should sit and meditate on the aura of the gemstones and metals.

"There are two sets of forces at work here. First, meditating on gemstones set in specific aspects has beneficial impacts on individuals. It is similar to a fighter psyching himself for a future fight by visualizing or meditating upon the fight. If one meditates on the aura of the gemstones, by the time it passes through the quartz screen, it actually then merges into the potential future events of that time period.

"A psychologist helps release problems buried in the subconscious mind from an individual's past. This cleansing, possibly in conjunction with other therapies, changes the present and has a direct impact on the person's potential future. The mandala pattern works in a similar fashion. This mandala is more of an artistic creation than a technology. It is a highly intuitive art form. To work with this mandala requires skills in astrology, mathematics, and spiritual attunement."

In the two charts or mandalas provided here, the inner wheel in figure 1 shows the natal chart for February 5, 1939. The outer wheel shows the transiting position of Saturn and Uranus for February 5, 1988, in relation to the natal chart. Figure 2 shows the translation of the astrological symbols into gemstones and metals. Professional astrologers would often make one mandala just listing the stones in their correct aspects.

With this example, the natal chart shows a 150 degree, or quincunx, relationship of Venus to the planet Pluto. Venus is the ruler of the chart and indicates a strong need for identification with others, peace and harmony, as well as comfort and security. In Sagittarius, sign of the seeker of ultimate understanding and growth, Venus can here eternally seek the ideal mate and never find him. The person may also want to help others by sharing her resources. The home base, family and emotional security, and ones past would also affect personal relations. In opposition to the Midheaven, the person may be so bound to the past and to her obligations to others, that she may struggle to achieve personal goals. The quincunx to Pluto intensifies all this, making the person obsessed with a need for acceptance by others. Thus, the person may be overgenerous, overextend herself, deplete her resources for others, and be easily manipulated. Physically, this conflict could express itself in glandular disorders, particularly of the thyroid and kidneys, and cause lower back problems or diabetes. There is also the potential for liver disorders, hip problems, or sciatica. These problems are associated with a conflict in one's needs in relation to the needs of others.

This person does maintain a financial dependency on her parents and has as yet not been able to actualize her own career goals. She is now in her mid-forties. She feels continually manipulated and abused by others. On one hand, she wants to be generous, while at the same time, resents the fact that she seems to attract others who expect her to share her fortune. She has had glandular imbalances and shows signs of a liver disorder.

On her solar return in 1988, Saturn and Uranus will be forming an exact conjunction to her natal Venus. This highlights the natal conflict with Pluto and provides her with ample challenge and opportunity to restructure and define herself in relation to others and to achieve new-found independence. But she is liable to experience much upheaval in the process. In the first place, her personal resources (Venus) and those shared with others (Pluto), i.e., in banks and institutions, may experience sudden reversals, perhaps as a result of some collective (Uranus) events. This would certainly threaten her security, but ultimately would force her to seek measures to realize her own goals. She may find that she can no longer depend on her relationships with others, either as benefactor or dependent. Either by choice or by being stripped of her resources, she may feel that she has nothing left to give and, for a time, until she creates a new and more genuine structure for her relationships, may feel alienated and depressed. All of the above ailments could certainly be aggravated, with the particular potential for kidney stones due to Saturn's hardening effect.

This person could begin to meet the challenges of this future time period by simply meditating on the dynamics of her natal chart, expressed in a natal mandala set to this time period in 1988, particularly focusing on the gems for Pluto and Venus and the houses that contain them, and on the metals for Sagittarius and Leo. A transit mandala could also be constructed showing the gems for Saturn and Uranus placed in conjunction to Venus and in quincunx to Pluto, within an outer circle surrounding the natal wheel. A third possibility would be to construct a solar return mandala and to use the gems and metals of that chart to meditate on the potentials of the year to come. Relevant remedies could be chosen to assist in this process and to enable her to manifest the highest expression of these planetary dynamics.

"A meditation with this mandala for people familiar with birth charts is to arrange the zodiac signs to correspond to the birth charts so that there are the twelve houses, arranged with the twelve zodiac signs. Thus, they correspond to the astrological chart at birth, and the planets fall in place in their usual order.

"In meditating on the mandala, some may want to start with the birthstone corresponding to their own zodiac chart. Place that stone in the center of the mandala to represent the earth, and meditate on it for one day. This helps one to attune to the entire mandala and gives the mandala a central focus point. Here, with the birthstone, the use of a cut gemstone is preferred, although it is generally best to use uncut stones for the rest of the mandala. After one day, leave that stone in the center of the mandala and move on to the next stone for twenty-eight days, proceeding around the zodiac chart.

"Some people may not feel attuned to their birthstones. Such individuals can, instead of placing the birthstone in the center of the mandala, place tiger's eye in that region. Because of the relationship of tiger's eye to the earth, that stone will also help one attune to the entire mandala, and give the mandala a central focus point.

"There are many other possible ways to meditate on the mandala. One can meditate on both the first house and the Sun sign and proceed outward, meditating on each planet and each successive house. Start with the Sun, Moon, Mercury, Venus, Mars, Vesta, Jupiter, Saturn, Chiron, Uranus, Neptune, and Pluto. If one is only meditating on the houses, start with the first house and proceed up the ladder to the twelfth house. Or proceed through each zodiac bracket in the mandala. If your birth sign is, for instance, Pisces, start meditating on the next zodiac sign, which is Aries. Proceed through the zodiac until you reach the last sign, which is your birth sign. Thus, it may take longer than a year to go around the mandala. While focusing on each sign, house, or planet in the mandala, the entire mandala should also be attuned to. If you are attuning to the mandala when there are several difficult aspects, it will often be best to focus only on one or two areas to first learn the lessons involved before proceeding to other areas of the mandala. Maintain your attunement for the normal transitory time of planets. For instance, when Saturn makes a transit to Jupiter over a two month period, maintain your focus on both planets during that period. Link the periods of meditation to the planets' transition. Then you stimulate your own potential.

"We are not stressing one system over another. Some may want to focus primarily on one part of the mandala, such as on the twelve houses, twelve planets, or twelve constellations. It is possible to meditate on the mandala with the eyes open or closed. Some may want to make the mandala three dimensional by hanging it from a string to have it spin by its own accord to show the front and back of the mandala. The mandala will slowly stop, and the individual will then meditate looking at one area of the mandala. What can develop in this process is a form of hypnosis, because the vibration of the stones and metals fills the environment as the mandala spins. If the mandala is worn, there can be a similar effect.

"Many will experience the powerful energy that is generated by meditating on this mandala. The heart will often open. People may want to focus their energies of love and healing on others. Occasionally, the energy generated will be too strong for some. Personal insights revealed at such times may be submerged in the subconscious. The proximity of the Moon to the earth, in terms of how the Moon rules the subconscious, may be a relevant factor. For instance, if one suddenly feels tension or starts sweating while meditating on the mandala, gaze within and examine the inner Moon, so that the messages which you are experiencing can be revealed. Soon you will appreciate that the characteristics of the planets, houses, and zodiac signs refer to many human traits. This understanding will increase as you deepen your meditation with the mandala.

"When you meditate with this mandala, we strongly suggest that the heliocentric viewpoint not be used, except by those who already understand astrology, because that viewpoint is fairly advanced in the soul's evolution. We recommend proceeding with the geocentric viewpoint. The heliocentric system places the Sun at the center, and the geocentric system places the earth at the center. With the earth in the center, start with the closest planet, which in this system is the Moon. Then proceed outward to the various planets, usually continuing with Venus, Mars, Mercury, Vesta, Sun, Jupiter, Saturn, Chiron, Uranus, Neptune, and Pluto."

Q How would someone cleanse the metals and gemstones used in one mandala before they could be reused in another?

"Place the metals and gems under a pyramid for at least two hours. If the stones have been on a mandala for one year or more, then for each year leave the stones under the pyramid for twenty-four hours. For instance, if a mandala pattern was established for three years, leave the stones under the pyramid for three full days or seventy-two hours. However, be certain that only the stones from one of the three levels are placed under the pyramid at one time. For instance, never place the gems that represent the houses under the pyramid with any gem that represent the planets. And be certain that the stones never touch each other while under the pyramid."

Q Speak on the future development of this technology?

"It is hoped that some individuals will create a large mandala and that they will do so in their house in full form with the actual gems and metals. They may notice a tranformation of the energy within their house. Hopefully, this will be done in a spiritual center, like a meeting hall. The mandala will probably affect the consciousness of many people as they meditate in their own ways, perhaps not even aware that the mandala is in the house or building. What would eventually develop from this is an amplification of energies that gives people new ideas about themselves. Some will perceive how to build structures with the mandala as an intrinsic part of it. Instead of the mandala being built as an afterthought to the house, some may design houses around the mandala.

"Many astrologers will have questions about this mandala system. This is part of the process, for many astrologers learned much of what they know about astrology in Atlantean times, when this mandala system was used. Some individuals will get new ideas about using this system while asleep, in cars, or at work. People should be encouraged to experiment with this mandala system and not be restricted to what has been said here. This mandala system offers a great deal of promise and indeed may become an important technology in mankind's immediate future."

Q Speak on the relationship of astrological charts to the Tibetan tankas, which often have a mandala pattern?

"While Tibetan tankas are often based on astrological information, we find no major discourse here."

Last year I attended a lecture given by Hunbatz Men, a Mayan who has spent many years studying ancient Mayan philosophy and spirituality. After his talk on the Mayan calender, I asked if he had ever heard of the Mayans using quartz crystals with any of their astrological calenders. He said that some time ago British archeologists, visiting an ancient Mayan observatory, had discovered a sheet of quartz crystal which may have been part of the observatory. They took it back to England to study.

The mandala has long been a sacred symbol in many cultures.[8] Some already suspect that the mandala and medicine wheel sites found among the native cultures served as astronomical observatories and lunar calendars. Perhaps the most extensive recorded use of the mandala is among the Tibetans with the tangka, in their religious and artistic endeavors.[9]

When projecting into the potential future, it will often be easier for people involved in spiritual work to use this mandala system. It is important to understand that projecting into the future also involves interpretation and does not violate one's free will. The future is partly determined by how we act in the present.

John also mentioned that the Lemurians used this technology and understood that their civilization would collapse when it did. Some in that culture understood the course of evolution for this planet for hundreds of thousands of years into the future. Sometimes, it was through the use of this mandala technology, while in other instances it was through inner spiritual development. Nostradamus used this same technology to see accurately hundreds of years into the future.

John said that because the Lemurians understood that there would be a collapse in consciousness, dolphins were created through mental energy to put all the teachings of Lemuria into the genetic code of those animals. This was done to preserve the teachings of Lemuria for the human race in the future. This is why there is increased interest in studying dolphins today. At the level of the collective consciousness, people intuitively understand that there is much to learn from dolphins. Studies to establish communication with dolphins have already begun. In the coming years, we will again learn how to have direct communications with dolphins, and then learn how to tap into their genetic code to release the teachings of Lemuria. This may also be done in conjunction with reestablishing the universal language on this planet.

1 Juliet Ballard, *Treasures From Earth's Storehouse* (Virginia Beach: A.R.E. Press, 1980),p.7-10.
2 Sarah Burnham, *Precious Stones In Nature Art and Literature* (Boston: Bradlee Whidden, 1886),p. 115-130.
3 F.F.C. Mees,M.D., *Living Metals* (N.Y: Regency Press, 1984).
Wilhelm Pelikan, *The Secrets of Metals* (Spring Valley,N.Y: Anthroposophical Press, 1984).
4 A.K. Bhattacharyya, *The Science of Cosmic Ray Therapy or Teletherapy* (Calcutta: Firma KLM Private, Ltd., 1976).
_____, ed., *Teletherapy* (Calcutta: Firma KLM Private, Ltd., 1977).
5 Anthony Aveni, *Skywatchers of Ancient Mexico* (Austin: U. of Texas, 1980).
Evan Hadingham, *Early Man and the Cosmos* (Norman,Ok: Univ. of Oklahoma Press, 1985).
Charles Gallenkamp and Carolyn Meyer, *The Mystery of the Ancient Maya* (N.Y: Atheneum,1985).
E.C. Krupp, *Echoes of the Ancient Skies: Astronomy of Lost Civilizations* (N.Y: Harper and Row, 1983).
6 Hilarion, *Astrology Plus* (Toronto: Marcus Books, 1980).
7 Dane Rudhyar, *The Sun Is Also A Star. The Galactic Dimension of Astrology* (N.Y: Dutton and Co., 1975).
8 Jose and Miriam Arguelles, *Mandala* (Boston: Shambhala Publications, 1972).
Jose Arguelles, *Earth Ascending* (Boston: Shambhala Publications, 1984).
Giuseppe Tucci, The Theory and Practice of the Mandala (London: Rider and Co., 1969).
9 Willy Fischle, *The Way to the Centre* (London: Robinson and Watkins, 1982).
David and Janice Jackson, *Tibetan Thangka Painting, Methods and Materials* (Boston: Shambhala Publications, 1984).

Aesar
P.O. Box 1087
Seabrook,N.H. 03874

Provides the 12 metals needed for mandala usually in powder and granule form.

Quartz Scientific, Inc.
819 East St.
Fairport Harbor,Oh. 44077

Provides quartz sheets and tubing.

American Quartz Co.
Bridge Rd. and U.S. Highway 202
Montville,N.J. 07045

Provides quartz powder. Natural, not fused quartz, is preferred. They also sell quartz sheets.

People can also check the Thomas Register of American Manufacturers in most libraries. Under the subject quartz, over 100 suppliers are listed.

I would be interested in hearing from people who build this mandala.

LIST OF GEMSTONES AND METALS
USED IN THE ASTROLOGICAL MANDALA

Zodiac signs and associated metals

Aries-iron or carbon steel
Taurus-copper
Gemini-molybdenum
Cancer-silver
Leo-gold
Virgo-magnesium

Libra-palladium
Scorpio-manganese
Sagittarius-tin
Capricorn-zinc
Aquarius-chromium
Pisces-platinum

Planets and associated gemstones

Sun-ruby
Moon-pearl light
Mercury-aquamarine
Venus-sapphire light blue
Mars-bloodstone
Vesta-topaz

Jupiter-amethyst
Saturn-garnet rhodolite
Chiron-diamond white
Uranus-ulexite
Neptune-jade
Pluto-herkimer diamond

Houses and associated gemstones

1 house-coral
2 house-lapis lazuli
3 house-agate picture
4 house-moonstone
5 house-jasper yellow
6 house-star sapphire

7 house-emerald
8 house-opal dark
9 house-turquoise
10 house-quartz clear
11 house-garnet-spessartine
12 house-opal light

CHAPTER V

HOW GEM ELIXIRS, FLOWER ESSENCES,
AND HOMEOPATHIC REMEDIES WORK IN PEOPLE

Exactly how gem elixirs and other vibrational remedies work in people is a complex process that has never been fully explained. Dr. Roberts, a prominent homeopathic physician, even stated that it will never be possible to understand how homeopathic remedies assist the vital force to conquer disease.[1] While the complete process is not described in this text, much new information is presented.

In time, it will be understood that many of the developing concepts of what is called 'new physics' will explain in great detail how vibrational remedies work with people. There does not yet seem to be much understanding of this in homeopathic circles, but there is an interesting examination of this relationship in *Space Time and Medicine* by Larry Dossey, M.D.[2] and *Health and Healing: Understanding Conventional and Alternative Medicine* by Andrew Weil,M.D.[3] Professor Tiller,Ph.D, of Stanford University has also done some interesting research into the relationship of modern physics and how homeopathic remedies work in people.[4] Many homeopaths are increasingly using the electroacupuncture machine that Dr. Voll has made available.[5] With this and similar devices a growing number of practitioners are developing a better appreciation of the subtle energies involved in the way vibrational remedies work in the body.

Recent findings in magnetobiology and biomagnetism offer a theoretical explanation of how vibrational remedies work. (Magnetobiology is the study of the effect of magnetic fields upon biological systems, and biomagnetism is the study of magnetic fields emanating from biological systems.) Several recent conferences and books, such as *The Body Electric: Electromagnetism and the Foundation of Life* by Becker, M.D. and Selden,[6] attest to the growing interest in the relationship between electric and magnetic energy fields and physiological activity.

It is understood that biological organisms emit specific electromagnetic fields associated with underlying physiological activity.[7] It is not so much the exchange of energy which is important in vibrational medicine, it is the exchange of information which is conveyed in very weak electromagnetic patterns. This is information in one of its most basic forms.

A cell is an open system. It must exchange matter, energy and information with the environment in order to survive in a balanced fashion. If a cell is denied a continuous and balanced exchange of matter, energy, and information with the environment, the cell develops aberrant behavioral patterns. The cell membrane regulates these exchanges between itself and the environment. A cell membrane can be defined as a dissipative structure, and its membrane properties may be understood in terms of far-from-equilibrium thermodynamics. Dissipative structures, sometimes called dynamic patterns, are those 'structures' which arise and are maintained by the continuous dissipation or consumption of available energy, matter and information imported from the environment.

A dissipative structure is a far-from-equilibrium thermodynamic system. There are three types of thermodynamic states. One is at equilibrium, the second is at near-equilibrium, and the third is far-from-equilibrium. Previously, it was felt that far-from-equilibrium thermodynamics would not play a role in explaining biological processes, but recently it has been discovered that far-from-equilibrium processes play a fundamental role in explaining how biological systems work. Previously, biological systems seemed to violate the second law of thermodynamics which states that the amount of energy available in a system must decrease over time, or that the system must become more disorganized over time. However, biological systems seem to, and actually do, become more energized and organized over time.

There are three types of thermodynamic conditions—isolated, closed, and open. An isolated system or cell is a system across the boundaries of which neither matter nor energy flows. A closed system is a system across the boundaries of which energy, but not matter, flows. This means that matter stays within the system in the same material content, but energy can be introduced into the system. In an open system both matter and energy can cross the boundary. For biological systems, not only are matter and energy needed in each cell, but information must also cross the cellular boundary.

The type and properties of an open system(dissipative structure) which come into being depend in an essential way upon the type of environmental conditions in which the structure is formed and continues to exist. Since there is a continuous exchange of matter, energy, and information with the environment, the cellular system co-evolves and changes with changing environmental conditions. Vibrational remedies change the environmental conditions of each cell; the cell is then able to transmute that change into a biologically significant response.

There has been a radical transformation in the way in which we view protein molecules. Due to a misconception brought about by x-ray crystallography, the idea arose that protein molecules had static or rigid structures. The physiological function that a protein molecule had depended on its rigid structure in order to change from one physiological function to another, it had to change from one rigid structure to another. Today we know that the atoms in protein molecules, which exist in every cell, are constantly vibrating and do not have a rigid structure.[8] One vibrational mode corresponds to one physiological function, and another vibrational mode corresponds to a different physiological function. This is a key link with vibrational medicine.

Protein molecules are the master energy and information manipulators in biological cells. Each cell has three protein molecules which are responsible for changing external signals into internal signals. These three molecules are called the receptor molecule, the transducer molecule, and the amplifier molecule. The receptor molecule, on the surface of each cell membrane, is a molecular antenna which receives or detects external signals from the environment and activates the transducer molecule. The transducer molecule translates external signals into internal signals, thereby carrying the signal through the membrane. The amplifier molecule or enzyme converts a precursor molecule into a second messenger that activates the internal workings of each cell. The first messenger in this process is the external energy, pattern such as a vibrational remedy.

The second messenger affects an internal effector which is usually a protein kinase. A protein kinase has two parts—a regulatory component and a catalytic component.

The second messenger usually binds to the regulatory component and activates the catalytic component. In this way, the protein kinase activates a cellular response.

Various cellular responses, such as secretion, metabolism, growth, and contraction are activated in this way. These cellular responses are created by the different type of vibrational remedy used. The vibrational mode of various gem elixirs, flower essences, and homeopathic remedies are affected in a very specific way outside of a biological system. Then, that substance is ingested or applied exernally to interact with and change the vibrational mode of the receptor molecule on the surface of each cell.[9]

There are several unexpected properties which may be associated with cells defined as dissipative structures or far-from-equilibrium systems. These properties allow for very small-scale environmental changes to be amplified to create large-scale physiological or psychological changes in biological organisms. For instance, dissipative structures have an inherent sensitivity to very small-scale internal and external environmental field changes. Moreover, dissipative structures have an inherent nonlinear relationship between the fields that interact with them and the responses that are elicited from them. These principles of electomagnetic phenomena and biomagnetism explain how vibrational therapies work in people.

This information was provided by an associate, Vernon Rogers. He is conducting research into new physics and electromagnetism to explain how vibrational medicines work. Hilarion and John have both noted the basic validity of his research. The reader should also understand that this explanation discusses how vibrational remedies work on a cellular level. Vibrational preparations also influence other aspects of the body. Hilarion had some further insights into how vibrational medicines work on the cellular level.

"In the usual vibration-changing mode of these protein molecules, certain sets of frequency patterns and vibration rates are easily perturbed by other vibrational patterns. The vibrational pattern from a gem elixir, flower essence, and homeopathic remedy is largely stored in an etheric vibrational pattern, sometimes called an etheric matrix. In this matrix certain transitory states are reached that are near the physical level. The protein molecule, because of the sensitivity of many of its vibrational patterns to etheric vibrations, can come into sympathetic resonance with the vibrational pattern of a gem elixir, flower essence, and homeopathic remedy. This altered vibrational pattern becomes the seed pattern that then is moved and amplified through the self."

Q Would you describe how vibrational remedies work in people?

"When a gem elixir, flower essence, or homeopathic remedy is ingested or used as a salve, it follows a similar specific path through the physical and subtle bodies. It initially is assimilated into the circulatory system.[10] Next, the remedy settles midway between the circulatory and nervous systems. An electromagnetic current is created here by the polarity of these two systems. Indeed, there is an intimate connection between these two systems in relation to the life force and consciousness that modern science does not yet understand.[11] The life force works more through the blood, and consciousness works more through the brain and nervous system. These two systems contain quartzlike or crystalline properties and electromagnetic currents. The blood cells, especially the red and white blood cells, contain more crystalline properties: the nervous system contains more electromagnetic current. The life force and consciousness use these properties to enter and stimulate the physical body.

"From midway between the nervous and circulatory systems, the remedy usually moves directly to the meridians. There is a direct link with the nervous, circulatory, and meridian systems partly because, ages ago, the meridians were originally used to create these two parts of the physical body. Consequently, anything that influences one of these systems has a direct impact on the other two areas. The meridians use the passageway between the nervous and circulatory systems to feed the life force into the body, almost extending directly to the molecular level. The meridians are the interface or doorway between the physical and ethereal properties of the body.

"From the meridians, the remedy's life force enters the various subtle bodies, the chakras, or returns directly to the physical body to the cellular level through several portals midway between the nervous and circulatory systems. Its path is determined by the type of remedy and the person's constitution.

"The three main portals for the remedy's life force to reenter the physical body are the etheric body and ethereal fluidium, the chakras, and the skin with its silica or crystalline properties.[12] The ethereal fluidium is the part of the etheric body which surrounds the physical body and brings the life force into the individual cells. Hair, with its crystalline properties, is a carrier of the life force; it is not a portal. Specific parts of the physical body are portals for the life force of a vibrational remedy only because they are associated with different chakras or meridians. The pineal gland, for instance, is directly associated with the crown chakra. The life force of a vibrational remedy usually gravitates toward one portal, but it may reenter the physical body through several portals. For example, vibrational remedies with crystalline properties gravitate toward the skin.

"When the life force leaves and reenters the physical body, it always passes through the etheric body. This body is not necessarily considered a portal, however, if it is not in some way especially affected by the process."

Q When a remedy's life force returns to the physical body, does it go directly to the injured area or must it first pass midway between the nervous and circulatory systems?

"After passing through one of the described portals, the life force always passes midway between the nervous and circulatory systems. Then it enters the cellular level and imbalanced areas of the physical body. This entire process takes place instantaneously, but it usually takes awhile to experience the results. In a similar fashion, if you get punched in the face, it may take several days to feel swelling or soreness.

"The vibrational remedy is carried to the imbalanced areas with the aid of the crystalline properties in the lymph. The fact that the lymph has crystalline properties aids in its function of removing toxicity from the body. Not only does the lymph draw out physical toxicity, but its crystalline properties enable it to remove the vibration of toxins from the body. Toxins also have a natural tendency to be drawn to the lymphatic system for their elimination."

Q Would you expand on your statement that there are quartzlike properties in the body?

"There are various quartzlike crystalline structures in the physical and subtle bodies that augment the impact of vibrational remedies. In the physical body, these areas include cell salts, fatty tissue, lymphs, red and white blood cells, and the pineal and thymus glands. These crystalline structures are a complex system in the body but are not yet properly isolated and understood by modern medicine. However, quartz is being used increasingly in medicine. For instance, in the last few years, it has become common for liquified quartz to be used to fill cleansed cavities.

"Crystalline structures work on sympathetic resonancy. There is an attunement between crystalline properties in the physical and subtle bodies, the ethers, and many vibrational remedies, notably gem elixirs and flower essences. There is a close attunement between the body physical and gemstones.[13] These properties in the body magnify the life force of vibrational remedies to a recognizable level to be assimilated. Indeed, these crystalline properties are relay points for most ethereal energies to penetrate the body physical. This allows a balanced distribution of various energies at correct frequencies, thus stimulating the discharge of toxicity to create health. In a similar fashion, vibrations of radio-wave frequency strike a crystal in a radio. The crystal resonates with the high frequency in such a way as to absorb it, passing along the audio frequencies which are preceivable by the body.

"The physical body is often exposed to ethereal-like properties, and the crystalline properties of the body and the organized patterns of the ethers integrate and amplify vibrational remedies to work better and faster in people. If vibrational remedies were not amplified, the physical body would eventually acknowledge over longer periods of time their cumulative effect.

"There is an attunement between individual cells and quartz crystals. Each is broken into patterns of three and six. The top of a quartz crystal always has six sides. The number three in crystals involves their breaking down mathematically into intersections of a triangular basis. Molecular structures are often based upon principles of a triangular structure that is part of the formulation within crystalline structures. Individual cells have a similar pattern of three and six through similar geometrical structures when there is an interlinking on the molecular level. It is the process of the triangular basis that allows for the interlinking of individual molecules of differing elements to make a proper interlinkage on a self-perpetuating basis. This specific information is provided not so much for the lay person but is to stimulate those who study molecular science.

"When vibrational remedies are amplified, their life force reaches the imbalanced parts of the body faster and in a more stable state. The remedies may cleanse the aura and subtle bodies so those imbalances will no longer contribute to ill health. If this sounds strange, remember that scientists have many times proven that subtle energies such as ultrasonics and microwaves can cause sickness. Why cannot other subtle energies produce health?

"The internal working of the ethers, which are forces that travel slightly faster than the speed of light, amplify energy that passes through a crystalline pattern. When the life force of vibrational remedies passes through a crystalline pattern, there is a slight amplification from a temporary expansion of mass that transpires as the energy approaches the speed of light. The property of amplification creates more stability in energy. The crystalline pattern also stores electromagnetic energy and amplifies thought projections.

"The pineal gland is a crystalline structure that receives information from the soul, higher self, and subtle bodies, particularly the astral body. The subtle bodies often act as filters for teachings from the soul and higher self. From the pineal gland, information travels to the right portion of the brain. If there is a need to alert the conscious mind to this higher information, it passes through the right brain in the form of dreams. Then the left brain analyzes it to see if the information can be grasped. This often occurs with clear dreams that offer messages. From the left brain, information travels through the neurological system, specifically passing through two critical reflex points—the medulla oblongata and the coccyx. There is a constant state of resonancy along the spinal column between the medulla oblongata and the coccyx; properties of the pineal gland resonate between these two points. Then the information travels to other parts of the body through the meridians and crystalline structures already described. The life force of vibrational remedies activates this entire procedure. This is a key process the soul uses to manifest karma in the physical body.

"The crystalline properties within the aura are stable fields of energy. Even as magnets carry fields that have a structure or core, so in turn are there energy patterns in the aura. The central point of consciousness for these crystalline properties is often in the body physical, such as in the glands. Certain organs have a higher concentration of crystalline properties. In addition, there are points and peaks of crystalline activity that extend beyond and independent of the physical body. These fields of energy extend into areas of the aura that become ethereal in their nature. These energy patterns are actually focuses of consciousness that extend themselves back into the physical form to activate that vehicle. Thus, the crystalline patterns in the aura extend into the physical and subtle bodies. These fields may be referred to as a matrix of energy or a matrix of consciousness that is self-actualizing and obeys natural laws. Even though this energy is beyond the capacity of the biological, it still fits within the natural laws and mechanics of physics.

"It is with these fields that gem elixirs first gain their influence and seek to resonate with and penetrate to the level of the body physical. Just as there are certain biochemical energies within the body physical's neurological tissues that activate and control the mass of muscular tissue, so in turn there are subtler fields that are influenced by gem elixirs. This matrix of energy is amplified and projected into the physical body; and eventually, with a cumulative effect, it stabilizes or crystallizes the gemstone's pattern to promote healing and consciousness. Eventually, there is a transformation of the personality."

Q Explain how to activate the crystalline properties in the body?

"Focus on the chakras with visualization and meditation. Using the musical scale project the OM with three different correct pitches for attunement with the solar plexus, heart, and brow chakras. Visualize white light in these chakras. This activates the entire body physical because these three chakras are the main points where the crystalline structures in the body have their greatest enhancement. This process naturally attunes the physical body."

Q Can you give further information on the crystalline system in the body that Western medicine has not yet isolated?

"No, this will be discussed in the future."

Q Why is there constant resonancy between the medulla oblongata and coccyx?

"First, there are two reflex points by which the body's responses are processed. Pulling back from a sudden shock exemplifies this. This area is in a continuous state of stimulation; therefore, it amplifies ethereal energy associated with the pineal gland. It also translates energy from the subtle bodies into the physical body, especially the nervous system. The kundalini energy is augmented by this constant stimulation."

Q Are people affected differently when they take gemstones internally as an elixir, externally on the skin, or by injection?

"All three systems still work through the same passageways as described above. There are some unique influences in each case depending on the particular needs of each individual."

Q Explain how a gem elixir focuses consciousness in someone?

"It is simply that a state of consciouness that exists in the mineral is transferred to the individual."

Q Is it correct to say that various gemstones have a vibrational rate similar to the vibrational rate of different emotional states and parts of the body and that this is a key reason why all vibrational remedies work in people?

"This we find to be correct. This is one of the basic principles of all vibrational healing."

Max Heindel noted that matter is crystallized spirit and that the blood contains cyrstals. [14] The crystalline structures in the body are also referred to in the *Book of Enoch* .[15] In the Tao, the crystalline structures in the body are referred to as the 'Pa Kua.' The pituitary gland is called the crystal cave. A number of physicians influenced by the teachings of Rudolf Steiner now do the capillary-dynamic blood test. The crystalline properties in the blood are used for the early detection of diseases.[16] Ehrenfried Pfeiffer has done much work in this area.[17]

Q What happens when toxins are pushed out of the body by vibrational remedies?

"Toxins are pushed to the outer limits of the aura for purification. Some toxins are pushed into the ethers where they are purified, while others are pulled back into the body by the mind. The mind does this because vibrational remedies only temporarily stabilize the physical and subtle bodies until there is a cleansing of consciousness and a release of emotional attachments and mental misconceptions.

"All energy is secondary to the energy of the ethers. The ethers exist and flow in a perfect state of harmony with time and nature. Toxins in the body do not share this harmony in their chemical composition and molecular structure. This makes them unstable and easier to transform. Study the patterns, for instance, of sand placed on the bottom of the ocean. If your hand disturbed the sand, the water would immediately become clouded. This symbolizes toxins traveling into the aura. Just as ethers affect toxins in the aura, after awhile water currents restore sand to its original pattern and the water is purified and stabilized.

"The physical body is a flow of energy in the flow of time-past, present, and future. Existence of disease means the physical body is dwelling out of synchronicity with the time flow, which crystallizes karma. Being in proper synchronicity with time means you are in perfect health."

Q Do herbs and various physical-level nutrients work in the body the same way to push toxins out of the physical body as you just described with vibrational remedies?

"All forms of natural healing preparations follow these general principles. The process is about the same with a slight distinction of various remedies starting at a different base in the physical or subtle bodies. There are some differences in where the toxins reenter the physical body, but this involves complex principles that will be reviewed in the future."

Q Do nature spirits work with and affect minerals and gem elixirs the same way that you described with flower essences?

"As previously discussed, in the same way that there are different wavelengths for sound, light, and other energy patterns, there are different wavelengths in the life force or ether fields. Nature spirits exist in a spectrum or frequency of life force similar to that upon which flower essences function. This sympathetic resonancy creates a background effect amplifying flower essences. As electromagnetic beings of pure consciousness, they especially amplify the nervous system, which is notably electromagnetic in its operation. Nature spirits also occupy a stratum of energy that is associated with the subtle bodies.

"Flower essences come from the living vehicle that holds the pattern of consciousness and are the actual shaping of consciousness. In contrast, gem elixirs merely amplify consciousness; they are not the actual consciousness. Thus there is a distinction between gem elixirs and flower essences because they work on different spectrums of the life force. This distinction is an important reason why gem elixirs work closer to homeopathic remedies than do flower essences. Homeopathic remedies do not have the capacity of amplifying consciousness. They merely hold the physical pattern. Because gem elixirs do not have so much life force as flower essences, nature spirits do not work with gem elixirs as much as they do with flower essences."

Q Why do certain substances block vibrational remedies from working?

"Certain toxicities block the passageway of the remedy's life force through the physical and subtle bodies. Stress, a lack of B vitamins, and a weak spinal column, especially in the coccyx or medulla oblongata, weaken the nervous system. Heavy metals in the system or a lack of iron weakens the circulatory system. It has long been understood by some that aluminum in the body is highly toxic,[18] and that it usually interferes with the action of homeopathic remedies.[19] Steroids block the nervous system, muscular system, spleen chakra, and heart chakra. Other chemicals block various parts of the passageway of vibrational remedies' life force.

"The effect of caffeine and nicotine on an individual is devastating. The cure is complete abstinence. Camphor and caffeine lodge in the etheric body and occasionally in the emotional and mental bodies. They sometimes irritate, but do not fully penetrate, the astral body. These four bodies have a special connection with the nervous system. While both substances interfere with the circulatory and nervous systems, camphor notably blocks the nervous system. In contrast, caffeine overstimulates the nervous system and causes a constriction in the meridians and circulatory system. Anything that irritates or overstimulates the nervous system also penetrates at least the emotional and possibly the mental body. This is because the substance usually stimulates these subtle bodies directly and these two subtle bodies are directly connected to and influenced by the sympathetic and parasympathetic nervous systems.

"Caffeine unbalances all the meridians, which causes a leakage effect in the etheric body and emotional instability in the personality structure. An imbalance develops between the emotional and mental bodies. This is why coffee upsets the emotional chakra and stomach, which is the main seat of the emotions in the physical body.

"Alcohol interferes with the astral and mental bodies and weakens the entire personality. The vital forces in the abdomen and heart chakra weaken, which breeds cancer, especially in the thyroid. It also creates tumors in the pineal gland, and there is a lengthening and lessening of the elasticity of the circulatory walls. It makes a person more selfish, so there is increased strain in the heart chakra. There is a withering of the thymus, with disorders developing in the thymus and heart including in the unborn and in the chakras of the unborn. When alcohol and caffeine are taken together, the heart chakra is especially damaged. All the chakras associated with these parts of the physical body are weakened."

I have received several reports of people taking the coffee or tobacco flower essences and then not being able to stand the taste or smell of coffee or tobacco. It would be interesting to conduct some double blind studies with these two flower essences.

"Other substances that can block vibrational remedies include a poor diet, mints, menthol, thymol, odor of garlic, and strong perfume, especially if it contains aluminum and other synthetics. The odor of garlic can block the throat chakra, the abdomen, and the base of the spine. Mints sometimes weaken the entire process of how vibrational remedies work in people, although they do not notably affect particular areas. With a few people, sulphur interferes with vibrational remedies because it interacts with ammonia in the skin. This only happens, however, when a deficiency of iron in the blood weakens the magnetic properties in the ethereal fluidium.

"While these substances can block gem elixirs and flower essences from working, they usually act merely as irritants. The problem is greatest with homeopathic remedies because these remedies are so imprinted within the physical body. When gem elixirs and flower essences are prepared into homeopathic potencies, these substances present greater problems if homeopathic potencies below 1M are used.

"Biofeedback, correct diet, creative visualization, herbs, hypnosis, meditation, and massage, including chiropractic and osteopathic adjustments, ease these blockages. Fasting especially removes caffeine from the body. These modalities seal the healing pattern of vibrational remedies."

Q Will you explain what blocks minerals from working as gem elixirs, in contrast to gems being prepared in traditional homeopathic potencies?
"There are no unique properties to each system beyond what has already been said."

It is increasingly understood that the well chosen homeopathic remedy does not work properly as it used to because so many people take numerous chemical drugs and radiation treatments. Environmental pollutants, such as chemicals in our food supply, also play a key role in interfering with how vibrational remedies work in the body.[20] All these modern pollutants comprise a key reason why the baths discussed in my previous book *Gem Elixirs and Vibrational Healing, Vol. 1* are so crucial.

Q Is it possible to prove scientifically that vibrational remedies work this way with people?
"Sophisticated medical devices can be used to monitor different parts of the body, including the meridians. This demonstrates that these remedies affect specific parts of the body. This can involve the simple placing of electrodes on parts of the body. The Voll electroacupuncture machine can be used."

64

Q Will you explain how gem elixirs, flower essences, and homeopathic remedies work differently in people?

"When the pattern of flower essences travel to the meridians from midway between the circulatory and nervous systems, its main effect is more on ethereal parts of the body such as the psyche. At the same time, when flower essences primarily affect the physical body, more of the life force moves directly back into the physical body from the meridians. Gem elixirs and homeopathic remedies work closer to the physical body; therefore, most of their life force also moves into the physical body from the meridians. When these remedies affect the emotions or psyche, however, some of their life force goes from the meridians into the subtle anatomies, aura, and chakras, rather than primarily into the physical body."

In the future, a number of other issues will be discussed concerning how vibrational remedies work in people. This is a complex and important topic. In the coming years, new physics will reveal much more information in this area.

1 Herbert Roberts,M.D., *The Principles and Art of Cure By Homeopathy* (Saffron Walden,England: The C.W. Daniel Co. Ltd.,1976),p.44.
2 Larry Dossey,M.D., *Space, Time and Medicine* (Boston:Shambhala Publications, Inc.,1982).
3 Andrew Weil, M.D., *Health and Healing: Understanding Conventional and Alternative Medicine* (Boston: Houghton Mifflin and Co.,1983).
4 William Tiller,Ph.D., "Homeopathy: A Laboratory For Etheric Science?" *J. of Holistic Medicine,* V No. 1 (Spring/Summer,1983), 25-53.
_____,"A Rationale For the Homeopathic Laws of Similars," *J. of Homeopathic Practice,* II No.1 (April, 1979),48-52.
_____, "A Rationale For the Potentizing Process In Homeopathic Remedies," *J. of Homeopathic Practice,* II No. 1 (April, 1979), 53-59.
5 Reinhold Voll,M.D., "Twenty Years of Electroacupuncture Diagnosis In Germany A Progress Report," *American J. of Acupuncture,* III (March, 1975), 7-17.
6 Robert Becker, M.D. and Gary Selden, *The Body Electric. Electromagnetism and the Foundation of Life* (N.Y: William Morrow and Co., Inc., 1985).
7 H.A. Pohl, *Electrical Dielectrophoresis: The Behavior of Neutral Matter In NonUniform Electric Fields* (Cambridge:England: Cambridge University Press, 1978).
8 Martin Karplus and J. Andrew McCammon, "The Dynamics of Proteins," *Scientific American,* CCLIV no. 4 (April, 1986), 42-51.
9 Stefi Weisburd, "Dissecting the Dance in DNA," *Science News,* CXXV (June 9, 1984), 362-364.
10 Rudolf Steiner, *The Etherisation of the Blood* (London: Rudolf Steiner Press, 1971).
_____, *The Occult Significance of the Blood* (London: Rudolf Steiner Press, 1967).
11 Alice Bailey, *Esoteric Healing* (N. Y: Lucis Publishing Co.,1980), p.46, 106,142, 165, 240,337, 628.
Rudolf Steiner, *An Occult Physiology* (London: Rudolf Steiner Press, 1983), p.38-49.
_____ and Ita Wegman, *Fundamentals of Therapy* (London: Rudolf Steiner Press, 1967), p. 48-53.
12 Ibid.
Rudolf Steiner, *Spiritual Science and Medicine* (London: Rudolf Steiner Press, 1975).
13 Juliet Ballard, *Treasures From Earth's Storehouse* (Virginia Beach: A.R.E. Press, 1980),p.10-11.
14 Max Heindel, *Occult Principles of Health and Healing* (Oceanside,Ca: The Rosicrucian Fellowship, 1938), p.28,186.

_____, *The Rosicrucian Cosmo-Conception* (Oceanside,Ca: The Rosicrucian Fellowship, 1977), p.120, 186, 247, 249.

15 J.J. Hurtak, *The Keys of Knowledge: The Keys of Enoch* (Los Gatos,Ca: The Academy For Future Science,1977), p. 80, 291, 498-499.

16 Otto Wolff and Friedrich Husemann, *An Anthroposophical Approach to Medicine, Volume I* (Spring Valley,N.Y: The Anthroposophical Press, 1982), 366-392.

17 Ehrenfried Pfeiffer, *Sensitive Crystallization Processes: A Demonstration of Formative Forces In the Blood* (Spring Valley, N.Y: The Anthroposophical Press, 1975).

18 Gary Null, "Aluminum: Friend or Foe?" *Bestways,* X (October, 1982),60-65.

19 H. Tomlinson,M.D., *Aluminum Utensils and Disease* (London: L.N. Fowler,1967).

20 T.D. Ross,M.D., "Miasmatic Thoughts," *British Homeopathic Journal,* LI (April,1962), 71-83.

A.T. Westlake,M.D., "New Factors In the Twentieth Century Disease Pattern," *British Homeopathic Journal*, LIV (July,1965), 180-189.

CHAPTER VI

THE RELATIONSHIP OF GEM ELIXIRS TO FLOWER ESSENCES, HOMEOPATHY, HERBS, INCENSE, AND ESSENTIAL OILS

Many people use other preparations and healing modalities with gem elixirs, so it is important to understand the relationship between some of these practices. This can avoid certain problems and improve clinical results. The primary focus of this chapter will be on vibrational therapies because there is not yet a proper understanding of the principles of these healing systems.

Q What is the relationship of gem elixirs to flower essences and homeopathic remedies?

"Gemstones function between flower essences and homeopathic remedies. When a physical gemstone is ingested after being crushed, it is closer to homeopathy and notably influences the physical body with medicinal, nutritional, and antibiotic properties. When a gem is prepared into an elixir, however, using the sun in a method similar to preparing flower essences, that remedy functions slightly closer to flower essences and is more ethereal in its properties.

"With either method of preparation, gem elixirs influence specific organs in the physical body; homeopathic remedies have a wider impact on the entire physical body. Gems carry the pattern of a crystalline structure, which focuses the physical body's mineral and crystalline structures on the biomolecular level; therefore, gems work more closely with the biomolecular structure to integrate the life force into the body. Finally, gem elixirs function between the other two systems of vibrational medicine because they have a stronger impact on the ethereal fluidium. Flower essences come from the living vehicle that holds the pattern of consciousness. Flower essences are a stream of consciousness, while gemstones are amplified consciousness. Gem elixirs are closer to the accord of flower essences because they focus, but do not actually possess consciousness. Flowers are a living vehicle that possess life force, not unlike people. Minerals, and to a greater extent homeopathic remedies, are more inanimate. Homeopathic remedies do not focus or actually possess consciousness. They possess a limited spectrum of information contained in a specific chemical order that can be translated into necessary facts by consciousness. Homeopathic remedies connect more to the subtle bodies by alleviating stress. Stress is more an interface between the mind and the physical body.

"Flower essences, and to a good degree gem elixirs, work through the subtle bodies to affect the pure consciousness of the individual. This first alters the individual's consciousness, which then alters the personality and integrates into the physical frame. In contrast, homeopathy seeks to alleviate the biochemical patterns that contribute to the personality. This then creates a birthplace for the consciousness to eventually evolve and proceed therein.

"Your scientists have isolated the fact that stress can allow disease to enter the physical body. Mental concentration can become stress that may affect isolated parts of the physical body and lead to disease. Consciousness is the next level above mind. The pattern is consciousness, mind, stress, isolated parts of the physical body, and then disease. The subtle bodies are in many ways representative of consciousness. This is partly how gem elixirs and flower essences affect the physical body by affecting the individual's consciousness. Homeopathic remedies work more on levels of the mind and stress, incorporating principles of consciousness."

Q How would you respond to the objection by some homeopaths to your statement that homeopathic remedies work more with inert matter on the physical level, but flower essences are more an expression of consciousness?

"Homeopathy seeks to increase the capacity of the conductor in the body physical upon biomolecular levels. Therefore, the importance of homeopathy should not be discounted for without, the proper conductor of energy, such energy would be unfocused. The channel speaking does not as set forth a principle that is necessarily in violent conflict, but merely seeks to present information to expand peoples' understanding."

Q Explain in detail the different properties released when a mineral is prepared as a gem elixir with the sun method of preparation, and the traditional grinding of a mineral into a homeopathic remedy.

"When the sun is used to prepare a gem elixir, that elixir is the bridge between the ethereal and physiological principles. The prepared elixir contains many of the properties of the physical mineral, for there is activation of the life force and transference of the pure elixir into its totally crystalline state. When traditional homeopathic methods are used, many of the mineral's properties are released, which bonds it closer in ethereal chelation to its mineral life properties. Homeopathic principles magnify the mineral's properties, which align to the corresponding properties and physiology of the body physical. Although gem elixirs penetrate to the level of the body physical, they have more impact on the ethereal levels. Homeopathically prepared gemstones are perhaps superior when applied to physiological levels, but they tend to lose some properties when as working with the higher subtle anatomies. A mineral's properties when released through the homeopathic method of preparation, are mostly transferred when that same mineral is prepared as a gem elixir. But the natural self-adjusting properties of a mineral are more activated when a mineral is applied as a gem elixir. This is one reason why gem elixirs work more on the spiritual and ethereal qualities in people.

"The homeopathic preparation of minerals is a bridge between vibrational therapies and classical medicine and its studies of the immune system. Gemstones are as a bridge between total vibrational remedies and homeopathic principles. Gemstones even occupy this position in thy society. Gem therapy is the linkage between the radical esoteric patterns of flower essences and the more accepted standards of homeopathy; therefore, it occupies a graduating spectrum of vibrational therapy between flower essence and homeopathic healing. Gemstones have medicinal and nutritional impact, especially when applied in the traditional homeopathic form. But when applied in an elixir or vibrational form, or as when used in bathing, these preparations then straddle the principles of consciousness as described in the application of flower essences and the physiological accords that make up the discipline of homeopathy. Gem elixirs work more so upon the cellular level directly through the ethereal fluidium, remaining in that state between the physical and the pure subtle anatomies. In contrast, homeopathically prepared gem elixirs penetrate to the molecular level."

Q Please comment on the ayurvedic use of minerals?

"In the ayurvedic tradition, we find that many of the vibrational properties of minerals are assimilated into the body physical. There are several principles at work here. First, the mineral's properties strictly interacting with the body's own physiological processes stimulate the nutrient effects of the mineral upon the body physical. There are also medicinal benefits that do not normally fall in the range attributed to the nutritional accord. This is because homeopathic principles also come into play. The mineral's properties, because of their crystalline state, are as broken down and assimilated into the body physical within the physiological or digestive processes. The crystalline properties in the mineral activate the vibrational principle. This also releases into the body physical the medicinal benefits stored in the mineral because the body itself is activating or animating the dilution process that is normally done in the traditional homeopathic method of preparation, as well as by the sun method of preparing gem elixirs. Thus, there are two factors. The minerals nutrient and vibrational qualities are being used by the body.

"Aside from the natural crystalline properties of minerals, the ayurvedic method of grinding and preparing minerals for application helps the body physical to dilute minerals naturally to release their medicinal properties. Through this natural dilution process, the vibrational benefits of the mineral interplay with the body physical. This is why there is sometimes confusion when it is sensed that the medicinal benefits of a gem go beyond its traditional nutritional makeup or identifiable mineral properties."

Q Will you explain in detail the difference between flower essences and homeopathic remedies?

"Homeopathic remedies usually come from denser inorganic material, while flower essences have a much higher concentration of life force. Homeopathic remedies often vibrationally duplicate physical disease within a person to push that imbalance out of the body. Homeopathic remedies integrates into the subtle bodies but still functions upon the vibrational level of the molecular structure.

"In contrast, flower essences adjust the flow of consciousness and karma that create the disease state. They influence the subtle bodies and ethereal properties of the anatomy, and then gradually influence the physical body. The fact that flower essences come from flowers, which are the most concentrated area of the life force in plants, is one key reason why there is more life force in flower essences than in other forms of vibrational medicine.

"The most efficient way to experience the effects of flower essences is through baths because they are more ethereal in their effects, and bathing makes it easier for nature spirits to assist in the process of assimilating the life force. Ingestion is best with homeopathic remedies because they work more directly on the physical body. Either method is superior with gem elixirs, but there is a slightly increased impact with ingestion."

Q Why can people take a number of gem elixirs and flower essences together, but only one or a few homeopathic remedies at the same time?

"Gemstones, when prepared as elixirs, have some of the self-adjusting properties of flower esssences. When prepared into low homeopathic potencies up to lM, they lose some of their self-adjusting activities and work closer to the level of homeopathic preparations. In the higher homeopathic potencies, of 1M and higher, gem elixirs have a higher degree of self-adjusting properties. Generally, gemstones which are ground up and ingested have fewer self-adjusting properties than gem elixirs prepared by the sun method.

"Flower essences work on realms of consciousness and are self-adjusting, so they can be assimilated at the same time in a coordinated fashion. The body selectively applies the various essences. Flower essences work more in ethereal areas and less directly on the physical body, as do homeopathic remedies, so it is easier to assimilate many flower essences at once. With the broad sweeping social changes and changes in consciousness in recent years, many people now have expanded and more complex subtle anatomies, so they can assimilate greater numbers of flower essences and gem elixirs. Most individuals can now take up to nine different gem elixirs and flower essences together. Some people meditating for some time can take more than this number.

"It is harder to take many homeopathic remedies together because of the increased stress placed on the physical body from the increased number of pollutants in society today. In addition, because homeopathic remedies work directly upon the physical and cellular levels and are less self-adjusting than gem elixirs and flower essences, too many remedies taken at once would tend to overstimulate the release of toxins from the system. This could cause sharp aggravations and a healing crisis that many people would find disruptive."

When homeopathic remedies are combined in neutral homeopathic potencies, it is easier to combine more remedies at once, especially when the individual preparations are united using quartz crystals and pyramids. This is one reason why homeopathic combinations are sold in low homeopathic potencies, which are also neutral homeopathic potencies.

Q Can gem elixirs, flower essences, and homeopathic remedies be taken at the same time without interfering with each other?

"Although it is relatively easy to intermix gem elixirs with flower essences, the same is not true with homeopathic remedies because they work closer to the physical body and are not as self-adjusting. Except for certain universal preparations such as lotus, quartz, pineapple, diamond, and jamesonite, only a skilled practitioner should prescribe homeopathic remedies with gem elixirs and flower essences. Gem elixirs and flower essences may not of themselves cause an interference effect but the by-products of their activities may stimulate such a reaction. To illustrate, a flower essence may release emotional tensions causing a physiological change that could interfere with homeopathic or gem remedies. At the same time because flower essences are organic compounds with self-adjusting properties, they do not tend to interfere with homeopathic remedies taken at the same time. Flower essences are the perfect blend of the interface between homeopathy and gem therapies.

"Some gem elixirs and flower essences are so ethereal and universal that they do not interfere with other vibrational remedies. These include jamesonite, diamond, quartz, cherry, larkspur, lilac, lotus, mango, papaya, pineapple, yarrow, and all rose flower essences. Gem elixirs and flower essences sprayed over the house or put into clothes will not interfere with other vibrational remedies. Gem elixirs, flower essences, and homeopathic remedies prepared into homeopathic potencies at 1M and higher or in the neutral homeopathic potencies-6x, 6c, 12x, 12c, 200x, 200c, and 10MM interfere less with each other. When these are prepared at stock bottle level or in homeopathic potencies below 1M, there is a greater chance for an interference effect. In addition, gemstones prepared into elixirs with the sun are slightly less apt to interfere with other vibrational remedies than are gemstones ground up for ingestion. It is important to remember these guidelines when vibrational combination remedies are prepared and used."

Q You also said that homeopathic remedies made from the same minerals and gem elixirs tend to interfere with each other when taken at about the same time because of the innate makeup of each. Please explain?

"Homeopathic remedies which contain mineral properties are not as coordinated and stabilized as are minerals prepared into gem elixirs with the sun. With the homeopathic process of dilution and succussion, the mineral loses some of its crystalline properties and stabilization. In addition, such remedies would tend to interfere with each other because of their similar mineral vibrations. They are too much like each other. However, this principle does not apply if the physical mineral supplement is taken when the same substance is ingested as a homeopathic remedy or as a gem elixir. For instance, it is not wise to take a homeopathic remedy of magnesium and magnesium gem elixir at the same time. But a magnesium mineral supplement can be taken with magnesium as a gem elixir or as a homeopathic remedy with no interference."

Q You also said that there are other areas where gem elixirs and homeopathic remedies interfere with each other, especially in relation to the subtle bodies and the soul's higher properties. Please explain?

"This cannot be given now. This has to do with the higher properties of the eight and ninth chakras, just above the crown chakra.

"Combining meditation, chanting, and creative visualization with various vibrational preparations lessens the chance of their interfering with each other. These practices particularly enhance the properties of flower essences and homeopathic remedies to thoroughly integrate into the body's biomolecular properties so gem elixirs can be used without interference.

"The main problem occurs when clients are treated by two different people or when they also take vibrational remedies on their own. In such cases, if this procedure continues, it is best to stop the treatment because it is difficult to be of assistance and disruptive aggravations could occur.

"There is a special meditation that can be done when taking vibrational remedies, so they will not interfere with each other. Sit on the floor or ground with the palms turned upward and the spinal column straight. The lotus position in hatha yoga exemplifies this. The head should be tilted slightly upward, and you *must* be aligned with true or magnetic north. Then visualize light from the center of the heart spiraling out to each of the seven main chakras, arriving at the base and crown chakras simultaneously. With this visualization do deep rhythmical breathing. Then concentrate on sending light to the imbalanced chakras and diseased areas of the body. These blocks in consciousness can be predetermined through diagnostic techniques such as pulse testing or use of the pendulum.

"This exercise should be done for at least seven minutes upon rising and before sleep for at least three days when taking different vibrational remedies. If this meditation is practiced when only taking one vibrational remedy, the remedy's effects are amplified.

"In using these remedies, it is sometimes wise initially to use homeopathic remedies or gem elixirs that primarily affect the physical body to alleviate chronic physical problems, before using the more ethereal gem elixirs or flower essences. This is one reason why the Bach flowers often take so long to treat certain physical problems effectively. The interference of physical problems can block flower essences from properly influencing the ethereal realms of consciousness.[1] Since many new flower essences work prominently or exclusively on the physical body, however, this principle is no longer as applicable as when only the Bach flowers were available. The Bach flowers usually have greater impacts on the psyche and personality, rather than on the physical body."

Q Elsewhere you said that a gem elixir given at 10MM would generally not interfere with other homeopathic remedies given at the same time. Is this principle also applicable with the other neutral homeopathic potencies?

"Yes, but care must be exercised here, especially when the lower neutral homeopathic potencies are being used. It is safer to give two different homeopathic remedies within the same time period when one of the remedies is at 10MM. You could also give stock bottles of gem elixirs and flower essences at the same time, but then there is an even greater chance of interference with a homeopathic remedy, even when that remedy is given in a neutral homeopathic potency. Skill is required here."

Depending on the strength and potency of a homeopathic remedy, as well as the health of the individual, the effect of homeopathic remedies can last for many months. It is understood in traditional homeopathic circles that a second homeopathic remedy can be given when the effects of the previous preparation have not yet fully worn off or when a new acute situation develops, but care *must* be used in such circumstances. The concept of neutral homeopathic potencies is also relevant here, and gradually homeopathic practitioners will understand this. It should be understood that 10MM is a neutral potency that represents a dilution and succussion of 10 million times, while 10M represents a dilution and succussion of 10 thousand times. Homeopathic remedies at these two different potencies are not to be interchanged. More information is provided on neutral homeopathic potencies in an appenidx in *Flower Essences and Vibrational Healing*.

Q Is any one neutral homeopathic potency best to use, especially in acute or chronic cases?

"All potencies have value. Each case is unique so there is no specific answer that can be provided."

Q What happens when you take too much or too little of a gem elixir, flower essence, or homeopathic remedy?

"If one takes too much of a gem elixir, there could be a mild healing crisis similar to what occurs with homeopathic remedies. This would rarely become a major problem, however, because gemstones maintain sufficient self-adjusting properties. When one takes too little of a gem elixir, its effects may be too weak to cleanse or assist the system. The crystalline structures of the body are then only slightly activated with gem elixirs because there is less life force in gemstones than in flower essences, and gemstones more often influence the physical body. The more ethereal vibrational remedies usually have greater impacts on the crystalline structures in the body.

"If one takes too much of a flower essence, the effects are cancelled because they are self-adjusting and work on realms of consciousness. If one takes too little of a flower essence, its properties are properly amplified and assimilated because the ethereal digestive tract is activated. This refers to the crystalline structures in the body that were previously discussed. These structures are similar to the digestive enzymes that break down and assimilate various nutrients.

"If you take too much of a homeopathic remedy, numerous complications and problems can develop. If you take too little of a homeopathic remedy, the crystalline parts of the body are only slightly activated; thus, there tends to be little or no cleansing from that remedy. The crystalline structures are not sufficiently activated because there is usually not sufficient life force in homeopathic remedies, and they work so close to the physical body."

Q Why are there different types of aggravations with gem elixirs, flower essences, and homeopathic remedies?

"Gem elixirs and homeopathic remedies work closer to the physical body and have less life force than flower essences, so there is an increased chance of aggravations occurring. If the wrong homeopathic remedy is given, the aggravation can at times be notably intense. This could also occur with gem elixirs, especially when gem elixir combinations are being used or when gem elixirs are being taken in accord with astrological movements, but such problems are extremely rare. If the wrong flower essence is prescribed, it will almost always pass right through a person. Greater clinical skill is needed to prescribe homeopathic remedies than is the case with gem elixirs and flower essences.

"Gem elixirs and flower essences do not negatively affect people. What some call negative influences are really healing crises. As ingrained emotions are released, points of confrontation may be experienced. This sometimes creates illusions that the remedy negatively affects the person. If some emotional problems are too difficult to face, the remedy gradually influences the individual. Gem elixirs very rarely cause aggravations, and flower essences work on levels of consciousness, so they are self-adjusting and do not violate the individual's free will. If there is an emotional blockage that should not be released at a particular time, the flower essence will usually cancel itself in that part of the person's consciousness.

"However, there is not a 100 percent guarantee that extreme emotional states will never be created as flower essences release emotional blockages. When people do experience aggravations with these essences, it is often because it is important to their psychological rigidity and paranoia that the remedy not work. People should have enough common sense to understand that if extreme reactions result from taking a flower essence or gem elixir that substance should probably be discontinued, at least for a while. The client and, to a lesser extent, the practitioner should take some responsibility in this process. Expert psychological counseling can be crucial in some instances.

"There can be abuses in this process even with positive personality changes. To illustrate, if a person gains a great deal of confidence, that individual may become loud and obnoxious. You cannot blame the remedy for such a response; it is the consciousness of the individual. Certain personality flaws were not properly treated in a therapeutic setting.

"Gem elixirs and flower essences gradually heal within the capacity and limitation of the individual to create stable changes in mind, body, and spirit. This is why the results with these remedies tend not to be instantaneous.

"Sometimes, when taking gem elixirs or flower essences, there is a sensation of negative energy attacking you. Released emotional tensions or physical toxins can trigger a concentration of orgone in the emotional chakra that your system cannot always easily handle. The released energy travels out the crown chakra through the kundalini process three to four feet into the aura and back into the emotional chakra. This is partly why there is a sensation of energy entering you. Demons and devils attacking you are usually your own emotional negativity. This sensation sometimes causes nausea, and it generally increases the white blood cells. This process is about the same, or more intense, with homeopathic remedies."

Q What is the relationship of herbs to vibrational remedies?

"Herbs have nutrient and medicinal properties, so they augment the body and repel invading toxins. Herbs and vibrational remedies which influence the same diseases and body functions can be given in unison to support each other.

"As for using herbs with gem elixirs, we find they are best aligned through the principles of astrology. Isolate individual minerals and herbs to their particular planet and predominant zodiac sign. For instance, we find that chamomile is ruled by the forces of Leo. There is a natural alignment of its principles to emerald or ruby. The herb valerian is aligned to the forces of Libra, as are opal and topaz. The student will find that many of the medicinal properties of gemstones parallel the medicinal uses of herbs. Gem elixirs often aid in the digestion of various herbs, and they act as natural enhancers for each other. The superior nutrient qualities of herbs are more easily assimilated into the system. With the Chinese five-element theory, the student will be able to isolate certain herbs to the seven main chakras. By studying which gemstones are as linked to the same chakras, the student will expand an understanding of how to apply gem elixirs and herbs together. It is best to take gem elixirs or flower essences with herbs to unify their properties. This is more true with flower essences than gem elixirs because flower essences are more self-adjusting."

Q Explain how to use gem elixirs with essential oils?

"Gem elixirs, especially when applied externally, can be used with essential oils for increased amplification. Isolate gem elixirs and essential oils that apply to the same chakras, meridians, and pressure points on the body physical. In this accord, it would be wise for the student to study the use of oils in ayurvedic and Chinese medicine. The elixirs and oils enhance and stabilize the impact of each other's vibrational qualities to be assimilated into specific anatomical, chakra, and meridian points when placed upon the surface of the skin. A suggested technique is to first mix together gem elixirs and essential oils, and then apply them on a meridian, while massaging other parts of the body. The individual would find that the other meridian points and chakras become self-adjusting to the dynamics, enhancements, and needs of the particular energy flow as represented by the applied gem elixirs and essential oils."

Q Can incense be used when gem elixirs and flower essences are taken?

"Yes, as long as there is no camphor in the incense. Sandalwood flower essence is especially valuable to enhance aroma therapy."

Q In homeopathy, the clinical effects of many remedies have been discovered by conducting provings. A group of healthy people over a period of weeks ingest a homeopathic remedy or placebo. The subjects who ingest the homeopathic remedy gradually develop symptoms that are carefully recorded in a diary and discussed or reviewed by an attending physician. The participants are not told if they have been ingesting the remedy or a placebo. The logic of this is that symptoms created under such conditions can also be treated by the same remedies when people become ill. Can these tests be conducted with gem elixirs to increase our understanding of their clinical effects?

"Yes, the tests could be conducted the same way they have traditionally been conducted with homeopathic remedies. This would be another way to validate the clinical value of new gem elixirs or to confirm the traditional folklore of many gemstones. However, depending on how ethereal the gem elixirs are, the initial symptoms that manifest might be shifts in consciousness and personality and then, depending on the physical effects of the elixir, changes in the physical body. For certain homeopathic remedies the same results could occur, but generally speaking, because they have more of a direct effect on the physical body, the initial symptoms tend to manifest there. In other instances, gem elixirs, more physical in their impact, would tend to affect the physical body immediately and directly.

"These provings are positive in their own right because by bringing to the surface symptoms, they often reveal dormant patterns within the individual that could ultimately lead to disease. Symptoms that result from provings with gem elixirs are usually milder than with homeopathic remedies, but stronger than the symptoms that develop from taking flower essences. They usually last for six hours after the elixir is ingested. While any potencies can be used to manifest symptoms during provings, 10MM and the mother tincture or stock bottle levels are best. There is a slight pattern for symptoms to be harsher when the remedy is below 1M and to be milder in the potencies at 1M and higher. Again, this is because there are greater self-adjusting properties in the higher potencies."

Q To what degree are the traditional homeopathic uses of various minerals the same when these minerals are prepared by the sun method and used as gem elixirs?

"Most of the homeopathic properties of minerals are as transferred when they are applied as gem elixirs. This is particularly true of the minerals traditionally used in alchemy because of their greater self-adjusting properties. This is partly why these minerals and metals are used in alchemy."

As originally stated by Dr. Hahnemann, the founder of homeopathy in modern times, miasms are the root cause of all chronic diseases and can be a contributing factor in some acute problems.[2] They are the vibrational foundation of genetically inherited diseases in the body, which are passed on from generation to generation. These miasmatic traits include viruses or bacteria that lie dormant in the cells for many years or entire generations in a delicately balanced symbiosis.[3] They occasionally flare up, which leads to chronic or acute illnesses, trauma, stress, and old age. As individuals age, their vitality weakens, which allows miasms to penetrate the physical body from the subtle anatomies. Many gem elixirs are extremely valuable in removing miasms from the body.

It is essential that holistic health practitioners understand the profound impact miasms have on chronic diseases. Underlying miasms contribute to making one susceptible to various acute illnesses. What usually happens today is that the client is treated with natural remedies, yet the underlying miasmatic problems are not even considered or examined. The overt symptoms are treated, but the underlying cause is not confronted. Today, only a few homeopaths consider the miasms in their clinical practice. Effectively treating the miasms is essential if the holistic health movement is to reach its full potential of restoring people to health in mind, body, and spirit.

"Miasms are stored in the cellular level of the physical body and in the subtle bodies, especially in the etheric, emotional, mental, and, to a lesser extent, astral bodies. Some miasms are passed on to the next generation genetically by inhabiting the molecular level of the physical body, which is the genetic code. A miasm is not necessarily a disease; it is the potential for disease. Indeed, miasms are a crystallized pattern of karma. The merger of the soul's forces and etheral properties determine when a miasm will arise in the physical body to become an active disease. This happens only when the miasm's ethereal pattern projects into the physical body from the subtle bodies. Miasms may lie dormant in the subtle bodies, aura, and cellular level for long periods of time. They are organized in the subtle bodies, and gradually, through the biomagnetic fields about the physical body, miasms penetrate the molecular level, then the cellular level, and finally the physical body. This often happens as people age and physical vitality lessens.

"There is a general misconception in homeopathic circles that miasms represent the imbalanced pattern that blocks the person's vitality and the life force of a vibrational remedy. This observation is not wrong; it is just incomplete. Miasms are not just darkness or tainted energy; they are more the lack of light or life force—the one true energy. It is the void or lack of life force that indeed is the miasm. The imbalanced pattern and blockage is the void and lack of life force. The life force is the causal element that arranges the pattern correctly; thus, healing occurs when the life force penetrates into the void. Many times, individuals remove blockages but still do not permit the light or life force to enter, thus recreating the circumstances."

Q How does a lack of the ethereal fluidium in the etheric body relate to the miasms and break down the genetic code?

"The ethereal fluidium is the connective tissue between the ethereal properties of the subtle bodies and the body physical. A lack of this substance leads to the miasms because this causes a weakening upon the cellular level opening the body physical to diseases because the karmic patterns stored in the subtle bodies enter the body. Diseases linked to past karmic patterns thus enter the physical body. This is often due to energy imbalances resulting from an improperly functioning ethereal fluidium. It is not necessarily due to psychospiritual causes. The ethereal fluidium is a conductor between the subtle bodies and the physical body, just as water is a conductor, and just as the neurological tissues carry information throughout the physical form. A lack of the ethereal fluidium as a conductor or relayer of information to the physical form in its functions with the karmic dynamics becomes not unlike a process similar to stress in the physical body.

"There are four types of miasms, including the planetary, inherited, acquired, and stellar miasms. Planetary miasms are stored in the collective consciousness of the planet and in the ethers. They may penetrate the physical body, but are not stored there. Inherited miasms are stored in the cellular memory of individuals. Acquired miasms are acute or infectious diseases or petrochemical toxicity acquired during a given lifetime. After the acute phase of an illness, these acquired miasmatic traits settle into the subtle bodies and the molecular and cellular levels, where they ultimately may cause other problems. These four levels of miasms can aggravate the body, preparing the system for more miasms to develop."

Hahnemann stated that there are three inherited miasms: psora, syphilitic, and sycotic. Most homeopaths today accept this principle. With the psora miasm, one manifests an imbalance in the rhythmic functions of the body, general mental and physical irritation, numerous skin disorders, congestive states, and deformities in the bone structure.[4] Such people are usually tired and mentally alert but often anxious, timid, and perhaps sad or depressed.[5] Hahnemann said psora is the mother of all disease.

The syphilitic miasm, which is partly caused by syphilis, has a destructive effect on all tissues, especially bones. Imbalances in the eliminatory functions often lead to ulcers. Cardiac and neurological symptoms abound. Meningitis exemplifies this trend. Such people are easily upset, sentimental, irritable, and suspicious.[6]

The sycotic miasm, which is partly caused by gonorrhea, produces disordered assimilation leading to deposits, congestion, and tumor formation. Disorders often occur in the pelvic and sexual areas, skin, digestive, respiratory, and urinary tract. Rheumatism of the small joints is another problem with this miasm. These people tend to be fearful, nervous, and morally degenerate.[7]

In the 1880's a debate developed in homeopathic circles concerning whether or not tuberculosis was a fourth inherited miasm.[8] Many today consider it a fourth inherited miasm, and the channeled guidance agrees. With this miasm one is prone to respiratory, circulatory, urinary, and digestive problems. Mental illness and cancer also develop. Chilliness and weight loss likewise occur.[9] Such individuals cannot make decisions or face the realities of life in a stable fashion. They have a lively imagination, an artistic sense, and a flight from material reality.[10]

One of the most important pieces of new information that I have learned in the channeling is that there are now two, and soon three, new inherited miasms. Except in a few instances,[11] this is not understood in homeopathic circles. These new miasms are the radiation and petrochemical miasms. The heavy metal miasm will develop by 1990, if present environmental trends continue.

"The radiation miasm is associated with the massive increase in background radiation, especially since World War II. It contributes to premature aging, slower cell division, deterioration of the endocrine system, weakening of bone tissue, anemia, arthritis, hair loss, allergies, bacterial inflammations, (especially in the brain), deterioration of the muscular system, and cancer, especially leukemia and skin cancer. Individuals are also subject to hardening of the arteries and the full spectrum of heart diseases. Females are prone to miscarriage and excessive menstrual bleeding, and men experience sterility or a drop in the sperm count.

"With the radiation miasm the capacity to reason is weakened. When first exposed to this miasm the reasoning capacity may increase, but then there is a noticeable deterioration. This miasm may actually increase the capacity to define the spiritual dimensions of the self. The sixth chakra is stimulated, which is why this miasm may sometimes be associated with spiritual growth. There is a general inability to integrate upon molecular levels which leads to skin lesions, neurological disorders, and other imbalances associated with radiation sickness. This miasm is mainly focused on the molecular level. There is also a notable impact on the etheric body, the astral body is moderately affected, and the nadis are mildly enhanced. This particular miasm is not necessarily associated with disease states. Indeed, moderate background radiation can be an enhancer to the individual."

Q Would you consider exposure to x-rays injurious or enhancing, as compared to background radiation that we are all exposed to?

"All overexposure to radiation is harmful. This is especially so when the radiation is synthetic, although too much natural radiation also will cause harm.

"The petrochemical miasm is caused by the major increase in petroleum-based and chemical products in society. Some problems caused by this miasm include fluid retention, diabetes, hair loss, infertility, impotence, miscarriages, premature greying of the hair, degenerative muscle diseases, skin blemishes, and thickening of the skin's tissue. Metabolic imbalances that cause excessive storage of fatty tissue may occur. It is harder to resist stress and psychosis, especially classical schizophrenia and autism. Leukemia, cancer of the skin, and lymphs also occur. Finally, it is harder to assimilate vitamin K, circulatory disorders result, and endocrine system imbalances develop.

"The petrochemical miasm may first enhance the mental faculty as the biochemical personality attempts to supersede the immediate chemical or even physical environment. The crown chakra is stimulated, which helps to spiritualize the biological personality, giving the higher forces more expression. Overexposure to petrochemicals leads to a deterioration of the biological personality which may lead to schizophrenia and wildly erratic emotional behavioral patterns, especially those associated with allergic states. The petrochemical miasm can thicken the density of the biological personality to the point where it supersedes the definable qualities of the spirit and its ability to pass through and enhance the individual's life. This is a detriment to individuals who seek full knowledge to make themselves whole. There is no great impact on the molecular level. The cellular level is enhanced or injured with the miasm finding its expression to bring about appropriate chromosomal exchange of genetic material, thus promoting and perpetuating the well-being of the biochemical existence of the self as a being. Cell mitosis is either enhanced or weakened. This miasm has little impact on the nadis."

Q You said no diseases are associated with the crown chakra so why does the petrochemical miasm affect this chakra?

"Remember a miasm is not a disease; it is the potential for diseases to develop. When the petrochemical miasm influences the body, and even when it has some impact on the crown chakra, that imbalanced energy pattern will enter other areas of the body such as the pituitary gland, portions of the brain, and various lower organs. It is like trying to balance a particular negative energy pattern on the edge of a razor blade, the razor sharp clarity and purity of the crown chakra. The crown chakra will split apart the energy pattern so that it will be transformed, or it will fall away, perhaps entering various parts of the physical body."

Q Can you suggest a treatment for people with the petrochemical miasm, especially for people with allergies?

"Since this miasm is only now arising as a major issue for humanity the treatment suggested is to isolate the exact chemical that is causing the problems. Petrochemicals are, of course, defined as man-made chemicals such as are found in chemical dumps. For instance, dioxin, the chemical in agent orange, could be given at the homeopathic potency of 10MM. Such a remedy would work not only on the isolated chemical but also directly on the miasm, since the miasm has such a wide and broad display, opening the body physical to the influence of many chemicals. Those who do not display the symptoms of the petrochemical miasm may have lived in an area long exposed to such chemicals, in contrast to those who display various symptoms and who have more recently moved into such an area. In addition, when someone gets cancer from direct exposure to a specific chemical, the ingestion of that chemical in the homeopathic potency of 10MM will weaken the cancer miasm, as well as the actual chemical that directly caused the cancer.

"At the present time, the heavy metal miasm is cross-indexed with other miasms. For instance, radioactive isotopes often latch onto heavy metals. The contents of this miasm include lead, mercury, radium, arsenic, sulphuric acid, carbon, aluminum, and fluoride. The symptom picture of this developing miasm includes allergies, especially from petrochemicals, excessive hair loss, excessive fluid retention, inability to assimilate calcium, and susceptibility to viral inflammations.

"The heavy metal miasm also causes senility. Study for instance the influence that lead has on the body with the deterioration that results in the mental faculty. As such density increases, it is harder for the higher forces to penetrate the physical to stimulate an evolution in consciousness as expressed in enlightened or animated personalities. Thus, the symptoms of senility are expressed even upon energy levels. With this miasm, negative personality traits develop. This individual seeks the survival of the self rather than the cooperation and enlightenment of others. The activities of this miasm are focused on the first chakra, for understanding and intuition are the key to the evolution of the soul's forces. This miasm has little impact on the molecular level of the body. All the meridians, along with the astral, etheric, and emotional bodies are weakened by the heavy metal miasm.

"It is taking longer for heavy metal problems to become an inherited miasm for the planet because these minerals have existed in minute degrees in people and in the water and atmosphere for thousands of years. Consequently, a tolerance has developed. This tolerance, however, is for elements that have traditionally existed in the water. The growing prevalence of these pollutants in the atmosphere is a key factor in this problem becoming an inherited miasm."

Conditions causing these three new miasms are very recent in their development. It is only in recent years that people have been excessively exposed to these pollutants. One has only to read in the daily papers about nuclear accidents, toxic waste dump problems and mass evacuations, or the debate over unleaded gasoline to sense the great concern over these issues.[12]

Most homeopathic research was conducted in the 1800's and early 1900's when these problems did not exist or were of little consequence. Practitioners have little understanding of these problems partly because they rarely recognize these issues as problems. In addition, except for an occasional recognition that chemical drugs can interfere with homeopathic remedies, there is no real understanding that these toxicities play a major role in blocking most vibrational medicines from working properly. This is one of the main reasons why clinical results with homeopathic remedies are not the same now as they were before these pollutants became so common.

In my private practice, when I used to treat people, and that of several associates who have incorporated some of these concepts, it is constantly found that these new miasms exist in a high percentage of clients. It should be realized that the well-chosen vibrational remedy will not work properly until these problems are dealt with. In our complex society, people typically have several of the old and new miasms in their system.

Q To expand our understanding of the other inherited and planetary miasms, will you please present a full symptom picture of their characteristics?

"With the psora miasm, there is repression of the acceptance of God and of there being method in the universe. The inner motivation to grow in spiritual understanding is blocked. There is a pattern of rejecting and even attempts to disprove all ideas relating to spiritual oneness. Sometimes this will manifest in the hardened skeptic who uses his intelligence to turn people off to spiritual ideas , but he awakens a few people to look more deeply for themselves.

"Partly because of this spiritual block to God's laws, the psora miasm adds strength to all the other miasms. The individual is not aware of any connected or overriding spiritual purpose in life. Gradually, irritability and an unwillingness to move forward in life manifests. This pattern depletes the physical body and lessens energy on many levels in the body. On the cellular level, this leads to reduced neurological activity, chemical imbalances in the endocrine system, and various glandular malfunctions. But remember, there is an overall reduction of energy on many levels of the body at the same time.

"While all the subtle bodies are affected by the psora miasm, the mental body, especially in its connection with the astral body, is most influenced. The heart chakra and the eleventh and twelfth chakras above the head are affected by this miasm. This is primarily because more balance develops to learn God's laws, as God uniquely manifests in the heart. In addition, the minor chakras in the feet are balanced. The psora miasm is directly associated with attuning to the earth because of humanity's coevolution with the earth, which is also under God's laws.

"The psora miasm affects the balance existing in the meridian meeting points in the hands. Regarding the meridian pairs that are associated with one another, it is typical that one meridian flows upward and another flows downward. With the psora miasm, the upward flowing meridian has its energy flow reversed; but the other meridian, in which the energy naturally flows downward, develops an increased intensity. Thus, energy builds up in the lower portion of the body. This does not always lead to obesity, but that may sometimes be the result. Such individuals usually have a great dislike of spirituality.

"With the tubercular miasm we find a complete polarity between mental and emotional expressions. The emotions overwhelm the mental capacity. There is often a setting aside of the spiritual, and the person may be an agnostic. An improved balancing of the breath is critically associated with a more balanced spiritual approach. Study for instance the idea of the holy breath, or use of the breath in yogic postures. Again, this miasm represents an imbalance in the emotions and may generate an agnostic or even an atheistic state within the individual. Those who inherit this miasm have often had many past lives of an agnostic accord. Thus, they may manifest many evolved spiritual properties but also manifest the tubercular miasm because they failed to present such a spiritual expression in many past lives.

"Upon the physical level, the impact of the tubercular miasm is of course obvious. There is difficulty in focusing breath along with lung problems. Upon the cellular level there is degeneration of tissue closely associated with oxygenation. This especially relates to the lymphs and thymus. Often, one of the keys to the active presence of the tubercular miasm is the rapid deterioration of the thymus, a lessening of the body's ability to produce hemoglobin, and a weakening of these areas. There may be sickle cell anemia or various problems with the plasmic walls of the blood tissues. There may also be a weakening of the diaphragm or even of the central nervous system. These effects all take place on the cellular level. Upon the molecular level these activities create an inability to reproduce harmoniously on chromosomal levels. In other words, genetic deterioration or genetic diseases develop. The etheric and emotional bodies and throat chakra are also affected."

Q Why do many homeopaths think that tuberculosis is part of the original three miasms and that it is not a new miasm?

"This is because of a linkage of symptoms. Indeed, one miasm may activate another, giving the illusion that there is one not two or more miasms. But even as each order of miasm is a progressive system of consciousness, so in turn their activities bring about obvious linkages.

"With the syphilitic miasm, paranoia develops which disrupts the mental faculty. Fears increase, and there is an inability to manage one's immediate environment or to create positive circumstances in one's life. Phobias are the inability to negotiate the immediate environment or the imagined environment. Thus, fear sets in. When the individual knows he can always negotiate any environment he inhabits, be it physical, mental, or spiritual, then phobias do not arise. This is especially true when the sexual or creative chakra is influenced because that chakra influences the ability of the individual to create an environment. The sexual chakra contains the ability and knowledge to be a creator.

"There is a sharp impact on the sexual chakra, the nadis in that chakra, and the sexual region of the body physical. There is also a weakening of spiritual activities associated with the affairs of the sexual chakra. Thus, there is a weakening of creativity, the ability to transform understanding into creativity, and the ability to proceed forward with, and to transform, spiritual aggression. The astral body is weakened, and on the cellular level, the presence of this miasm may create a genetic defect in the next generation. For instance, this miasm may be present in those who produce a mongoloid child. Thus, on genetic and molecular levels the syphilitic miasm may injure the next generation.

"With the sycotic miasm, the sexual and fifth chakras are affected. There is a general mental deterioration, although the presence of this miasm may initially enhance the mental force. The existence of this miasm without the disease state will often stimulate individuals to spiritualize their intellectual force. There is an alignment of the spiritual, etheric, and astral bodies. The very presence of this miasm sets up a resistance to it. The homeopathic principle applies to the miasm by its very presence. It is only when there is a rejection of that with which the individual is confronted, or a blockage, that the miasm becomes a detriment to the individual. Remember, the miasm is originally but as a characteristic of the individual; it is not an active disease penetrating the body physical. Those with this miasm may display mediumistic and clairvoyant faculties, but eventually there may be a deterioration of the mental faculty with the possible development of schizophrenia. On the molecular level, genetic difficulties may be passed on to the next generation, although the seeds of this miasm may not actually be present in the physical body of either parent."

Planetary miasms were first discussed in 1953, in *Esoteric Healing*, by Alice Bailey,[13] but this concept has had no real influence in homeopathic circles. The three planetary miasms are cancer, syphilis, and tuberculosis. Syphilis and tuberculosis have settled into the cellular level of individuals to also become inherited miasms, but this has not happened with cancer. It remains stored in the planetary collective consciousness and ethers, not in the cellular memory of individuals. When someone has the inherited miasms, especially the sycotic, heavy metal, petrochemical, or tubercular miasms, they are more susceptible to developing cancer. While some homeopaths consider cancer a separate miasm, most who study the issue consider it a combination of one or more miasms.[14]

"With the cancer miasm there is a lethargic state. There may be a lack of will power as in the death wish. In some instances, too much will is expressed as there is a focus on survival of the self, the ultimate density of the ego. In its spiritual expression, the cancer miasm offers the individual the opportunity to develop an understanding, acceptance, and knowledge of the self as a spiritual being. This is the test of the cancer miasm. This miasm is associated with the third chakra, which is usually directly related to the emotions. There is a weakening of the etheric body, which is the connective tissue of the subtle anatomies. Often cancer enters the body physical through an imbalance in the hara. On the molecular level, there is a breaking down of the genetic code and of the capacity of the body physical to correctly identify itself."

Q Speak on the debate in homeopathic circles as to the relationship of cancer to the recognized inherited miasms? I refer to the psoric, syphilitic, sycotic, and tubercular miasms.

"Cancer can indeed enter the physical body more easily when there are already present the currently recognized inherited miasms. These miasms are chronic in their presence, while the cancer miasm is a planetary miasm. It is the planetary chastiser. Cancer represents the final breakdown of an isolated area of consciousness upon which the individual is not working, and to which the individual may be prone. For instance, a concentration of the tubercular and psoric miasms may open the individual to lung or skin cancer, thus bringing about a predominance of the broad symptoms displayed by the traditional disease and by the actual symptoms induced by the miasm itself. The miasm is not specifically isolated to the disease that it is associated with. The principle of the miasm opens the body physical, perhaps to broader ranges of various disease states. These principal miasms are as isolated according to the symptoms that blockages of consciousness would bring into the body physical itself. Thus, in relationship to cancer, if any of the inherited miasms are diagnosed to exist within the subtle anatomy of the individual, symptomatically, as in character, personality, karma, and physical makeup, the person is open to experiencing such a diseased state as cancer by an expression of consciousness."

Q Why is cancer a planetary miasm?

"It is a planetary miasm in the sense that it is the consciousness of the individual that generates it, but it comes from the collective consciousness and then proceeds down to the genetic levels. Cancer is also a planetary miasm partly because its actual formation and influence has been known since the days of Atlantis. The inherited miasms have developed more recently."

Q Is it true that planetary miasms cause inherited miasms and that inherited miasms cause planetary miasms?
   "Yes."

Q Please describe how this occurs?
   "First, without giving a complex answer, they may aggravate each other often preparing the physical vehicle for the development of disease states. One or more miasms may be present along with other disease states associated with other miasms. This principle may be expanded upon in the future."

Q At the present time, the other two planetary miasms, syphilis and tuberculosis, have settled into the genetic code to become inherited miasms, but cancer has not done this. Will this happen with cancer as well in the future?
   "Cancer is the chastiser of the individual according to the individual's consciousness. It is also the disease by which there is the greatest bond of healing through the use of the pure mind. This is always dependent upon the individual. There will always be forms of cancer genetically attached to the physical vehicle but not truly as an inherited miasm."

Q Why?
   "Any general weakening of cell tissue opens the individual to cancerous influences. Cancer can also develop from the activities of the other miasms, but this is not a true inherited miasm."

Q You also referred to the stellar miasm. Would you discuss the characteristics of that miasm?
   "Generally, there is constant low vitality. The individual may not even be aware of this because it is such a constant pattern. But there is an overall sense of loss. The loss seems unconnected to the forces that bring an individual into existence, as if they are being told to go back to sleep, leave physical existence, or stop what they are doing. Such people will feel this as a general malaise. This miasm will be a profound problem in certain geographical areas where there is a high degree of background radiation. People moving to such areas will often experience these changes. There will be a more difficult state of mind. This miasm also notably weakens the respiratory system. The assimilation of oxygen and the removal of waste products in the body are sharply affected by the stellar miasm. The brain, which is very involved in these processes, is quite imbalanced by this miasm. The stellar miasm is related to the five chakras above the head.
   "It is also important to understand that stellar background radiation is an important energy that can transform people. It is an energy of tremendous force once it is understood. Its source is in the same place in which gravity is created. Therefore, as one evolves in consciousness and understanding, it is not a matter of purging radiation

from the body but of coming to use and accept it. Indeed, it is quite possible for individuals, once they have reached a certain frame of mind, to exist on such a radiation level as if it is an energy source. This will gradually be an important step in the evolution of many individuals.

"Elsewhere in this manuscript, when discussing the mandala and astrological information, we presented twelve different gems and twelve different metals that are associated with the twelve constellations of the zodiac. These two separate combinations can be ingested as protection against the stellar miasm as well as to alleviate the radiation miasm because of the relationship between these two miasms. People should generally take the gem combination for naturally occurring radiation, while the metal combination should usually be used for radiation exposure from artificial sources, such as in mining or from x-rays. In most cases, natural background radiation is associated with the stellar miasm, and artificial radiation is connected to the radiation miasm. The difficulty is that background radiation can be from both natural and artificial sources. In such cases, it may be wise to take both combinations."

Q What is the suggested dose to use when taking these combinations?

"Follow the general dosage patterns that we have previously suggested for various imbalances. Generally, take up to seven drops of the combinations several times a day at the stock bottle level or at the homeopathic potency of 10MM. If the two combinations are taken together, mix equal amounts into one bottle. Or take one of the combinations for two weeks, wait a week, and then switch to the other combination for two weeks. However, people will often need to take one or both of these combinations for up to six months because of the pervasive effect of radiation in the environment. While it is usually best to take a homeopatic remedy or stock bottle preparation for one or two months to weaken and gradually dislodge a miasm, that is often not enough for treating the stellar miasm.

"Taking one or both of these combinations could be repeated once every two years. Use diagnostic techniques, such as the pendulum, to check every two weeks to see if the stellar or radiation miasms are weakening. Treat background radiation as if it is an overall stress pattern in a person's life. Gradually, the individual will feel more connected and attuned to the environment and to all of nature. To illustrate, someone quite affected by the weather would feel more comfortable in different climatic conditions. Indeed, when someone is notably influenced by the weather, they may have the stellar miasm, although it could also relate to the impact of the syphilitic miasm on the bones or to the psora miasm and a need to understand structure."

Q In the book, *Diseases From Space,* by Hoyle and Wickramasinghe[15] it states that virus and bacteria-related diseases on this planet often reached earth from space. Is this true, and if so, is this part of the stellar miasm?

"There are many parts of this concept that are correct. And this is indeed one more aspect of the stellar miasm. You must remember the powerful action that all thought forms and miasms have in attracting and allowing viruses to take hold. The actual sources of these life forms are often selected by mankind's guides to serve specific purposes."

The stellar miasm is a major fourth category of miasms that was not discussed in the material on miasms in my previous book, *Flower Essences and Vibrational Healing.* That we are influenced by the stars is one of the key foundations of astrology, and is also discussed in the writings of many metaphysical teachers.

Q Are there any other levels of miasms besides the four categories that you have described?

"We will for the present only focus on the stellar influence. Indeed the stellar miasm expresses the understanding that miasms go above and beyond the capacity that miasms are as isolated points of diseases. Miasms are more so the portals in the subtle bodies to which the whole of the very symptoms and very characteristics or foundations of individuals come into manifestation. We offer only this brief discourse at this time as a clue to the student, for to go into the vast hierarchy of miasms is not that which is desired at this time. We wish to expand and build upon the definable principles of miasms as understood by both the orthodox and the esoteric student. Other levels of miasms may perhaps be hinted at and even explained in the future, but they will not be presented within this manuscript."

Q What percentage of the United States population now has the seven inherited miasms?

"At this time 35 to 42 percent of the populace have the syphilitic, psora, and sycotic miasms, and 27 to 32 percent have the tubercular miasm. Concerning the developing new miasms, 10 to 15 percent have the heavy metal miasm, but in the next generation that percentage could rise to 46. Presently, 23 percent have the radiation miasm, but in the next generation that could rise to 48 percent. Currently about 11 percent have the petrochemical miasm, but that figure could rise to 23, 37, or 42 percent in the next generation."

Q What percentage of the population has the stellar miasm?

"As many as 60 percent of the population now have this miasm."

Q Comment on the debate in homeopathic circles that one must first have the psora miasm before developing the syphilitic, sycotic or tubercular miasms?

"This expresses the theory that an individual must be exposed either in ancestral lineage or in direct experience to a specific function or level of stress before the person can open to the activities of other disease states. The channel speaking would contribute to this debate the concept that there may be the symptomatic existence of the psora miasm for other miasms to manifest. It is not that the whole of the psora miasm must be displayed. If the potential for that miasm is displayed, then there is also the potential for these other miasms to exist in someone. But remember, there is often an overlapping of symptoms with these miasms. Therefore, the issue is more that there may be parallel symptoms rather than the actual existence of the psora miasm itself on the physical or ethereal levels of the body."

Q Please give a discourse on specific miasms joining together to become like a combination miasm?

"The major features of joint miasms can usually be easily diagnosed or linked according to the succeeding properties of the chakras to which they are linked. Each of the miasms has a tendency to be prevalent according to the functions of the individual chakras to which they are associated. You would not find any divergent pattern, except that some of the miasms may be detected as being linked when they have a similar impact upon similar or identical internal organs."

Q Would you suggest any general treatments for joint miasms?

"No, except that it is usually best to treat the miasm linked to the lowest chakra first, and then treat the miasm identified with the next higher chakra."

Q Are there any new combination miasms that will tend to develop in the coming years?

"Here we find none. In fact, the tendency within the race as a whole is for just the opposite situation to develop. Individual prevalent miasms will show through and be focused on by individuals. Generally, miasms are not found joined together. They aggravate each other, with individual miasms being found in individuals who desire to remove from themselves karmic conditions that again can be analyzed by their relationship to the chakras."

Q Give a talk on the historical origins of the inherited, planetary, acquired, and stellar miasms and how various societies have treated them?

"The complexity of the stellar miasm will be reserved for a future discourse. Each of the miasms have developed as though in a context of as arising to express personal needs within individuals. The essential nature of the psora miasm has been on earth long before mankind arrived. However, its full development on the planet did not take place until the mid-Lemurian period, when some conflict with God's laws began to be a problem with mankind. All the miasms associated with sexual gender arose mostly in the time periods of Atlantis, where individuals first began to develop most of the activities for using sexual expression. This was when the body physical was first divided into two sexes. Towards the close of Atlantis and the rise of historically recorded civilizations in India and China, there developed the cancer and tubercular miasms. The rise of these miasms was associated with the increased development of individuality and the greater capacity of the emotions. The cancer miasm was initially formed before any of the inherited miasms, but it did not directly begin to affect the human race until the latter days of Atlantis. Finally, the heavy metal, petrochemical, and radiation miasms are developing in these days in accord with various emotional states and a need to master and overcome the environment.

"Note that the overall activities of each miasm contributed to the development of the individual, for they arise not only as though as a disease but also as an indicator and marker of evolvement of the human condition. Historically, in Lemuria there was as the perfect balance of individuals within the collective consciousness. Therefore, miasms had little or no degree of influence within the general populace and only occasionally arose as a pattern unique to certain individuals. Or miasms were created through impure practices of consciousness.

"In Atlantis there began to arise the inherited miasms as they are known in these days, for herein there began to be the development of issues of sexuality and the development and thickening of the astral and emotional bodies, which are, of course, the key to the treatment and understanding of most disease states because most diseases arise from both karma and emotional patterns. The thickening and activities of these bodies made individuals accountable for the karmic actions and deeds committed on the earth plane, setting up the vehicle of focus for the purpose of reincarnation. As activities and miasms began to find a more personal expression through the development of diseases in people, people inhabited physical bodies that were in an inherently weakened state because of various diseases. This opened people to diseases that neither arose directly in connection with the main disease with which each miasm is associated nor to diseases or emotional patterns of a similar nature. The complex disease pattern of each miasm settled into the physical body. For instance, someone would develop a set of symptoms that would be considered tubercular in nature, although that imbalance would not necessarily arise directly from a tubercular bacteria. Such individuals might experience sleeping sickness, difficulty in drawing the breath due to a decentralizing of neurological impulses in the central nervous system, or even the acute tubercular miasm as experienced in the sudden death syndrome, where there is the complete collapse of the neurological tissues and an inability to draw breath.

"Here we find the faculties of the expression that each of the miasms is indeed as linked or associated with the conscious progression of the soul itself by being either active or inactive within each person. Note that the capacity to activate each of the miasms is present within all individuals, although this may not always be detectable. Many seek to define the miasm within the context of the disease model or the order of the disease itself. But the true activities are to define balance as a model of progressing orders of consciousness. This is how people in past cultures related to and treated individuals. People were not examined for their particular disease or disorder but for their progressed levels of consciousness. Historically, it was considered the causal format that consciousness was the critical issue rather than as though the healing of a physical disease was of key importance."

Q Are you saying that a miasm represents an evolutionary step that a person has fallen to and that the treatment in essence is the raising of their consciousness to a pure state?

"Correct. Remember that consciousness is always present. There is a blockage of the self which may find its focus or expression through disease in the physical body. Only when a miasm is rejected or blocked is it a detriment. If one is willing to learn the lessons offered by a miasm, then it can be a positive factor."

Q Explain what blockages the miasms represent?

"Rather than as giving a full discourse, it would be better for the student to study the information already given concerning individual chakras and their relation to the miasms. In examining the diseases associated with each chakra the self-evolutionary pattern of the individual as expressed by the miasms becomes clearer. The miasms are also linked to the minor chakras in that, although their point of focus in the body physical is with specific main chakras, the miasms also affect areas of the anatomy where various minor chakras are isolated. Isolate what parts of the body physical tend to be affected by each miasms, noting what minor chakras are also located in that part of the body. The individual seven rays also unify the energy between the chakras and the miasms. The miasm is transferred to an energy level by which its inner lesson can be understood and experienced by the individual. Thus, at the various chakric levels, the energy of the miasm is received. If the lessons offered by the miasm are not understood, then there will be problems."

Q Speak on the miasms in relation to mankind's spiritual growth?

"The miasms collectively reflect peoples' wish to return to spirit in that diseases arise from blockages in accepting and acknowledging being divine. This, of course, may lead to various levels of stress that may activate the miasms and create disease. Miasms crystallize mankind's struggle toward spiritual evolution. First, there is the need to rise above base sexuality, which includes overcoming syphilis and gonorrhea. Next, there is the use of breath to draw upward and overcome tuberculosis. Then there is the need or attempt to overcome and master the environment. Thus, there are now the radiation, petrochemical, and soon the heavy metal miasms. The cancer miasm allows humanity the opportunity to learn life's lessons as symbolically expressed in the body. The psora miasm is allied with an overall understanding and integration of the structure in the universe and of God's laws. Overcoming the psora miasm means living in harmony with all of creation, leading one closer to being one with the universe. Miasms reflect blockages in conscious growth that mankind has not yet overcome."

Q As one miasm is removed from the body, another may come to the surface. Is it usually best to focus on removing the initial miasm before focusing on the next one that surfaces?

"This is most wise, especially as the practitioner learns the drainage system of removing miasms. The drainage system of removing miasms is most effective because then you are cleansing the organs where the miasms are established in the body physical."

Q Discuss in detail the drainage system of removing miasms from the body?

"Each of the miasms may be treated by simply isolating a simple disease state that functions and is traceable to that miasm. For instance, tuberculosis is linked with the tubercular miasm. Regarding deeper levels, we find the sycotic miasm, which generates venereal disease. Each disease state traditionally associated with the miasmic compounds could be isolated. Any of the disease spectrum associated with each miasm is a portal for other disease states to develop within the individual. Therefore, the individual or general practitioner could homeopathically prepare these disease elements, as has traditionally been done in homeopathy. This is one simple way to treat the miasms.

"Another means of treating the miasms is but to as obtain a classical medical text to examine a disease state in each of its levels of manifestation and to examine how it affects the body in a progressive order. For instance, with tuberculosis, the early manifestation is in the lungs, but as the disease progresses there is some influence on the heart. Eventually, there is pressure on the kidneys with a gradual increase in blood pressure and a mild swelling of the lymphatics.

"Perhaps the purest example of this is syphilis, for it has a very specific graduating progression and anatomy to it as a disease. After affecting the genital region, it then affects the central nervous system, graduating to skin lesions. Drainage through each of the graduating organs affected by this disease would stimulate the removal of this miasm when it is detected in the system.

"The student could isolate and trace the natural course of the disease from its point of initial symptom and the increasing symptoms, throughout the body physical, to its advanced stage. Then apply a system that would purge the miasm from the body by cleansing and purging the internal organs that are affected by the miasm. Generally, first deal with the most internal and vital organs. As each organ is cleansed and purged upon homeopathic principle in a graduating progression that would coincide with the progression of the disease, this would alleviate the miasm. By using various vibrational drainage remedies to drain or cleanse the organs affected by the miasm, each miasm can in a progressive order be purged from the body. Isolate a single disease associated with a miasm and then examining its graduating effects on the body physical and its progressions through each organ until it runs its full course as a disease. Then institute the principle of drainage.

"The student should understand that it is not just that a general total cleansing of the internal organs, in a proceeding order as imbalanced by the disease pattern, would necessarily totally eliminate all miasmic tendencies. Such a method could bring the miasms to the surface to be as more clearly examined. One should use the drainage method linked specifically to knocking out or removing the miasms that are linked to the internal organs that miasm is association with."

Q When one treated the liver, for instance, is it true that the average person could have several miasms lodged in that organ and that cleansing that or many other organs would dislodge several different miasms?

"This is correct, but ye must remember that to remove the miasms fully, the treatment should follow the progressive order in which the internal organs are affected by the miasms. It would be wise to apply Hering's law in using drainage remedies to treat the miasms. First, usually treat the miasms, and indeed diseases in general, associated with the lower chakras and then move to the miasms affecting the higher chakras."

Q In Hering's law, it is stated to treat diseases from above downward and from the more internal and vital organs to the lesser organs. This seems to conflict with your statement to first treat the miasms that affect the lower chakras.

"Remember that the chakras are not directly related the physical body. It is thus not a conflict to use Hering's law to treat the miasms and also treat the miasms that affect the lower chakras first, for you are dealing with energy centers in treating the chakras. In addition, the lower chakras relate more directly to the internal organs; the higher chakras are more associated with the external affairs of the body. The higher chakras are also felt more physically on the skin.

"However, the course of the miasms can be very complex, and a homeopath must certainly use quite a bit of judgement to understand what areas are most important to treat in their proper time. For instance, an abdominal or intestinal difficulty can deplete energy from the overall system when the actual area that is of greatest importance is the head, when the person's full self conception is not clear. Sometimes it is more appropriate to treat imbalanced energy patterns to alleviate the miasms. This is the guiding light."

Q Can the doctrine of signature be used to discover which drainage remedies should be used to cleanse various organs?

"Correct. The doctrine of signature can give insights into those particular homeopathically prepared herbal and even nutritional elements to act as appropriate drainage remedies for the internal organs to remove the miasms. Thus, the doctrine of signature is linked appropriately to the internal organs and, of course, the empathy that exists between the internal organs and those particular herbal, mineral, and even vegetable compounds that have the necessary signatures and sympathetic linkages. Correlate traditional knowledge already available, such as the use of walnut because of

90

its obvious shape, to bringing about drainage in any activities involving the cerebral cortex, such as in the more advanced stages of syphilis. Homeopathically prepared walnut or the flower essence can be used for such conditions. Indeed, gem elixirs and flower essences can also be used as drainage remedies. The doctrine of signature has already linked many gem elixirs and flower essences to isolated portions of the anatomy. To illustrate, bloodstone and bleeding heart are linked to the affairs of the heart.

"Already within the apothecary system drainage, remedies are well established. For instance, a prime drainage remedy for the brain and nervous system is mercury. For draining the lymphatics, use homeopathic calcium, the simple cold virus, or combine them together. This technique will broaden the student's knowledge and perhaps institute a new theory of approach to the drainage system for treating the miasms. The channel speaking desires more so to present these general concepts and principles than to provide further details. It is sensed that with these principles the generally knowledgeable student and, above all, the advanced practitioner will be able to see the new principle of drainage as applied to the miasms."

Q Is the rather developed system of drainage remedies that have been used in France sufficient for this work?
   "Correct."

The use of drainage remedies in the French school of homeopathy has gone on for some years. This technique has rarely been used among homeopaths in the English-speaking countries. Perhaps many homeopaths would benefit from examining that literature. One interesting text in English is *Drainage In Homeopathy* by Dr. Maury.[16]

Q Explain how miasms block vibrational remedies from working properly. For instance, it is increasingly understood in homeopathic circles that certain chemical drugs such as steroids tend to block homeopathic remedies from working properly.
   "Again, this is primarily linked to the activities of consciousness. Biochemicals integrate into the body physical primarily either to stimulate or to disrupt the conscious ability of the individual to function in a clear or overly stimulated fashion. These forces may ultimately block the enhancing influences of homeopathic remedies. The rejection by the individual from levels of consciousness is the ultimate blockage. Note that any of the stimulants currently understood to block homeopathic remedies, from simple caffeine to various chemical drugs, are all primarily things which tend to have a direct influence upon someone's behavioral patterns or on one of the major seats of consciousness in individuals. For instance, steroids, in their capacity to promote muscular density, indeed stimulate the muscles which are a direct major seat of consciousness in the body physical. Any stimulants that cause a disruption of consciousness in the body physical will tend to block or at least not enhance homeopathic remedies."

Q So you are saying that it is not the drug or stimulant but the state of the person that blocks the homeopathic remedy?
   "Ultimately, yes. It is not so much a physiological process as much as it is a vibrational process."

Q Is this why homeopathic remedies often do not work with extremely depressed people or with people who have severe mental illnesses such as schizophrenia?

"Correct. In such cases, we recommend using drainage remedies. They work somewhat independently of consciousness because they work directly on the seat of consciousness itself. It is quite difficult to explain what the seat of consciousness is, but primarily we are look at the principles by which an individual is brought into existence. This, to some extent, relates to the concept of the permanent atom, which has largely been superceded by the idea of an etheric thought form that is actually the creative spark that begins an incarnation. This incarnation holds within it the seat of consciousness, the idea of bringing into action those things that need to be learned and created to actually have a physical body to accomplish these things. These principles are open to deeper acting remedies, such as drainage remedies, because they work in harmony with the original principle and plan to have a physical body in which to learn and grow.

"Moreover, people extremely depressed should take a simple dry sauna to release toxins in the sweating process to cleanse the system. This should be done twice daily for twenty minutes each time. That people are willing to do something for themselves can be an important aid in the healing process. Eventually this will create a state of enhanced well-being so that general homeopathic practices can be applied."

Q In such cases, would psychotherapy or love be appropriate?

"Love, of course, is superior. Psychotherapy perhaps as spiritually practiced would aid the process, especially if combined with meditation. Massage therapy would also often be helpful."

Q Would this explain why some people, no matter what you do, do not seem to improve with homeopathy?

"Correct. Give the case history you are reflecting on."

Q An associate who is a physician is treating someone who had hepatitis in Latin America twelve years ago. It was so severe he almost died. He was involved in spiritual work for five years, but since the hepatitis attack he has had continual health problems and has stopped meditating or working on himself to grow spiritually. He has seen many doctors and tried numerous approaches with very little improvement. He had hypoglycemia for a while, but that seems over and the doctor now treating him has also found that his liver seems clean. That physician has worked with him from the heart level, and the sense of pessimism seems to be gradually lifting now.

"This case would indeed exemplify the great role of consciousness in adequate health care. The liver is the ultimate confrontation of one's innermost fears."

Q Is this a key reason why it is wise to use flower essences, and to a slightly less degree, gem elixirs in treating the miasms because they work on realms of consciousness more than do homeopathic remedies?

"Correct."

Q When one sees that homeopathic remedies or perhaps other natural remedies such as herbs or nutritional supplments are not effectively working on the individual, should one use flower essences and gem elixirs to directly affect the person's consciousness?

"Yes, along with love and possibly spiritually orientated psychotherapy. This should alleviate the factors that are blocking the remedies from working."

Q Explain how miasms become diseases in the body. For instance, you said miasms, when diversified, become portals for different diseases. How does this process develop?

"Here we find again that the miasms correspond to the different chakras. When miasms are introduced into the body physical, they become portals for other disease states. All diseases have a graduating order or progression and the miasms, as is already somewhat understood in traditional homeopathy, correspond to the body physical's natural five levels of defense.

"In this discourse, we shall discuss the levels of miasms in relation to the five levels of the body's defenses. The first defense in the body exists with the skin as it resists the first penetration of a disease. Then there is intestinal and mucous membrane resistance. Ultimately, the disease penetrates to the cellular level. The next level of defense in the body includes the electrical properties and energy stimulus of the body. The neurological tissues attempt to regenerate cell memory. There is the capacity of tissue regeneration as has been given in past discourses. This is somewhat understood in some aspects of chiropractic theory. Finally, there is the role of the subtle bodies in the way they protect the body physical. That a disease may ultimately again pass through the skin, which is the first point of entry for a disease, is also symbolic of an individual's connection with other people and the environment.

"Each of the miasms eventually moves deeper and deeper into the body physical. Thus, it also activates deeper levels of defense in the body physical. It may accurately be said that gem elixirs, flower essences, and homeopathic remedies activate all five levels of defense in the body physical. However, they have a natural sympathetic resonancy with different levels of defense in the physical body. Therefore, miasms are portals to other diseases because they break down the different defenses in the body physical, thus allowing deeper and deeper levels of various disease states to penetrate more easily into the body physical.

"For instance, the defenses of the skin's tissue are injured in those people who are subject to lesions or allergic responses upon the surface of the skin's tissue. This makes it easier to develop problems with the body's next layer of defense in the mucus membrane and sensitive linings of the lung's tissue so that deeper allergic responses may develop. The tubercular miasm may ensue opening the body to deeper levels of disease states. Simple viral attacks as found in pneumonia may materialize which could allow the development of cancer-causing leukemia viruses in the body physical. That allows the cancer miasm to enter the body physical. As each of the body physical's natural series of defenses are broken, that opens the body physical to deeper levels of disease. Therefore, the miasms are portals through which a wide variety of diseases could develop.

"Eventually, diseases could be isolated so that if one or more miasms were present, the full spectrum of diseases present in the individual could be isolated and a profile of potential disease states could be presented. This could be done by simply analyzing the levels upon which diseases function. For instance, simple tetanus enters the body through the skin's tissue. Tetanus then quickly penetrates to the body physical's second level of defense where true resistance to it begins, especially upon the cellular level. In the final phase of tetanus, it eventually penetrates to the body physical's first initial defenses causing a gradual rigidity in the muscular tissue often causing mild neurological inflammation and increasing difficulty in the original level of skin penetration. It thus animates all levels of the body's natural defenses."

Q How do gem elixirs affect the miasms?

"Gem elixirs function along similar lines and principles as homeopathy, but also integrate more closely to the level of the subtle anatomies working directly with the functions of consciousness and karmic patterns, not unlike the properties and activities of flower essences. Gemstones balance the physical body and subtle anatomies more than homeopathic remedies, so they weaken the miasms slightly more than homeopathic remedies. The key way to use gem elixirs to treat the miasms is to focus on the chakras. Identify the chakras affected by different gemstones and miasms and diseases associated with each miasm.

"The crystalline makeup of many minerals parallels the mineral makeup of specific organs. Gem elixirs penetrate from the subtle anatomies into the physical body promoting health usually through specific organs, which then stimulate a form of immunology. They are similar to herbs which also promote general health by stimulating portions of the anatomy. Miasms are integrated throughout all levels of the genetic code and spread throughout many levels of organs. Miasms are as spread throughout the entire pattern of the body physical's rejuvenative capacity. For instance, the syphilitic miasm is not necessarily just concentrated in the spinal column and genital areas. It is spread throughout the general pattern of the DNA. Therefore, gem elixirs alleviate miasms, not only by activating the chakras, but also by rejuvenating isolated organs and glandular tissue and the genetic code in specific parts of the body. In contrast, homeopathic remedies rejuvenate the entire body physical more than isolated spectrums of the anatomy."

Q Will you further explain how flower essences and homeopathic remedies affect the miasms, in contrast to what you have just said about gem elixirs?

"Flower essences do not so much directly abate the miasms; they merely create a clear state of consciousness, which then affects the personality, the physical body, and the genetic code and may entirely eliminate miasms from the physical and subtle bodies. This is also true of certain gem elixirs that are especially ethereal in their effects. Gem elixirs and flower essences that notably influence the crown chakra and the subtle bodies weaken all the miasms, although this is more true with acquired miasms. Gem elixirs and flower essences work along the same passageways in the physical and subtle bodies. This action naturally weakens the miasms. Moreover, gem elixirs and flower essences can be ingested and be applied externally or in a bath to alleviate the miasms.

"In treating the miasms, first isolate the main diseases caused by different miasms. Then combine several gem elixirs, flower essences, or homeopathic remedies and sometimes herbs into one remedy to eradicate the various miasms. However, it is not always necessary to combine these different types of remedies to eradicate the miasms. Sometimes it is best to take only gem elixirs or only flower essences or homeopathic remedies. This gradually releases the miasms from the genetic code and subtle bodies, so they can be discharged from the system. This procedure, however, requires skillful treatment.

"Because the activities of miasms extend into the subtle anatomies, they can be treated from that level. Flower essences, working on levels of consciousness, first alter the individual's consciousness. Then the individual's consciousness is able to flow more smoothly through the body physical as an instrument. Slowly, these energies are applied and redirected into the body physical to remove from the biomolecular and cellular level the energy that represents the miasms. This energy is pushed into the ethers for its eventual dissolution from the physical form.

"Homeopathic remedies attempt to duplicate in the physical body a vibrational frequency similar to the miasm to expel it. They work directly on the same levels as miasms—the etheric body interfacing with the genetic code. This is where miasms tend to get rooted in the physical body. The effectiveness of homeopathy in these areas is that it integrates closer to the physical levels and indeed is the interface between the cellular structure and the etheric body. Homeopathic remedies work closer to the principles of the ethereal fluidium and the etheric body and influence in varying degrees the subtle bodies, while flower essences are closer to the patterns of energy that indeed are the subtle bodies. Homeopathy is not so much more effective against the miasms; it is but that as a science it has been isolated as working specifically within the frequencies that the miasms inhabit. Those originally working with homeopathy thought of it as a pattern and system of stimulating the body's own biochemical immune system and were puzzled by the vibrational aspects."

In recent years, some homeopaths have accepted the fact that miasms can also be acquired by numerous infectious illnesses, especially the childhood diseases. This view was first presented by Dr. Tyler in 1933.[17] These infectious toxins settle into the cells as acquired miasms where they often remain dormant for many years before producing symptoms that seemingly have nothing to do with the original infection.[18]

In 1969, United States scientists working at the National Institute of Health discovered that a rare brain disease that killed about 200 people a year was caused by measles that these people had years ago.[19] Today, it is widely understood in orthodox medical circles that many chronic degenerative diseases are caused by slow or unapparent viral infections.[20] Extensive medical research is now being conducted to discover which acute infections tend to relate to which degenerative diseases many years later.[21] The relationship of measles to multiple sclerosis is one such example. Miasms are a predisposition within the vibrational makeup of the individual that these viruses find a sympathetic resonancy to. In time, orthodox medical practitioners and classical homeopaths will discover the relationship between slow viruses and miasms.[22] As with inherited miasms, difficult cases are relieved when acquired miasms are isolated and treated.

Q Why is an acquired miasm connected more to the physical body rather than to the subtle anatomies?

"Miasms are as passed on through the genetic code. An acquired miasm is attached to the physical body through the DNA level."

Q Explain the different effects that gem elixirs and flower essences have on acquired and inherited miasms?

"Acquired miasms generally develop during interaction with the environment during one's current life. It is how the consciousness and its acts of being free flowing or being suppressed can impact with the environment during one's life. The acquired miasms may develop from a suppression of karmic paths or patterns in the flow of everyday life. There are the dynamics of the personality and the personal choices of the individual to consider. These activities then become the acquired miasms that may be passed on to succeeding generations. These activities are as cumulative.

"Gem elixirs and flower essences are most wisely applied in treating acquired miasms as preventive activities in a fashion similar to preventive medicine. This allows for the taking of these vibrational preparations to monitor the general state and well being of one's consciousness and spiritual reality to expand the spiritual dynamics of the individual. This creates more balance than just to seek to isolate and treat various miasms. It is better to use gem elixirs and flower essences to promote the spiritual well-being of the individual. Even though many have various acquired miasms in these days, meditation and the partaking of gem elixirs and flower essences focusing on spiritual growth can often alleviate and remove these miasms. This is not so true with inherited miasms, which have generally settled deeper into the body. In addition, homeopathic remedies generally do not work on realms of consciousness, so they will not usually be sufficient to treat acquired miasms by raising one's consciousness, although they will often be effective in alleviating the physical efects of acquired miasms.

"With the activities of the inherited miasms, there are both the karmic patterns and the actual circumstances by which the miasms were inherited directly from the physical form from the parents. Usually when the soul overshadows the physical body the forces of the soul may shape the activities according to karmic dictates so as to open the physical form to various miasms that have come from past lives. However, inherited miasms may also be contained directly with the genetic biomolecular and cellular levels carried with the individual as part of the hereditary pattern inherited from the parents. The hereditary miasms must be detected through analysis, then brought to the surface and removed from the body by the institutional use of vibrational preparations. These preparations should be applied to specific diseases, especially when the disease pattern is directly related to specific miasms. These activities bring forth balance not only to strengthen the individual to remove the miasms but also can manifest complete and total healing because karmic circumstances are always equivalent to the activating or causal force for activation of the disease state. The final principle here would be to bring forth balance and understanding that it is the promotion of the individual's consciousness that should be the original causal element and the understanding of the lesson gained. This, of course, comes from meditation and a balanced use of vibrational preparations, not from specific resistance to disease states."

Q If one is born with any inherited miasms, does that make the person more prone to developing any of the other miasms, such as the acquired miasms?

"The inherited miasms are more directly linked to the individual's consciousness. By the word 'inherited' it is implied that the body physical is somehow subjected to the planned ancestral lineage of the individual to find as a karmic focus within a particular physical body. Inherited miasms and various diseases are reflective of many of the soul's activities. Thus, these imbalances are karmically originated as the soul expresses or activates itself in a physical body. The inherited miasms become a portal, particularly as they align with the chakras, through which other miasms become active expressions of either blockages or enhancers to the progression of the soul in its quest to obtain knowledge of itself as a spiritual being by as placing itself under the discipline of the body physical. Thus, the inherited miasms are linked more closely with the personal

96

consciousness of the individual, having been inherited as an expression of the collective soul group or the soul force. This takes place both individually and collectively in the soul group itself."

Q Speak on the view that the tubercular miasm makes one more prone to developing the other miasms?

"Since all disease enters the body through the measurable results of stress, the lungs are the most sensitive of tissues that bring about the most measurable results. The lungs are the one autonomic response that brings about focus and centralization of regulated consciousness in the body physical. The tubercular miasm centrally locates the deterioration of that critical autonomic response that links consciousness with the physical body itself—the lungs, breath, and emotions. The lungs have been associated as though in many systems of thought, such as with the Chinese five element theory, as being the center of emotions. Thus, when there is disruption of emotional patterns, stress is immediately centered. And the lungs are immediately associated with mortality and with the deep inner fears of people. Thus, since breath is a critical autonomic response to which there is direct conscious control and conscious expression that links ye with the autonomic responses of the body physical, the tubercular miasm is indeed the grand portal through which many of the diseases and miasms enter the body physical. The disruption of that central regulator of consciousness in the body physical is why that miasm is especially associated with the other miasms."

Q Explain how acquired miasms are passed on to the next generation as inherited miasms?

"This is purely dependent on the degree to which the miasm has thoroughly integrated into the biomolecular structure. In the biomolecular structure, as the individual accumulates through consciousness a continuous practice, ultimately the miasm becomes such a prevalent state with the individual that it becomes interlinked with or could eventually be considered pathological behavior. This particularly transpires in the first seven years of life. Thus, when studying pathological behavior, that can indeed accurately be said to have been acquired in childhood. One can also link that behavior pattern consciously with the various internal organs. One can even predict the potential miasm that may then become an inherited miasm passed on to the next generation.

"For instance, there may be turmoil in early childhood such as with sibling rivalry wherein the lungs become involved. These sibling rivalries may remain unresolved within the individual and contribute to a pathological behavior pattern towards other people that remind the person of the various siblings that they were in association with. Ultimately, there may be an effect on the person's general state of well-being as connected with the lung's tissue. This karmic pattern could be passed to succeeding generations to wherein another soul for its purpose of reincarnation could then pick up the line of that particular karma as passed on physically and then act out these affairs in a later generation. Thus, acquired miasms can be connected to a pathological study of individuals in their behavior patterns, wherein the behavior is not so much simple conditioned response but indeed has become pathological and has a direct influence on specific internal organs. Then the pattern of the internal organs and the consciousness linked can be directly traceable to the patterns associated with the miasms. Thus, one can predict which acquired miasm will become an inherited miasm."

Another category of miasms to consider is the remedy miasm. A remedy miasm can occur if someone takes too many doses of a remedy. The vibration of a remedy can attach itself to the individual, and there can be problems releasing this vibrational frequency. It is easier for this problem to occur at high homeopathic potencies—200x or 200c and higher. This is one reason why only a few doses are prescribed for homeopathic remedies at high potencies. However, 10MM is a neutral potency in a separate category. Remedy miasms can be considered a subcategory of acquired miasms in that both develop during a given lifetime.

Q Can gem elixirs and flower essences cause remedy miasms?

"As with flower essences, constant exposure to a gem elixir creates not so much a remedy miasm, but a change in the individual's consciousness. When the actions of a gem elixir or flower essence release emotional tensions, this sometimes seems to be associated with remedy miasms. In addition, some very sensitive or spiritually aware people sometimes seem to experience remedy miasms with flower essences and gem elixirs because such people are almost pure consciousness and usually less in need of physical treatment. Consequently, the subtle bodies are usually temporarily aligned, and the properties of the remedies are almost immediately activated into the consciousness and physical body.

"It is easier to create a remedy miasms by taking too much of a homeopathic remedy than with other vibrational remedies because they work more directly in the physical body. With homeopathic remedies, and to a lesser extent with gem elixirs, remedy miasms do not necessarily disappear right away when you stop taking the remedy. Remedy miasms created from using gem elixirs would be quite mild and would rarely last longer than seven days once the elixir was stopped, although proving symptoms could continue for thirty to sixty days but never beyond that. However, it is extremely rare to create a remedy miasm with gem elixirs. If it did occur, exposure to blue, indigo, or violet for thirty minutes would supersede the vibrational patterns of the gem elixir. These colors activate and synthesize the crown and pituitary chakras to restore balance. And what someone thought was a remedy miasm from a gem elixir could just be temporary discomfort from toxicity being released.

"What can also occur is that the remedy will pull to the surface various miasms that have been held in check. Some may not yet be ready to receive their karmic significance. Individuals are awakened to certain issues before they are ready. This is more true with flower essences and least true with homeopathic remedies, because of the spiritual significance of flower essences. As is often the case, gem elixirs function between flower essences and homeopathic remedies in this process.

"Sometimes people using flower essences experience positive changes in consciousness which tear down certain barriers in the psyche of the individual. The resulting stress from an inability to let go and experience greater balance can sometimes seem like a created miasmatic pattern. Some people are so attached to existing in a state of imbalance that they feel more secure perpetuating negative feelings. Therefore, they deliberately intensify their situation to be left alone with the condition. Thus, the uplifting in consciousness that these individuals feel may not be synchronistic with the ability of their consciousness to assimilate the more positive aspects that can be brought to them. Such individuals need only exercise their free will to take advantage of the more positive states of consciousness that can be experienced."

More information could be presented here on the miasms, especially the new ones, but to do so would go beyond the scope of this book. Much of this information, including strategies in treating the miasms, has already been channeled for a future text on homeopathy. There is also much information on the miasms in traditional homeopathic literature[23] and in *Esoteric Healing* by Alice Bailey. Hopefully, in time, holistic health practitioners will jointly use gem elixirs, flower essences, and homeopathic remedies. For toxicity to be cleansed from the body's cellular level, vibrational medicine or spiritual healing must be used. Only then can all miasms be eradicated and true health prevail.

"These activities can become the foundation upon which to develop the principles with which to use vibrational therapies to treat and eliminate the miasms. This would have to be a gradually developing art and science through a system of testing and observation. Or it could be a completely independent system of study through a body of channeled information.

"A full understanding of homeopathy will develop when that science aligns itself with effective psychotherapy and the true laws of physics which govern this plane. The joining together of quartz crystal technologies with homeopathy will also be an important feature in the future."

1 Aubrey Westlake,M.D., *The Pattern of Health* (Boulder,Co: Shambhala Publications,1974),p.14-15.

2 Wm. Boericke,M.D., *A Compend of the Principles of Homeopathy* (Mokelumne Hill,Ca: Health Research,1971),p.73-74.

3 Aubrey Westlake,M.D., "Miasms," *Psionic Medicine*, I (Winter,1969),71-72.

4 T.D. Ross,M.D.,"Miasmatic Thoughts," *British Homeopathic Journal*, LI (April,1962), 71-83.

5 George W. Mackenzie,M.D., "The Principles of Psora," *British Homeopathic Journal*, XXVIII (October,1936), 392-415.

6 A. C. Gordon Ross,M.D., "Chronic Disease," *British Homeopathic Journal*, LI (April,1962),85.

7 Ibid, 85.

8 T. D. Ross,M.D., "Miasmatic Thoughts," *British Homeopathic Journal*, LI (April,1962), 72,78.

9 Aubrey Westlake,M.D., "Miasms," *Psionic Medicine*, I (Winter,1969), 21-22.

10 Victor Bott,M.D., *Anthroposophical Medicine* (London: Rudolf Steiner Press,1978),p.108-110.

Dr. Fortier-Bernoville, "The Tuberculinique States and Hanhemann's Psora," *British Homeopathic Journal*, XXVIII (October,1936), 358-391.

11 Aubrey Westlake,M.D., *The Pattern of Health* (Boulder,Co:Shambhala Publications,1974),p.145.

12_____, "The Contribution of Psionic Medicine to Hanhemann's Miasmic Theory," *Psionic Medicine*, XI (Winter,1974),24-25.

13 Alice Bailey, *Esoteric Healing* (New York: Lucis Publishing,1980),p.221-242.

14 T.D. Ross,M.D., "Miasmatic Thoughts," *British Homeopathic Journal*, LI (April,1962),75-76.

Aubrey Westlake,M.D., "Miasms," *Psionic Medicine*, I (Winter,1969),22.

15 Fred Hoyle and N.C. Wickramasinghe, *Diseases From Space* (N.Y: Harper and Row, 1979).

16 Dr. E. A. Maury, *Drainage In Homeopathy* (London: Health Science Press, 1965).

17 Dr. Tyler, "Hahnemann's Conception of Chronic Disease, As Caused By Parasitic Micro-

Organisms," *British Homeopathic Journal*, XXIII (January,1933), 1-56.

18 Aubrey Westlake,M.D., "Miasms," *Psionic Medicine*, I (Winter, 1969),16.

_____, "The Contribution of Psionic Medicine to Hahnemann's Miasmic Theory," *Psionic Medicine*, XI (Winter,1974), 26.

19_____, "Miasms and Smoldering Virus," *Psionic Medicine*, I (Winter,1969), 23.

20_____, "The Contribution of Psionic Medicine to Hahnemann's Miasmic Theory," *Psionic Medicine*, XI (Winter,1974), 27-31.

21 John Holland, "Slow, Inapparent and Recurrent Viruses," *Scientific American*, CCXXX (February,1974), 32-40.

22 Aubrey Westlake,M.D., "The Contribution of Psionic Medicine to Hahnemann's Miasmic Theory, *Psionic Medicine*, XI (Winter,1974), 27-31.

23 Herbert Roberts,M.D., *The Principles and Art of Cure by Homeopathy* (Saffron Walden,England: Health Science Press,1976).

J.H. Allen,M.D., *Chronic Miasms* (Calcutta,India: C. Ringer & Co.,n.d.).

Samuel Hahnemann, M.D., *The Chronic Diseases-Theoretical Part* (New Delhi,India: B. Jain Publishers,1976).

Proceso Sanchez Ortega, *Notes On the Miasms or Hahnemann's Chronic Diseases* (New Delhi,India: National Homeopathic Pharmacy,1983).

CHAPTER VII

BATH THERAPIES AND GEM ELIXIRS

All gem elixirs can be used in baths. In fact, bathing with gem elixirs tends to activate the higher properties of the mineral. Bathing with gem elixirs is always superior to just bathing with a gemstone. But a bath is even better if taken with both the gem elixirs and the gemstones. The best effect takes place when a gem elixir is ingested and placed in the bath along with the gem. These techniques also sensitize the body to adjust to the proper wearing of gemstones. It is best, if possible, to take a bath in the morning before noon because the life force is strongest with the rising sun. And it is best to not use soap during these baths. Usually put four to seven drops from the gem elixir into the bath. For greater spiritual awareness seven drops is superior because it helps you attune to the seven ethers and seven dimensions.

Generally, you should stay in the bath for at least thirty minutes, with one hour often being best. Cover as much of your body with water as possible, and except for very young children, take these baths alone. Wait at least six hours between taking these baths; indeed, one a day or every several days is usually fine. The water temperature should be at body temperature or a bit warmer. If you are pregnant, the water temperature should not be hotter than just below body temperature. Never take warm baths after the fifth month of pregnancy. And do not use soap when bathing with gem elixirs and flower essences. After the bath, lie down for a few minutes so the blood recirculates.

Q Will you now discuss the main principles involved in using gem elixirs and gem stones in bathing?

"Before taking a bath or shower with gem elixirs, cleanse your body. Instead of just filling the tub with water, put five gallons of water into the tub. Then step into the tub and rinse your body with a pure sponge, preferably a clean linen or some substance like cotton with a form of crushed white, rose, or amethyst quartz. If possible, use homeopathically prepared quartz at 10MM or 30c. The crushed quartz, which stimulates the properties of gem elixirs, goes inside the pure linen. It would be wise to put only five gallons of water into the tub initially because this focuses the initial cleansing on the lower extremities where many toxic energies are stored. After five or ten minutes of such bathing add more water. In five gallons, as well as in a full tub, an average of four to seven drops of the gem elixir is usually sufficient.

"Try to use spring water or distilled water for the bath. If you must use city water, add a quarter cup of lemon juice because this cleanses the water. Next, the enamel in the tub should be thoroughly scrubbed, preferably with a mildly abrasive action, possibly using baking soda or lemon juice. To potentize the water a bit more, especially if using city water for the bath, leave some of the water under the sun or put it under a copper pyramid for about thirty minutes. In either case, add a small amount of lemon juice to the water. These techniques cleanse and enhance the qualities of the water so that it can better receive vibrational elixirs.

"There is a peculiar enhancing effect of water as a conductor for activating the properties of gemstones. Water is highly conductive and has an immediate affinity with the electromagnetic and biomagnetic forces of the body physical. Water acts as a conductor for all electromagnetic energy. Bathing distributes the influence of the gem elixir immediately into the aura and then into the subtle bodies. This also occurs because the aura is in a constant state of movement so it is easier for the aura to be penetrated and cleansed by water. This process bypasses the need to penetrate first into the physiology of the individual. These patterns also mean that gem elixirs placed in baths become much more self-adjusting, almost to the level of flower essences. The effects move directly into the activities of the aura, alleviating and activating karmic patterns within the capacity of the subtle anatomies. Bathing with gem elixirs is an attempt to distribute the properties of the elixir with the conductive properties of water, its immediate and equal displacement throughout the water, and above all its continuous exposure to the individual while the person bathes. In fairly pure water or in distilled water, the properties of the elixir are immediately and evenly dispensed."[1]

Q Elsewhere you said ingested gem elixirs vibrationally function between flower essences and homeopathic remedies, but that gem elixirs usually act closer to the vibration of homeopathic remedies because such elixirs tend to have greater impact on the physical body like homeopathic remedies, rather than on the psyche and emotions like flower essences. Are you now saying that because the water further dilutes gem elixirs such preparations, when placed in water, work closer to flower essences?

"Correct. The vibrational effect of the water upon the gem elixir and on the aura and subtle bodies creates this distinction."

Q Would there be any difference in using a gem elixir in a bath on the stock bottle level versus a homeopathic level?

"No, the influence would be about the same. Occasionally, there would be the slight enhancing effect on the homeopathic level. With bathing, it is more a matter of just getting the energy of the elixir into the water. Ingesting an accurately prescribed gem elixir homeopathically prepared, however, is superior to giving that same elixir on the stock bottle level.

"An interesting showering technique is to take a pure piece of linen, soak it in lemon juice and quartz powdered or granules, then soak it in one or more of the elixirs that you want to bathe in. Next, place the quartz powder or granules in the linen. If possible, remove the front of the shower head and tuck in the linen, or simply tie the linen to the shower head. As the water flows out, the lemon juice neutralizes the impurities in the water and the quartz amplifies the effects of the gem elixir. Take this shower for around thirty minutes."

Q How would the quartz be purified to reuse in future baths?

"Put the quartz in a bottle of distilled water and seal the bottle. Then set the bottle in some sea salt. Twenty-four hours in the distilled water and sea salt would be a sufficient cleansing. Or put the bottle under a copper pyramid for at least six hours, but the pyramid is not essential here."

Q How could gems and gem elixirs be used in a bath for healing purposes?

"One technique that could be used is to calculate the course of a disease and the time period in which that disease would normally run its course. Then construct a mandala based upon your astrological chart and place that mandala within the bath. Individuals bathing in that water would as draw in the time flow of future ethereal patterns that would be affecting them. This speeds up the time flow of the disease affecting the individual so that the disease runs its course much quicker. Further information on the use of mandalas is presented in other parts of this text.

"Bathing with a gem elixir always works better if the actual gemstone is also placed in the water. This works even better if the water is first filtered through quartz crystals with the above described technique. Gemstones were embellished in the bathing pools of many past cultures including Lemuria, Atlantis, Egypt, Rome, Greece, Persia, India, China, the Incas, and the Mayans.

"A particularly valuable technique is to obtain and place seven oils in the bath along with the actual gemstone. Individuals can research what would be especially valuable to their unique needs, but the seven oils recommended for the general populace to activate the seven chakras include olive oil for the crown chakra, jojoba oil for the brow chakra, clove oil for the throat chakra, sunflower oil for the heart chakra, cotton oil for the third chakra, peanut oil for the second chakra, and safflower oil for the first chakra. People experimenting with other oils should feel free to use intuition and other modalities such as the pendulum to understand what chakra each oil is affecting.

"Oils fully strained to the point of clearness with as little coloration as possible are best. Otherwise, colored oils would manifest color healing and a given color frequency might be discordant with and interfere with the color vibration and healing frequency of a given gemstone. These oils should also be organic, preferably not including any animal fat or petroleum products."

Q How would these oils be mixed with the gemstones in the bath?

"First, experiment to isolate the level of natural suspension and buoyancy of each oil. One possible test is to take a tumbler half filled with pure distilled water and gradually place each oil into the tumbler. There would be a slight differentiation in buoyancy and density for each oil; each would float at a slightly different level in the water. You could then see what level the oil was influencing to better understand how each oil was working. The goal is to obtain seven different levels to activate each of the seven main chakras.

"In a tumbler or in a bath, the denser oils that settle closer to the bottom of the water have an attunement to the lower chakras and associated lower chakra influences, while the finer oils that settle closer to the top of the water have more affinity to the higher chakras. For instance, contrast the settlement of heavier castor oil with lighter almond or myrrh and frank oils. Castor oil is often used over the abdomen, while oils from frank and myrrh are traditionally used to anoint the brow and other facial areas, thus affecting the higher chakras. When used in bathing, the heavier oils have a greater affinity with gems that have an attunement to the lower chakras such as dark pearl and dark opal. Lighter oils intermix with gemstones that activate the higher chakras such as quartz and diamond. Approximately five drops of each oil should be placed into the average size bathtub. However, more oil could be added to the bath so that the entire surface of the water was covered with oil.

"The properties of these oils penetrate into the skin, which is, of course, part of the body's digestive system. The assimilation of these properties into the system cause increased harmony and balance within the self. Gemstones influence the person more by stimulating the subtle bodies through the meridians, which find a heightened quality upon the skin's surface. It is better if the gemstones used to correspond to the chakras are of a more porous nature. Because of this porous nature, it might be wise to use some of these gemstones only once in this process. While it is not crucial, greater amplification is achieved in bathing with gem elixirs, gemstones, and oils with distilled water. If the water used is first passed through crushed powdered quartz as described above, the properties of the oils and gemstones will then extend to the levels of the subtle bodies, stimulating a mild nutrient like property.

"In Lemuria, this same bath was often used with the gemstones then being suspended in the water at the approximate level of the seven oils being used. Individuals then completely submerged themselves in the water entering a state of suspended animation not unlike the yogis of today. While this total submersion is not crucial, it does enhance the effect of the oils and gemstones on the chakras. People today would need special breathing apparatus to submerge themselves under the water beyond very short periods of time.

"A further recommended amplification to use in any gem baths is to expose yourself to certain colors while in the bath. With the information on many of the individual gem elixirs, it is often suggested that the properties of particular minerals are amplified when they are exposed to certain colors. Exposure to those same colors while in the bath using that gem elixir and gemstone is wise. For instance, the properties of aventurine are amplified through exposure to blue light. If taking a bath with aventurine, try bathing in blue light as well. However, when ultraviolet and infrared light is recommended to amplify the properties of an elixir such as with apatite, only expose yourself to each light for five minutes while in a bath. During this procedure try to illuminate the entire perimeter of the bathing structure.

"Mud baths are perhaps the most advanced form of bathing because the crystalline particles in the mud activates the crystalline structures in the body and greatly enhance the effects of gem elixirs and flower essences. Advanced principles involving the physics of mud bathing will be presented in a future text."

Q Why would one take the mud bath versus an oil and gem bath?

"This depends on the unique needs of each individual. If there is a relatively simple condition, than the gem bath might be sufficient. Complex problems tend to require bathing with oils or mud being added to the bath along with the gem elixir and gemstone. But one would not necessarily take a mud bath before or after taking a bath with gem elixirs. Again, it depends on the unique needs of each individual."

Q What is the basic difference in taking a bath with a gem elixir versus using the actual gemstone in the water?

"Bathing with just a gemstone in the water more closely approximates the effect of ingesting a homeopathic remedy in that the physiological processes become more directly involved. In contrast, bathing with only a gem elixir mainly affects the aura and chakras and then moves into the physical body."

Q Do these bathing and showering techniques differ from the ingestion method concerning the effects of gem elixirs on people?

"Showering or using an atomizer with gem elixirs is the most effective way to augment the aura and subtle bodies. Bathing with gem elixirs is often superior in clinical effects to ingestion, although ingestion is more convenient. A combination of ingestion and a quick shower under the same elixir is just as effective as a full bath or shower with the elixir. The baths are the equivalent of larger doses. This is because bathing dilutes and energizes the elixir and spreads it over the entire skin surface. The skin is a natural assimilation point for the life force to enter the system through the pores, and the water brings you closer to the vibrational frequencies upon which the nature spirits reside. But nature spirits are not so drawn to bathe with gem elixirs as with flower essences. However, meditation does draw them to such baths."

Q Why is it often recommended that a gem elixir first be mixed with distilled water before it is added to the full bath?

"Distilled water is a neutral vehicle or conductor and thus a general potentizer."

Q Some people, rather than feeding the remedies orally to their children because of their resistance to taking them, just flick the elixir water onto their bodies. How effective is this method?

"This is a good method, but it is not superior to ingestion. A method similar to ingestion in its effectiveness would be massaging the soles of the feet because they are incredibly sensitive. Rubbing it on the palms of the hands or on the forehead is also excellent."

Q Would it be wise to hang a pyramid from your ceiling above the bathtub?

"It could be done, but do not make this a permanent structure because it could have negative effects. Pyramids tend to magnify whatever is put under them. If you enter a tub in a bad mood, that negativity could be amplified."

It has long been understood that some healing properties of gems are transferred to water or another liquid in which the stone is immersed.[2] Indeed, bathing and showering with gem elixirs are quite powerful. The gemstones can be added to the water, but it is usually sufficient to add just the elixirs to the water. The various amplification techniques offered in my previous books should also be used, if possible.

1   Max Heindel, *The Web of Destiny* (Oceanside, Ca: The Rosicrucian Fellowship,1975),p.114.
_____, *Occult Principles of Health and Healing* (Oceanside,Ca: The Rosicrucian Fellow - ship,1938),p.182-183.
2 George F. Kunz, *The Magic of Jewels and Charms* (Philadelphia: J.B. Lippincott Co., 1915),p.155-157.

CHAPTER VIII

GEM ELIXIRS WITH VARIOUS TECHNOLOGIES: BIRTHING, ANIMALS, AGRICULTURE, SOUND, AND COLOR

Gem elixirs can be used in many other ways besides healing and spiritual growth. Using minerals for birthing and to treat animals represents specialized areas of health care in which this work can be applied. Treating animals in a holistic fashion is another way to restore balance to the environment. As has been done for some time in bio-dynamic gardening, gemstones can also be applied in agriculture. There is also much room for research into the use of gemstones with sound and color technologies.

Q Will you now give a full discourse on using gem elixirs during pregnancy and the birthing process?

"First, use the astrological, not the birth stone, for each month starting with when the woman first learns that she is pregnant. The astrological stone is the gem for each month from the twenty-first to the next twenty-first. For each month, clear quartz gem elixir can also be ingested with that month's astrological stone for increased amplification. Quartz also aids in linking together all the elixirs used during this period. For instance, suppose you discover that conception occurred in July. Start with quartz and ruby for that month from the twenty-first to the twenty-first. Elsewhere in this manuscript we have provided a listing of the gemstones associated with each month."

Q Why is it better to use the astrological gems and not the birthstones?

"The astrological stones provide a broader degree of accuracy to appeal to the sympathetic needs at the point of birth. For instance, for May the astrological stone is malachite while the birth stone is emerald. We suggest only using malachite for May."

Q Would it be wise to have these stones physically present during the pregnancy or birth?

"We find no great point of urgency here."

Q What is the recommended dosage during this period?

"Add up to seven drops of each gem elixir to sixteen ounces of distilled water and ingest a full glass once to three times daily. Each time you take the elixirs, fresh drops should be added to distilled water with the entire contents then ingested. Once a day at noon is often sufficient but three times daily is superior. The preparation should usually be taken upon awakening, before noon, and before going to sleep. Each day visualize white light about the parts of the body that month's gemstone is attuned to.

"This process attunes one to the developing fetus and aids in its growth. One can also take other relevant gem elixirs, flower essences, and homeopathic remedies during the first six months of pregnancy, but it is usually recommended not to take vibrational therapies during the last three months of pregnancy unless the individual profile calls for it. Then greater clinical sophistication is needed. If a person is highly sensitive to homeopathic remedies, it is often best to use flower essences and gem elixirs in the final trimester of pregnancy. Certain flower essences such as squash, watermelon, and pumpkin, which specifically enhance the state of pregnancy and birthing, can generally be taken by most people during the entire pregnancy. During the last three months of pregnancy, the primary focus should be pure consciousness and meditation between the birthing couple. Such practices should of course take place during the entire pregnancy.

"One should continue taking astrological stones for three months after the child is born. Then many of the gems' nutrient properties and stimulating qualities go into the infant's milk. It is not necessary for either parent to take any other gem elixirs during the actual birthing."

Q Women will not learn that they are pregnant for a while. Will this interfere with the cycle of taking the gem elixirs?

"No, not at all. From the moment of discovery, follow the program with the gem elixirs. The final three months of ingestion after the child's birth may be considered as post-natal care for the physical form."

Q Steiner said that the etheric body is somewhat discoordinated with the physical body during pregancy. Please comment on this process.

"Even as the infant draws upon the mother for as nourishment and nutrition and grows within the context of drawing from the mother's tissue, so in turn does the fetus draw on the first resources of the mother for its own etheric substance. This causes a tear within the mother's etheric body so that the fetus is restored and still protected somewhat in a womb-like nature. This is the origin of the first emotions that the fetus experiences in association with the mother. This is what causes disalignment to the mother's etheric body. There is a temporary phase of inactivity of the infant's own etheric body because it is then drawing on the mother's etheric substance. Severance of this process comes with severance of the umbilical cord. Then the infant's etheric body becomes much more functional."

Q Explain how the miasms are passed on to the next generation in the birthing process?

"Even when the miasms do not exist in the physical form, they do indeed usually exist in the subtle bodies as a vibrational pattern. Fetal tissue is formed partly from the etheric bodies of the mother and father. This is how the miasms are passed on vibrationally to the subtle anatomies of the fetus during pregnancy. However, a level of susceptibility is necessary on the physical level for the miasm to actually enter the physical body.

"Ways to alleviate this problem include aura cleansing and bathing the newborn child in pure water, especially when that water has certain gem elixirs and flower essences such as clear quartz, lotus, and other more evolved vibrational preparations such as star sapphire and rose flower essences added to it. Because of their aura cleansing properties, myrrh and aloe vera flower essences could also be quite beneficial. Pennyroyal would often be indicated because of its capacity to regulate and affirm the reproductive process. Individuals may be drawn to use other vibrational remedies from their own natural attunement and the ability that certain preparations have to ease various miasms. The available literature can be examined.

"However, the effect of these preparations is reduced to some extent if too many of them are used in a bath. The reason for this is that there is a deep connection with mother earth at the time of birth. Therefore, the individual is very attuned to earth substances and to the earth's ways. Using too many of these vibrational preparations can upset this balance because of the deep changes that such preparations manifest. Thus, it is usually best to not use more than five vibrational preparations at once in a bath."

Q Should this quantity vary if the parents have been involved in spiritual practices and are relatively clear of toxins and miasms in contrast to parents who are rather toxic with at least several miasms?

"Correct. Parents involved in spiritual practices and who are relatively free of toxicity and the miasms could use up to nine vibrational preparations in a bath at once, but still five such preparations would usually be best."

Q Give further information on when to use the flower essences and gem elixirs that you just named?

"Lotus is indicated when there has been a struggle with consciousness during conception and the birthing process. There may be an evolved soul having difficulty incarnating onto the physical plane. The newborn child may have some difficulty eating any food. Clear quartz may be indicated for the baby when the mother has much physical pain during the birth process or during the last trimester of the pregnancy. There may have been continued morning sickness. This pattern does not necessarily indicate that there is only a physical problem. Such conditions often refer to the vibrational shift that takes place when the child's consciousness enters the consciousness of the mother. Pennyroyal should be used in the newborn baby's bath if the mother feels especially weak during the pregnancy or birth. Pennyroyal regulates the circulation.

"Myrrh flower essence seals holes in the aura. When this problem exists the mother may have sudden cravings for unusual foods, shifts in behavior such as with waking or sleeping patterns, sudden periods of weakness, or problems with bowel and urinary processes. The mother may continue experiencing these difficulties for a while after birth.

"Aloe vera flower essence may be indicated if the person has a family history of physical difficulty in a specific part of the body. For instance, if there is a history of developing cancer in the same part of the body over several generations, this flower essence may be needed. There is a cellular tendency to certain diseases, and aloe vera essence's use in sealing holes in the etheric body may be quite beneficial in resolving this inherited pattern. The mother can take these preparations while pregnant if any of these patterns are present."

Q Would it be wise to use diamond elixir as a universal cleanser if a newborn baby is very toxic?

"This is a tricky question because diamond sometimes acts too quickly, and it has a very deep effect on the individual. So its use with the newborn must be carefully regulated. Do not use diamond elixir with any other vibrational remedies. Use it in alternation with other preparations so that its effects can be studied."

Q How long should these baths last, and for how long should they be taken after the birth?

"These baths should last from fifteen minutes to two hours. As to how long they should be taken after the child is born, this varies greatly depending on the unique needs of each child. If the parents, especially the mother, have taken various drugs, smoked or taken alcohol, or been especially exposed to environmental pollutants during the pregnancy, then the baths should often continue for two weeks after the birth. One bath a day for such babies may be sufficient. But if the child still seems lethargic or weak, then a maximum of two baths a day for two weeks could be taken. If there has been no such exposure during the pregnancy and the pregnancy was relatively easy, then as little as three baths may be sufficient."

Q Regarding the gem elixirs and flower essences that you recommend for some newborn babies, should the mother generally take the same preparations if she has similiar symptoms while pregnant?

"No, not as a general rule."

Q Please give a full discourse on the historical background and principles of using minerals and gem elixirs to treat animals?

"In Lemuria the citizens meditated on gemstones placed in specific mosaic patterns as one method of remaining in a state of balance with nature. This was not sympathetic magic as was found in cave paintings for the purpose of hunting. These mosaics were used to activate the thought form amplification properties of gemstones to explore the realms of consciousness. This was partly done to experience a state of balance with the natural order of animal forms. Thy current society at times interbreeds various animal species for enhanced usage. The Lemurians also did this but in a more conscious fashion. They moved closer to and integrated with nature to scan with their psychic faculties the conscious evolution of various animal species. In comparing their results, they found that when there was a critical transitory faculty in a species, if that species had as begun to reach the outer limits and perimeters of its ability to function in the evolutionary chain, there was conscious intervention on the part of the Lemurians to seek that species' mutation into a new life form. This new life form was created to be fully adaptable and akin to the environment and standards of the day. Gemstones were used to advance the animal species into new evolutionary patterns and to make a smoother transition. In Lemuria gemstones were used in many ways to aid the animal forms for greater integration with the natural order of things, because that society's existence was based on a total balance with nature.

"With the fall of Atlantis and Lemuria, certain tribes developed the tradition of attributing to various animal forms specific gemstones and colorations. These were arranged into patterns so that the hunters could experience greater understanding and attunement with different animals. This was a primitive expression of the gemstone's thought form amplification ability for telepathic communication with various animals. These Lemurian traditions were transformed into a shamanistic tradition. The application of healing properties and thought form amplification properties of gemstones unto animal forms developed only when those animal forms were of service basically to the social unit of man.

"Aside from Atlantis and Lemuria, the accord of treating animals with gemstones reached its most developed form in ancient Egypt, Babylon, India, and China, with some minor activities found in the Greek and Minoan civilizations. Then the actual gemstones were usually used, not gem elixirs. Often those things, which have been observed as simple ornaments as though enhancing the beauty of animals, were actually used to enhance certain natural properties that were considered points of worship or points of focused consciousness within the animal form. These ornaments were not traditionally used to propagate health within animals, but were more so used to enhance certain natural properties within animals. For instance, when animals were used in hunting, certain colors and adornments were placed upon the animals to increase their senses for the purpose of hunting. This was applied with hunting animals such as the various cat forms. Later, when certain prized animals became personal pets in the royal households, there began to be used systems of gemstones that were then normally applied to promote healing and conscious growth amongst humans.

"In certain ancient civilizations animals were a key part of the nation's agriculture and were even vital to the nation's defense. Often at times elaborate armor with highly decorative gemstones was designed for beasts of war not only to protect the animals but also to enhance their reflexive actions. This was done with conscious understanding. For instance, when the chariot was introduced amongst the Hittites in Asia Minor, that vehicle and the animals that led it became crucial to the nation's defense. This inspired the development of a system to use gemstones to heal animals. It was essential that certain animals be kept healthy. There has been the discovery of certain jewels embedded within the skull structure of certain animals sacred in the temples, or that were pets of the noble classes. This was done by surgery. Sometimes these gems were applied to treat diseases that the animals developed.

"Most of the principles of gem therapy that can be as studied and applied to the human form are also significantly applicable to the animal form. While the animal and human forms have many variances, they also have numerous similarities. In the Orient entire meridian charts have been developed to treat certain animals. A recommended therapy for treating animals with an evolved form of healing includes the following suggestion. Review all the gemstone technologies and their application to various acupressure and acupuncture points within the human form. Animals can, in many respects, be treated in a similar fashion because of their similar anatomical form.

"As has already been done to varying degrees by thy veterinary physicians, scales should be developed comparing the life span of humans to various animal forms. For instance, each year of a human life is equivalent to seven to ten years of the canine form. This allows for the development of a scale to increase proportionally sevenfold the quickening of the physiology of that animal form. This enhances experiments and makes it easier to validate research. To treat the quickened animal metabolism in the most enhanced manner, expose gemstones or gem elixirs to the corresponding animal anatomical point through a meridian point that may be obtained through a study of oriental traditions. Then it is easier for practitioners and researchers to set up scales and to apply the channeled information presented for humans to animal forms.

"As practitioners work with various meridian points and seek to heal various animal forms, there will be advancement and evolution of the human spirit and a gradual return to balance with the entire ecosphere. This is achieved not so much on biochemical levels; there must be sensitivity through the entire energy patterns of the ecosphere, especially on mental and empathetic levels. As conscious and natural methods are used to treat animals in accord with the technologies as originally given in discourses concerning Lemuria, there will be a return to the original chart of the spirit, which is to have evolution and power over all forms native to the earth plane. The introduction of more spiritual energies into the healing of various animal forms will prove significant in the evolution of the return to consciousness of those original charges and duties as dictated in Genesis."

Q Please give a full discourse on the historical use and principles of using minerals and gem elixirs in agriculture.

"Not only have individual gemstones been used in agriculture, but at times soil rich in minerals that were pulverized became a natural source of fertilizer to supply basic nutrients and to critically enhance the ethereal needs of plants. This of course contributed to evolutionary change. Not only were chemical changes stimulated from the enhanced nutrient values ingested, but general changes in the ethereal patterns were also activated. The physical always follows the ethereal.

"There was the taking of basic topsoil, or its creation through a basic mixture with simple sand and then the accumulation of various decayed organic substances. This was then intermixed with pulverized rocks and stones from mineral substances not unlike that which ye today term diatomaceous earth. This was used by the ancients with the soil often being of volcanic origin.

"The intermixture of the soil with these substances became the basis for working sparingly with the direct pulverization and implantation in the soil of fine thin substances of various semiprecious stones such as lapis lazuli, emerald, and many others. This was especially true when the soil was volcanic. Minerals were used that were able to promote the ethereal patterns of individual plant forms. A simple way to make such discoveries is to study the relationship of certain astrological signs to various plant forms. These astrological signs are also attuned to various minerals. For instance, corn and sunflower are often attributed to being governed by the sun. Corresponding stones, astrologically derived, are garnet and ruby. If these minerals as elixirs or in their pulverized or original form were placed in the soil with such plant forms, the growth would increase from 5 to 23 percent. Not only does this enhance the mineral qualities of these plant forms, but it also brings forth balance and promotes their growth because the ethereal properties of the plants are enhanced. The plants' properties are also enhanced if they are exposed to emerald or quartz when there is a carrier or base such as volcanic soil. Volcanic soil acts as a cleanser as well as an amplifier. Much of this agricultural knowledge was developed to a heightened degree in Lemuria, but it was also developed independent of Lemurian knowledge by many indigenous populations."

Q Explain how individual gemstones and gem elixirs can today be applied to various plants?

"Quartz should be looked upon as a major amplifier in agriculture because it magnifies all the properties present.[1] For instance, if a gem is prepared homeopathically or by the gem elixir method and then included in the soil, there would be an amplification of all those positive forces present. This allows for maximizing the assimilation of various nutrient properties. Quartz is a major stimulator of the life force which extends to the biochemical level of plants.

"Emerald is an important and general enhancer for all plant forms because of its natural affinity with the sun and with the heart. However, it has a special affinity with all fruit-bearing trees, especially the citric varieties. Vine-growing plants, avocado, and spirulina are also greatly enhanced by emerald. Boji stone is also a general amplifier for all plants.

"When pearl in combination with oyster shell is pulverized and placed in the soil, one treatment acts as a fertilizer that enriches the soil for many generations. Pulverized oyster shell is perhaps the richest source of fertilizer. The oyster shell is a carrier of other stones' influences; thus, various gemstones could be combined with pulverized oyster shell. However, some plants may not benefit from the high amount of calcium and magnesium in the oyster shell. Pulverized oyster shell can also be used with pearls that remain in their original state. If one pearl is placed in the soil, the soil for a radius of 160 acres is enhanced by the properties of the moon. Pearl could be used with specific grains that are ruled by the moon. These include barley, millet, and rice. Abalone and kelp have properties similar to oyster shell as important fertilizers."

Q Does it matter if light or dark pearl is used?

"There is no critical distinction, although plants notably affected by the full moon would be enhanced with dark pearl.

"Lapis lazuli encourages the growth of plant forms that are found mostly in arid areas. This is especially true for desert plants with healing properties. It encourages the growth of the plant's root structure. Obsidian is also good for treating plants in barren soil. It makes these plants more resistant to disease and encourages root growth.

"Diamond should be used with plants that need much sun light, not with plants more comfortable in the shade. It increases the foliage. Amethyst activates certain grains such as wheat and oats. Amber also aids certain grains, along with trees whose sap gives forth medicinal properties. The maple sugar tree exemplifies this. Jet should be used for any root diseases, for plants that need shade, and for fungus-type plants such as mushrooms. Jadeite activates an attunement to devic realms and is a general amplifier for plant forms. It was often used in Lemuria."

Q Does it matter if gems are used in agriculture as gem elixirs, in their original form, or pulverized into the soil?

"There is no cricial distinction here. Perhaps in the future some general guidelines will be offered."

Q Can you provide some general guidelines as to how much of a gemstone should be mixed with so many acres of soil?

"This is not a critical issue, although we find that seven drops from the stock bottle of a gem elixir should be added to twenty-five gallons of distilled water. This should usually be used to treat approximately five to ten acres. One carat of a gemstone tends to treat a radius of ten to twenty acres. One carat of a pulverized mineral, if spread over the soil, treats thirty-five to sixty acres. The range depends on the strength and quality of the gemstone and how well the pulverized mineral is scattered over the soil.

"Broad general principles are provided now to stimulate activities on the part of students to increase their knowledge for more advanced works to be given at a later point in time. In time this will become a more complete system of agriculture and horticulture. A fruitful avenue of research is to examine astrological stones in association with specific plant forms. This is perhaps the most organized body of knowledge presently available to many students. This will allow for an expression and merging of botanical, mineralogical, and astrological skills."

Oyster shell has been used for some time as a fertilizer. The bio-dynamic farming originated by Rudolf Steiner has also recommended the use of various minerals such as quartz or silica, clay, and limestone to enrich soil for increased crop yields.[2] In time many different minerals will be used to enhance crop yields. Some of this work is already taking place with bio-dynamic farming, which is one of the most evolved form of organic gardening currently practiced.

Q Explain the historical background and principles involved in using gemstones with music?

"The Lemurians, of course, developed sound and resonancy with gemstones to its most heightened properties. In Lemuria, sound frequencies were used for both healing and heightened consciousness. Gemstones were arranged in acoustical patterns to activate the stones' healing properties. Quartz crystal flutes were often used in Lemuria. This instrument has a high degree of resonancy for healing. The use of minerals to construct certain instruments extended through Atlantis to India. Gemstones and sound were not so much interconnected in Atlantis for conscious growth, except amongst the priesthood. In Atlantis the populace used sound and gemstone frequencies for either weapons or industrial tools, rather than for the promotion of consciousness.

"The Lemurian tradition of using gemstones and sound frequencies together was well preserved in Egypt, Nubia, India, Babylon, Greece, Minoa and amongst the Zoroastrian and Melchizedek schools of thought. Some rudimentary forms were preserved about Stonehenge. Its most heightened faculties were preserved in Peru and neighboring areas amongst the Incas, Mayans, Aztecs, Olmecs, and Toltecs. Until the Spanish conquest, Peru had the most advanced of these art forms. In many ways they directly preserved the Lemurian techniques. The growing popularity of Peruvian flute music and whistling vessels exemplifies this tradition. They also had an exact science of quartz crystal technologies, knowledge of metallurgy, and knowledge of the mandala arrangement of gemstones. Only the sound patterns preserved in India and the Buddhist countries rivals that of Peru. That of Tibet with the Tibetan bells is perhaps the most superior in accord with Peruvian music today, but only in the sense that it has been maintained to this day.

"In the 1700's Benjamin Franklin, under the inspiration of some Egyptian guides, built a musical instrument involving quartz crystal technologies. The working of resins against the edge of the glass bells created ringing sounds that stimulated healing. It looked something like a harpsichord or piano. A horizontal rod had the glass bells attached to it with the rod turning when a connected pedal was pressed. Franklin used glass bells with lead paint in his instrument. He also used some glass made with lead. This is why, when people were constantly exposed to this music, some developed nerve diseases. The vibration of lead was being broadcasted.

"This instrument is extremely powerful to open the chakras and to attune the musical scale to the chakras. When playing this instrument, it would be wise to have glass bottles by your side with distilled water and gem elixirs and flower essences that activate each of the chakras. As the different notes on the music scale are played dip your fingers into the water when attuning to the different chakras. When playing this instrument one needs to wet one's hands every so often to create the friction necessary to create the sounds. This can be done with the twelve main chakras. For instance, use royal azel gem elixir when playing the musical note that activates the crown chakra. This also broadcasts the vibrational patterns of the various gem elixirs and flower essences."

The origins of this instrument, the glass harmonica or armonicum, as it is called, is believed to have been derived from the tapping of glasses to produce musical sounds. It gradually reached Europe from Asian sources, especially from Persia in the 11th century. The glass harmonica became quite popular in classical music circles, reaching the height of its popularity around 1830. Prominent composers such as Beethoven, Handel, Mozart, Strauss, and Schultz composed pieces specifically for this instrument.[3] For a while Mesmer used the glass harmonica to calm people in mental hospitals and to induce a receptive state in his hypnotic subjects.[4] Gradually, when people realized that illnesses were developing from listening to this instrument, it passed out of popularity. The police in some German cities even banned the playing of the glass harmonica.

In 1982 Gerhard Finkenbeiner in Massachusetts was inspired to rebuild this instrument, but he only used natural quartz crystals. Thus, a much higher spiritual and healing vibration was created with no dangerous side effects because no lead was used. People today using lead quartz as pendulums or on windows to create rainbow effects should reflect on this. Staring into lead quartz crystal balls can be especially dangerous. That brings the vibration of lead into the body. Finkenbeiner has been building quartz crystal church bells since 1956 so building a glass harmonica with natural quartz was a natural extension of his work.[5] He now sells several varieties of this instrument and a demonstration tape is available.(Mr. Finkenbeiner can be reached at 33 Rumford Ave. Waltham, Ma. 02154) He and several associates are available to present concerts with this harmonica. In fact, just as this book went to press I learned that Mr. Finkenbeiner and an associate were going to give a talk and concert in June 1986 at a conference in San Francisco on quartz crystals. I look forward to the day when many New Age composers incorporate Finkenbeiner's new instrument into their compositions. Many of us will derive great inspiration in our healing and spiritual growth. And if enough people express an interest in purchasing a quartz crystal flute, I believe that Mr. Finkenbeiner will consider producing them.

According to Finkenbeiner, the instrument is played by rotating a series of quartz bowls of decreasing size mounted on a horizontal spindel that are placed in a cabinet and rotated through liquid by means of a foot pedal. Several factors are involved in producing a satisfactory sound. These include the speed of the revolving cups, the amount of moisture on the fingers or gloves, and the amount of pressure against the rims of the cups. The larger cups work best with a slow rotation, while the smaller cups need more speed. A variety of liquids can be used, but alcohol seems to work best. People with sensitive hands may want to wear gloves.

Today in classical music circles the glass harmonica is again experiencing a revival. Bruno Hoffman, from Germany, has conducted many concerts around the world and other performers are now coming forward. In my seminars I have found that literally no one in the New Age community is aware of this work, but this will soon change. Quartz crystal music is going to achieve great popularity and prove to be of great value in healing and spiritual growth. It will, for instance, become a valuable tool for treating mental illness.

"Quartz crystals and other gemstones that have been interlaced synthetically stimulate healing by coordinating that particular gemstone with its own particular note,

Glass Harmonica

pitch, or octave. The individual resonances of various gemstones could also be duplicated by their specific octave or pitch resonating within the quartz container. Ruby, for instance, is attuned to the key of A. Thus, the key of A duplicates the healing properties of ruby. Physical gems or their elixirs can be placed in different quartz containers for amplification of the gemstones and the note. By studying astrology and the works of Rudolf Steiner, one can match the appropriate note to the appropriate gemstone to allow each note to be played upon the crystal harmonica. Individuals can examine the planets and constellations to learn which note each one emits. By learning which gemstones are also attuned to these planets and constellations, one can match the musical scale to the chakras and gemstones. Individuals will notice that their alignment by octave will sometimes vary by season. In the summer months, for instance, there is a deepening effect and in the winter months there is a heightening effect. The octave ranges that are selected in the winter are often higher.

"In the precepts of sound it would be easiest to align with the activities of the seven primary notes as would be given in graduating octaves. These are found to be as aligned with gemstones in that they activate, release, and enhance the vibrational qualities of gemstones. That which is most desirable to totally release the impact and to enhance the qualities of stones would be to expose the stones to the ultrasonic pitch at the sonic resonance frequency that would shatter the stone. Keep the loudness level of this sound just below the decibels which would actually shatter the stone. This notably enhances the stone's healing properties because that frequency remains indelibly imprinted upon the gemstone's crystalline structure, even to the point of recapturing that sound with certain sensitive instruments. The correct frequency to use can be calculated by the carat, gem quality, and purity of different gemstones. There should be the correct isolation of the pitch in relationship to individual stones through mathematical calculus of volume, weight, and structure against the individual internal characteristics of each mineral. These can be calculated by the gemstone's atomic weight so that there can be exposure to the necessary decibels without the stone shattering. This exposure increases a stone's healing qualities because it creates a storage of the individual vibrations of pitch, sound, and temperament. The sound, even though it is a vibration that is only projected through the atmosphere, achieves resonancy with the very molecular structure of the gemstone. This is a fusion of two forms of healing on vibrational levels. The vibrational frequency of a sound can be very similar to the vibrational frequency of a gemstone. When this matching occurs, the sound and mineral are each enhanced.

"Gemstones exposed to this sound have a closer attunement to the principles of the ethers. Rather than there being the need to stimulate the ether fields from two separate sources, the sound and gemstone become fused as a single element enhancing the qualities of each. If the pitch can be obtained from organic sources such as from various levels of the human voice or from recordings of ultrasounds used in marine life, it will carry higher properties for healing organic tissue. This is because there is bound within such organic sounds a capacity of resonancy closer to the ethereal fluidium of the etheric body, which stimulates the healing process. This is not unlike the difference between synthetic and organically bound nutrient sources. Organically bound nutrients are much better and healthier for the body physical to absorb. Sound is not only vibration as it passes through the atmosphere, but should also be thought of as kinetic energy which passes through mass itself. Therefore, it has a resonancy and harmony with the ethers, with mass acting as a bridge or portal to those levels. So it is possible for the individual human being to create sounds that have an empathetic resonancy with the ethers through the manipulation of mass on a vibrational level. Gemstones are the highest refined substances for obtaining such resonancies."

Q It is said that when jade is struck it emits a particular melodious sound.[7] Many gemstones have been found to emit different sounds.[8] Please comment on this?

"This is one reason why various minerals can be used to construct musical instruments as noted earlier. More will be presented on this later. Sound may be obtained from various crystalline structures by their own resonant properties."

Q Does the vibration of different mineral names have an effect on their usage?

"If each mineral could be coordinated with a particular mantric sound pattern and that sound pattern became the name of that mineral, this would be of great value. This is a technique that could go into the organization of all languages and is part of the universal language."

Q Please recommend some spiritual practices to discover what information is stored in different minerals?

"First, there should be the isolation of the stone to its corresponding chakra. Then meditate upon that stone and chakra, perhaps with quartz being present. This technique amplifies the properties of the stone and enhances its ability to further integrate with the forces of the chakras. If certain musical properties are also isolated with the forces of the chakras, this brings about balance to such a degree that the individual has complete resonancy with the stone. Pitches for activating the stone could as come through manipulating the vocal chords to the specific pitch and quality of the stone by striking each octave vocally with the OM that corresponds to each stone according to its chakric implications. Chant OM with the seven note scale to match the pitch with the chakra that the mineral is attuned to. The student should understand that there is not so much the peculiar linkage between sound and gemstones, except that they enhance each other according to the principles and properties described.

"The mantra that corresponds with individual gemstones could be deciphered by associating the stone with its astrological properties and the corresponding note or pitch which governs the stone according to its house property. On the eight note scale the lower pitches are associated with the lower chakras and certain color schemes. Thus, the lower pitch of OM we find attuned to Aries and diamond. Diamond is attuned to the pitch C natural or 256 cycles per second. The house, sign, and planet all have common denominators in the sense that, for example, the first house is ruled by Aries, and Aries is ruled by Mars. Whatever pitch rules Aries also rules Mars and the first house. There is an important set of octave correspondences that have to do with transformation in the human being. However, they do not directly relate to this particular system of pitch and astrological correspondences."

Since I am speaking about music I want to take this opportunity to alert readers briefly to the music of Alan Hovhaness. As John has noted, his music will in the future be of great value for stimulating New Age consciousness. Having studied music in Japan and India as well as in the West, and being born in Boston of Armenian descent, his music represents a unique and profound mixture of Eastern and Western spirituality. Many of the compositions of this contemporary composer are available in classical record shops. Hopefully, in time the New Age music distributors will sell his music along with that of quartz crystal music. Many now attuned to New Age music will appreciate the spiritual depths of this visionary.

Q How can color therapy be used with gemstones and gem elixirs?

"We have elsewhere already discussed the relationship of various colors to individual gemstones. Thus, we will here explore color therapy and its application to gem therapy. The system advanced by the channel speaking is to coordinate individual color tones with the seven chakras. The full color spectrum from red to violet are attuned to these chakras. As previously discussed, each gemstone has a sympathetic resonancy with these chakras and associated internal organs. When the individual primary colors of the color spectrum are anchored at the neurological points in the spinal column sympathetic to each chakra, the color spectrum in relationship to individual internal organs may be discerned. As individual colors are correctly coordinated with the chakras, this enhances gemstones and their resonancies.

"For instance, ruby and the color green are coordinated with the heart charka. Ruby and green can be applied in color therapy in several ways. Ruby elixir can be exposed to green filtrations that either represent the accurate scientific reality of green as measured by angstroms, or that which is the color reality perception of a given individual. These perceptual realities may be isolated through a series of tests, by showing someone a spectrum of green that appeals to them in their own perceptual reality of that color. This may also have beneficial psychological impacts on the individual. If ruby is exposed to green for approximately twenty to thirty minutes, the elixir carries the properties of green when it is applied to the heart chakra in any manner.

"There may also be an individual system of color therapy and perceptual reality that introduces the properties of gemstone healing as a meditative force and actually instigates some principles almost of a homeopathic accord. For instance, you will find that when meditating on ruby and then moving the eyes away from it to meditate on a pure white surface, the color green is held in the after vision upon the retina, introducing some similar principles of homeopathic stimulation by the process of the ruby's natural red coloration. Similar principles may be found by coordinating the chakras. This is but one of the other sources that are as stimulated by colorations in the amplification of gemstones."

Q So is it true that green stones have an association with the eyes, as some claim?

"Yes. This is because green stimulates many of the activities of the midbrain."

Q Does the color have much relevance when you have the same mineral in more than one color?

"It can make some difference. The darker colors have a more masculine orientation, while the brighter colors have a more feminine influence. But the different colors do not necessarily alter the areas of the anatomy affected by the gemstone."

Q Alexandrite and some other minerals have the ability to change colors when different colors are shone on them. Do minerals with this ability have a special relation to color therapy?

"Studies of what gives minerals their coloration has revealed that when gemstones are placed upon various isolated polarized lights, the activities bring forth the balance

120

and brilliance of the different colorations. Certain techniques, which involve creating filters with individual gemstones and then shining various polarized lights through them, to measure out their angstroms as being different portions of the color spectrum, will eventually be obtainable. These filtrations passing directly through the gemstones increase the magnitude of color therapy because they will as pass through an already crystallized structure, also carrying with them the activities of the life force."

This information has been presented partly so that people will appreciate the many areas in which gemstone technologies can be applied. In the future, more material on these five areas may be presented, but it is hoped that others will be inspired to conduct research in these areas.

1 George Kunz, *The Magic of Jewels and Charms* (Philadelphia: J.B. Lippincott Co.,1915),p. 26.
2 Rudolf Steiner, *Agricultural Course* (Spring Valley,N.Y: The Anthroposophical Press, 1972).
3 Horace Ervin, "Notes On Franklin's Armonica and the Music Mozart Wrote For It," *Journal of the Franklin Institute*, CCLXII No. 5 (Nov.,1956), 329-348.
Stanley Sadie, ed., *The New Grove Dictionary of Music and Musicians*, 12 vols. (N.Y: Macmillan Publishers, Ltd., 1980), p.823-5.
4 H.P. Blavatsky, *Isis Unveiled* (Wheaton,IL: The Theosophical Publishing House, 1972), p.215.
5 Jeffrey Carmel, "Franklin Invented It, Mozart Wrote For It: The 'Armonica' Returns," *The Christian Science Monitor*, (Nov. 29.1983,), p.5.
6 Max Heindel. *Occult Principles of Health and Healing* (Oceanside,Ca: The Rosicrucian Fellowship,1938), p.164-166.
_____, *The Rosicrucian Philosophy in Questions and Answers*, Vol. I (Oceanside,Ca: The Rosicrucian Fellowship, 1978),p. 314-315.
7 Arthus and Grace Chu, *The Collector's Book of Jade* (N.Y: Crown Publishers,Inc.,1978), p.7,16.
8 Wm. Corliss, *Unknown Earth: A Handbook of Geological Enigmas* (Glen Arm, Md: Sourcebook Project,1980), p. 529-544.
George Kunz, *The Magic of Jewels and Charms* (J.B. Lippincott Co: Philadelphia, 1915), p.1-3.

CHAPTER IX

NEW PHYSICS AND GEMSTONES

In order to use vibrational preparations properly it is wise to have some understanding of esoteric physics or the developing science of new physics. These concepts explain how we exist on this plane and how preparations such as gem elixirs work. Some information is also presented on the potential industrial use of crystals. In time the technological use of quartz and other minerals will become much more common than is now the case. We will not need to be so dependent on fuels such as oil, coal, and gas.

Q Give a full discourse on the seven rays?

"The seven rays are a function of physics integrating with the chakras and their extensions into the universe. The rays are the functions of physics that create and correlate holographic physical existence of individuals on this plane.[1] These principles may be correlated with the concepts of the physics of consciousness.

"The relationship of the seven rays to gemstones will also be thoroughly explored. The seven rays are isolated spectrums of the ethers that create biological life upon this plane. They find their focus and activities within the body physical, and various gemstones isolate and amplify these frequencies. Gemstones seek to harmonize the functions of the seven rays to create the reality of the subtle bodies. To isolate the relevancy and relationship of gemstones to the seven rays, it is wise to explore the material or physical level of the stones first and then to have a separate exploration of the functions of gem elixirs. Each gemstone is aligned with one or more of the seven rays. This can be discerned by the relationship of the rays and gemstones to the seven main chakras. So the inquiry will be limited to the enhancement of the seven rays in stones. This involves a discussion of esoteric physics, interweaving the principles of the ethers and the three states of mass. These principles shall in part be given so that there can be an understanding of the known spectrum of physics and conceptual realities and how the seven rays create the perceptual reality of the individual on this plane.

"There will be an examination of how a unity in mind, body, and spirit promotes physical health, especially through the chakras through an interplay with the individual's mental and psychological forces. This helps shape the perceptual reality of the individual. There is not so much the desire to as explore the element of the seven rays regarding physical diseases, as this would be better to explore in more advanced works. Later, there will also be a linking of the seven rays to the planets as points of harmony.

"To understand the seven rays, there must be a point of focus as to the distinction in their purpose and priority in creating the physical form. These properties, as attributed through the channel speaking, will find both complete synchronicity and complete diversity in interpretation with other sources. There are many different authorities as to the functions and purposes of the seven rays.

"There should first be an understanding of the forces that make up the individual rays and their coloration and uniqueness. These personal functions contribute to the personal dynamics of spiritualizing or actualizing the personality and help to create a linkage to the individual's perceptual reality.

"In red, the first ray, we find the initiator and vitalizer. Here there is the ability to focus and function on the earth plane as a dimensional aspect to be able to resist the movements of gravity. Gravity is more an expansionary force, rather than as a pulling force. Just as an object experiences pressure when it is set into motion, all things are in a continuous state of expansion. Therefore, when red is thought of as the great initiator, so in turn is it the first of the seven rays. The ability to have a basis and function on the earth plane comes from the great initiator which is indeed an expansionary force. But this is an expansion that begins with all things in a state of existence for in the stasis of existence all things move at an identical rate of expansion. This is the capacity and force of the ethers.

"These forces shape the dynamics of the individual in the desire to bring forth the conscious self. This is the activator of consciousness. In their perceptual reality, many times individuals display great frustration in their incapacity because they feel themselves not able to learn. These are the railers who cry out for justice. These were the classical prophets of old who flagellated themselves in a psychospiritual sense because they felt unworthy of those things that they felt and could not give expression to. This is the archetypal personality within the psychospiritual dynamics for this ray.

"Such individuals are at times the revolutionaries. They give forth from the depths of feeling, emptying themselves out. These are the students who constantly seek to grow spiritually. They hunger after spiritual growth. But it is only when they discover that it is through the calming of frustration and anger and the channeling of such negative states into higher creative healing that this greatly amplifies the capacity for spiritual growth. This particular ray integrates itself into the physical forces through the adrenals and coccyx with its influence extending to the testicles and ovaries.

"Orange, the second ray, expresses the creative energy. This is created as a separate force only as a synthesization of the two primary forces, red and yellow. Orange is the first creative force because it is a mixture of the initiative and the mental forces. These two forces manifest creativity and the ability to extend the self into other areas. It is the first act of consciousness. Activated creative consciousness contributed to the development of the mental forces. This is where consciousness first began to integrate or filter into the curvature of time and space to an in-depth level. There then began to be the focus and activity with the material plane of the higher ethereal forces. The ethers, which are energy traveling beyond the speed of light, integrate into mass in its three states of light, ethers, and matter.

"Here we find the artist, the creative outlet for red the great initiator. There is the alleviation of frustration and unbridled joy. There is the discovery and release of tantra and the perceptual realities associated with sexuality. All of these forces are of a positive nature that stimulates joy, intimacy, and outreach in individuals' perceptual reality. These individuals may empty themselves out charismatically speaking in tongues. Here we have the poet, no longer the railer.

"In yellow, the third ray, we find that the pure mental forces and mass are completely transformed. In this level there is the function of pure mental forces integrating fully into mass and having the realization of consciousness. This is where the ethers have fully awakened into intellectual awareness, not the totality of spiritual awareness, but intellectual awareness. This differs from the properties of the active consciousness in that active consciousness is creativity. Creativity at times does not necessarily have total awareness of its purpose, for the artist seeks awareness but does not necessarily obtain it. However, the artist is a seeker of truth. Here we have the spiritualized intellect. The not totally realized individual has come to a state of awareness in the path of illumination to where he is now conscious yet still in the material state. From the active mental state come science, philosophy, and similar perspectives.

"These indeed are the seeds of the mental forces. In the higher forces these seeds are called the emotions. They are the seeds of sensitivity and seeds of learning. Here the capacity of memory may develop. With yellow, the creative forces are organized into permanent and indelible forms. Order and joy are now brought to the conscious student. Here we find the archetypal form of individuals such as Socrates, Plato, and others of the philosophical concern.

"Green is the color of the fourth ray. Here we find the properties of healing and the ability to transcend the baser self. This is the first true step in the totality of that direction, for it is applied and carried awareness. This is the first step to the selfless state. Green is the first key to that development and indeed is the intellectual, philosophical, and healing process towards the altruistic state, which is the higher state of the conscious being. It is the inquiring state, the state that gives forth healing and balance of love. It is that which transforms the intellectual properties into the psychic faculties, shaping and tempering that awareness with the higher forces of inner peace. The key focus of green is the spiritually realized intellect. It is at this point that the individual is beginning to become the actualized force of inner peace.

"In green we find the perceptual reality of seeking forces beyond just those of joy and sorrow or of just the mental forces or the scrutinization of the material. Here we find the kindling of divine love, a love that goes beyond the individual. This is the capacity to love all. Here the individual for the first time begins to see the totality of the higher forces, the totality of the higher self. There is an attempt to integrate and spiritualize the forces and faculties of the three baser perceptual realities. Here we find the archetypal perceptual reality of Jesus and Buddha. Study these individuals, for here we have the spiritually realized intellect seeking the divine above and beyond personal ethics. The mental forces bring order but cannot, without the higher forces, give further direction and inspiration.

"In blue we find the true altruistic state and the total expression of the true self as can be realized through the dynamics of the human personality as it functions in the three dimensions. In blue one experiences inner peace, and a stabilizing effect for this particular dimensional aspect allows for the existence of awareness in time and space, yet still holds the presence as it is within the capacity of physics. There is the realization of one's true position in time and space and, of course, in relationship to other individuals. And there is the capacity to give expression in these areas. In developing the true altruistic personality one experiences inner peace, for in the ability to serve others the individual has completely mastered all the elements of the physical plane. It is only in the altruistic state that there is the complete mastery of the elements of the physical plane. This is complete altruism, which is total service to others. Yet one still maintains awareness of thy own position in time and space. This makes the individual the perfect servant in the earth plane.

"Examine the later years of service of Buddha and Jesus to understand the archetypal pattern of this ray. Then there was the complete servant, the total giving of self. Some, for instance, today seek to serve and preserve thy environment and to learn the ways of the dolphin. These are people who function on this particular ray and who seek to translate these things into a social force to be totally altruistic.

"The sixth ray, indigo, expresses the ability finally to seek the truer self. The forces or rays previously mentioned were more so the properties of realizing the self as it functions in harmonics within the physical plane. Here the individual fully activates the properties of the divine self and projects those energies to bring into total alignment the perceptual forces of the other five rays. A person in the five states or dimensions of existence may seek to have total mastery over the four basic dimensions and is gaining mastery over the fifth. However, there must still be a clear perceptual reality of true divine nature and complete harmonics in all states of existence. To experience this, one must be in attunement with the ethers. The ethers are but energies which travel beyond the normal time-space curvature. In comparison with the normal curvature of the universe, the ethers are closest to that which would be considered the ability to as travel between two points in a true straight line. This gives the ability to as experience greater sums of the whole.

"In indigo the perceptual realities are those which would be described as forces which bring the individual close to the activities of samadhi, the pure element of joy, service, and ecstasy. Study the patterns attributed to samadhi and the life of St. Francis of Assisi.

"With violet, the seventh ray, there is an alignment of all these capacities with the higher forces. Here we have the complete harmonics of the totally realized spiritual being. In this force we find constant upliftment and constant higher properties because this force is the merging of the great initiator and the altruistic nature, as found in violet. Therefore, violet is the perfect balance in harmonics of the full spectrum of the five baser dimensions or rays, yet still in frequency it transcends even the aspects of indigo. Thus, with this force, the key word is transcendence. It is the capacity of transformation and the ability to integrate the higher forces into aspects of the perceptual reality of the individual personality and its harmonics.

"This perceptual reality is usually obtained in states of meditation, where the individual has total oneness with all forces and a completion of all processes. This is usually the perceptual reality of the ascendent being. There is an attunement with all time and space, the ability of total prognostication, and an ability to see into all the dimensions. This is not so much a psychic force, for the psychic faculties are an attunement with various dimensions, but it is more so a knowing because of being at one with all the elements.

"These then are the perceptual realities and properties of the seven rays. These perceptual realities are aligned with the chakric forces and some of their psychodynamics.[2] The rays are forces that are pure in their own right. It is only resistance to these forces that as brings about the illusion of unnatural behavioral patterns. This is not unlike the healing crisis as the body physical seeks to eliminate that which is toxic within the self by the presence of a positive force. Then, in turn, there is activity as though there is imbalance and resistance to the positive influence. Thus the rays can lead to stressful behavioral patterns upon the level of the personality. This is not unlike an individual who would resist conversion to a positive system of behavior, believing that the limited self, or the negative self, is the true expression. Therefore, the individual feels that it is wiser to continue in the behavior that is known rather than perhaps risk the loss of what the person considers to be clarity.

"The rays are a constant progressing element. They are a force that comes down from the soul level itself to become self-actualizing in its own construct. No individual is under the influence of only one ray. The ray preference expresses a heightened faculty, but the rays are also self-actualizing. Study the patterns of the personalities to be given shortly in trilogy and ye shall indeed see how they are self-actualizing.

"It is also wise to understand some of the physics of the seven rays. In the first ray there is the element of grounding. But the process of grounding is more so the process of initiation or activation, the actual resistance to gravitation. If there is not a resistance to gravitational fields, these forces become a depressive element. Therefore, the actual uplifting and evolving into more complex forms, indeed perhaps the life force itself, involves the red ray. Life in a biological sense is the ability to as resist gravity and to expand at higher rates of expansion than the normal time-space continuum of the gravitational forces of the planet. This is why the forces of orgone can resist and demonstrate anti-gravity.

"The rays are not a typical electromagnetic vibration partly because they function more in the fourth dimension. These rays are not a vibration similar to what you call color or light. They are a pure vibration that is only sensed by individuals who ascend to higher planes.

"In orange we find not just the pure biological process of resisting mass that has then organized into living matter. Here we find the beginning of the sparks of consciousness. In its pure strain, this consciousness is that which extends and gives empathy throughout all things. This particular force is a key element in the dimensional state, that as all mass passes through the ethers, this becomes in part the origin of consciousness. The ethers occupy all time and space simultaneously. As mass passes through time and space, there are glimmerings that are organized into the current level of reality based upon the past, present, and future. By this process, after exposure to this force, comes the attempt to organize this energy into a linear three-dimensional perceptual reality.

"The mental forces associated with yellow attempt to stabilize exposure to the ethers and their element of existing in all time and space simultaneously. It is the ability to stabilize these forces in the current time and space frame, i.e., between absolute gravitional zero and the higher frequencies of the ethers, the great creative forces.

"In the forces found in green there is the ability to extend beyond the process of stabilization. Once the individual has stabilized the self in time and space, he can then move comfortably to those forces that are the ethers. Here the individual begins to initiate psychic perception such as telepathy and clairvoyance. Early phases of this are prognostication and the ability to as see, perceive, and interpret energies. This is the ability to as begin to move through forces and frequencies to extend the self to greater energies in the time-space flow continuum or the ability to move outside the curvature of the fourth dimension.

"In the forces of the fifth ray we find the ability to stabilize the self. Here there is the ability not only to have perceptual glimpses but also to as activate the forces within the personal reality of the individual. This is why it is found that those individuals who are totally altruistic and humble in behavior become as worthy of higher gifts that are observed in the psychic capacity, such as prognostication and healing. These gifts express the ability to stabilize the self in the ethers. The properties or descriptions of the two higher dimensions cannot be given at this time because they go beyond the currently known laws of physics."

Q With the first ray you said that gravity is more an expansionary force than a pulling force. Explain this statement?
"Gravity is the result of all forces expanding at right angles to each other, rather than being a pulling force. Gravity is a process of acceleration."

Q What did you mean when you said that the red ray explains why the forces of orgone resist and demonstrate anti-gravity?
"Orgone is the point at which there is the interlacing of the ethers' activity into the physical dimension. This is also true with the red ray. The ethers are the forces which continue to have all mass expand at a continuous and constant rate. This allows anti-gravity properties to intermix with the forces that exist beyond the speed of light and then enter into mass. Orgone is such a force. Since the red ray is the first point of entry into mass it allows for the equivalent measurement."

Q With the orange ray you said there is not just the pure biological process of resisting mass that has been organized into living matter. Expand on how the rays form matter?
"This is direct reference to the biochemical processes where there is the translation of inanimate matter into the potential building blocks of life. The student should look to the references where there was the lifting up of inanimate matter from the mineral kingdom to evolve eventually into more complex life forms through the processes observed in Darwinian evolution. This may be linked to the discourse given of the planet as a living entity, where simple life forms became more complex."

Q With the yellow ray you said the mental forces have their origin in an attempt to stabilize exposure to the ethers and their element of existing in all time and space simultaneously. Expand on this statement?
"This is the desire of the ego or mind not to assimilate into all quadrants of time and space because the mind is so identified with the three dimensions."

Q What about the belief that there are other rays besides these seven? [3]
"There are other rays, especially five key ones that are related to the five chakras above the crown chakra and to the subtle bodies. All these rays are now in existence, but it is only now that the consciousness is expanding sufficiently for people to tap into these higher energies.

"One could easily hold the mistaken belief that the seven rays are the end all in understanding, but the seven rays do not take into account all the facets and potentials of humanity. New concepts that do not fit into the old patterns of humanity are now manifesting that often reflects these higher ray patterns. This is why, though the idea of a total of twelve rays has been around for many thousands of years, the idea is only lately gaining more acceptance."

Q Are there other rays besides the twelve main ones?
"Yes. In fact there is a direct relationship of each ray to another ray so that one could say there are twenty-four primary rays. Beyond these twenty-four rays there are other rays in the higher planes. We have no set number of total rays to present because, while

there may be a limited number of rays, as an understanding of that number is reached so is the understanding of dimensions transformed so that the limitation appears arbitrary—as arbitrary as matter appears to you, as you begin to awaken from its hold on you."

Q Explain the relationship of the seven rays to the seven ethers.
   "Not at this time."

Q How do the rays affect the personality, the spiritual self, and the individual's perceptual reality?
   "First, there must be a brief discourse as to the functions and dynamics of the rays to remove any difficulty concerning their perception. The seven rays are dimensional states of existence, even as ye have height, width, and depth in the time-space curvature in the seven dimensions in which ye exist. The seven rays are aligned with the perceptual reality of the four dimensions plus the other three dimensions that make up the totality of thy actual existence.
   "The three dimensions allow for the existence of time and space to give a framework and context in which to exist. None of the dimensions could exist without the others. In the original creation all the dimensions came into existence in complete synchronicity. All rays came into focus and influence upon the earth plane simultaneously, but they did not have their critical function developed within individuals until the seven main chakras had developed. The fourth dimension, for instance, exists within the framework of the perceptual reality of the three dimensions. Each dimension is like a quality that has been isolated to describe a perceptual reality. All the higher dimensions exist relative to the position of the three dimensions. This is why the aspects are self-actualizing. They exist only in their point of relativity to penetrate to the level of the three dimensions. The higher dimensions would not exist and would be an entirely different state of existence if the perceptual reality of the three dimensions did not exist as a point of observation. The seven dimensions are seven levels of consciousness within the mind of God. The mind of God is apparently relative to the position of the observer on the earth plane, which is represented by the three dimensions. Note the different interpretations of the seven planes of existence. This is relative to the observer in his own state of consciousness.
   "The seven rays are a perceptual reality in the sense that the colors ascribed to them have a synchronicity and a bearing upon the seven-color spectrum of light. But this is not light within the laws of thy physics. It is only that the ancients attributed the sevenfold color spectrum to the seven rays as a point of visual aid, because there is also a degree of synchronicity and forbearance in behavioral patterns both spiritual and psychological with the forces of light stimulated within the self. Light can indeed be a vehicle for the activities of the seven rays, but light is not their total activity. The seven rays are states of existence or dimensional qualities. They perceptually have been assigned colors as a visual aid in learning their content and meaning as energy. There is not the desire to proceed beyond this point in this volume because of the complexity of physics that is involved."

Q Give some examples to explain how the seven rays affect people.
   "Individuals do not attune to just one ray. An individual may favor one ray in the creation of the physical body and the actions that extend forth from those activities to

find balance.[4] For instance, there were the individuals known as Washington, Jefferson, and Franklin. These individuals found themselves working within the purity of the indigo ray, which focuses on activating the brow chakra. Jefferson was most potent in this regard. The individual known as Washington functioned more upon the level of orange and yellow to wherein these rays merged to become almost divine. Washington represented a focus for bringing forth the visionary capacities of the other individuals in this trilogy. Franklin was the balancer, the pragmatist, and the diplomat. He functioned upon the accord of emerald(green) and blue rays. These are, of course, the forces of the heart and throat chakras. These three individuals formed a key trilogy to manifest thy own country. They had constant interactivity with each other, which brought forth balance at all times. However, there is not the representation of the base chakra or red ray and of the crown crakra and violet ray in this triology. This is because these forces were left to the people to have activities in either of these two polarities.

"Washington was critical to the element of grounding and taking direct action and will as found in the yellow and orange rays, represented from the center of the hara. He put that energy to work almost as a divine intellect bringing forth higher principles. We speak of democratic rules and their application as a direct force and will to lead the continental armies. Jefferson had the higher capacity of being indeed the spiritually realized intellect having many visions on the level of the intellect. Indigo is the expression of the higher visionary, and Jefferson was able to give dictation and articulation here. Franklin was the negotiator between the other two individuals who also traversed within the courts of Europe. He was stimulated by the intellect yet channeled the hara and aided in the preparations needed to attain armaments for the revolution. Franklin received inspiration from the indigo, red, and yellow rays. These three individuals functioned within the principles of a trilogy balancing each other. Jefferson represented the spirit, Washington the physical, and Franklin the mind. These three forces integrated, activated, and heightened each others' properties.

"There were other individuals such as Thomas Paine who functioned mainly on the isolated vibration of the blue ray with great and impassioned oratory skills. He manifested some connection to the red ray and was very influential with the people.

"Another individual, President Andrew Jackson, manifested pure power and abused this form. There was the desire to carry democracy to the people but also the double-edged sword of cutting away other fellow human beings in the mass genocidal policies towards the Indians. There was an attempt by this individual to attain mastery of the yellow and orange rays, but he slipped into the red ray and sought total power. There was the burnt orange, rather than an ascendency to the level of gold and wisdom. His activities polarized the people, setting the stage for the final element that would be traceable to the activities of the Civil War. He was a key figure who did not reach his potential.

"There was then the intervention of Lincoln who represented the higher vision, the desire to again spiritualize the forces. He represented another part of this trilogy functioning along the indigo ray and approaching the violet ray. He attempted to offer a new vision to the people, for people without a vision are dead. This was the desire to free and liberate and thoroughly integrate, not in a hypocritical manner, the principles that the nation had claimed to represent in its vision, that all men are indeed created equal. It was then that there could be balance in the perception of these forces to advance them to their highest accord. But this light was indeed struck down, and again these forces returned to the people.

"The other figure in this trilogy was Andrew Jackson Davis.[5] He had the capacity to work amidst the people, representing the opportunity to spiritualize the intellect by as counseling both great and small. It was felt that this individual would raise up the vibration to unite all, appealing to the rising science of the rational school of thought and balancing the existing empirical school of thought. His teachings were presented to the people as a revelation. This helped develop mastery of the heart chakra, which was indeed the advanced principle of the Christ in those days. This was reflective of the consciousness, in those days, of both the common man and those in positions of prominence. Davis did such counseling from his rise to prominence in the 1840's until his physical passing in the early 1900's. So massive was the outreach and influence of this individual in those days that he was a key balancer and inspiration to the people during this period. This individual played a key role in seeking to unite science, mind, social forces, and many other activities, even offering a blue print for forces that are still advancing in these days. Davis was attuned to the emerald, blue, and violet rays.

"The reason this light left in the time period of the early 1900's was that there was again the rise of one individual who could have united all if he had succeeded. Here we speak of Woodrow Wilson. Here was the idealist who sought to take on and represent the integration of the whole of the trilogy and then to give forth unto the entire world balance within the political mainstream. He was the idealist who was attuned to the yellow, blue, and emerald rays with some attempts to manifest totally the indigo ray. There was also an alignment with the works of Steiner and Krishnamurti, which represented an aspect of a trilogy in those days which, of course, did not find its culmination. These are examples of how the forces of the rays helped shape specific patterns of history and are associated with specific individuals."

Q What rays was Steiner attuned to?
"This will not be given because this would touch on sensitive fields of thought concerning an established individual. We will also not discuss the rays associated with the life of Krishnamurti. These are left to the speculation of the student."

Q It sounds as if certain rays focalize for a while around certain individuals and then they move back into the general populace. Is this true?
"Yes, this general pattern often takes place."

Q How does this information on the seven rays relate to gemstones?
"Gemstones, in part, have empathy with these different states. They are portals to various states of different time-flow continuums. When arranged in harmonics, gemstones activate and give focus or emphasis to the properties described above. Early in the creation of gemstones, their properties and attributes aligned with certain natural forces in the earth's gravitational fields. Gemstones are the very cut and angle of crystallization on the molecular level. They act as a pattern to which the ethers are stabilized, as when a light passes through a system of prisms or lenses and becomes stabilized, at times perhaps even polarized. So in turn is it with the ethers. Their influence crystallizes along the curvatures of activity mentioned, activating and penetrating the mass in which activities are acted out. The key to these things when they are translated into biochemical activity is the DNA. These are the points of resonancy. The properties and dimensions of the five rays obey the laws of light, yet they also violate other principles of the laws of light by traveling beyond the speed and frequency

of light. The primary element is that certain gemstones have empathy with the physics of the ethers, identical with the principles of light, giving such stones the ability to focus and isolate these attributes in the biomolecular activity that is becoming the spiritually realized being."

Q How is the DNA the key to all of this, and how does the RNA tie in here?

"First the DNA is as the activator. In the RNA you have the memory of the activity. In the DNA you have the translator or the building block of these activities to penetrate from the cellular to an anatomical level, to where they are acted out in the three dimensions. They are patterns that have crystallized in a true spiral form. It will be found that all crystalline structures work along a spiral framework. It is the empathy of creating an ether field that has a resonancy or frequency with those states of mass.

"You are constantly passing through the ethers. If your mass came to a total rest and there was no such thing as the ethers, you would collapse in on yourself like a black hole. Just as the wind moves window shutters in specific patterns, you are constantly moving through the ethers at high velocities. This is why the DNA structure is observed in set spiral patterns. This is like the ether winds constantly affecting the molecular structure in an intelligent pattern. Vibrational preparations are treating the time flow which you occupy so that you will be in perfect unison with the universe. The vibration that is transferred in a gem elixir is a higher velocity of a localized time flow which can be used to attune the individual's time flow into a more unified whole.

"The clairvoyant who sees the rays usually observes them as extending from the chakras, although they may be offset and function with other portions of the anatomy. Or they may be seen as centralizing from the subtle bodies and then extending off, usually towards the horizon into infinity. There is this perception because the soul is an omnipresent force; thus it is in all quarters of the known physical universe. However, since it also occupies the limited three dimensions, it gives the illusion that the soul's forces working in the three dimensions are penetrating from a distant place. In other words, the soul's presence is indeed right here within the physical frame, but at the same time, being an omnipresent being, the perceptual reality of the clairvoyant is to see the rays extend into infinity. You are literally at one with the universe."

Q Is the seventh ray replacing the sixth ray as the dominant ray on this planet?

"The seventh ray is now moving more to the fore as an expression of higher consciousness. However, the channel speaking does not state that one ray is replacing another. That approaches the concept of absolutes. The channel speaking would more so address the concept that there is an integration of the sixth and seventh rays' forces."

Q Does the increased influence of the seventh ray on the planet relate to the growing influence of St. Germaine?

"Yes, this is already happening. Witness the transformation now taking place in medicine. Medicine is the outer extension of the science of alchemy. St. Germaine is very associated with alchemy, and holistic medicine is again becoming a major social force."

Q Is it true that the different rays merge together in different combinations causing different states of consciousness?

"Correct. The lower rays are also part of the higher rays. Each higher ray balances and refines the elements of the baser ray."

Q Is the fourth ray a balance between the three lower and more practical rays and with the three higher more evolved rays?
    "Correct."

Q Is the seventh ray especially related to the mineral kingdom, the sixth ray to the vegetable kingdom, and the fifth ray to the animal kingdom?
    "There is this point of focus. A merger of all the rays focuses the consciousness of humanity."

Q Do the first four rays focus on a particular life form?
    "This information cannot be given at this time."

Q How do the subtle bodies relate to the seven rays?
    "In the etheric body we find the red ray, the great initiator. The emotional body aligns the orange ray, the mental body contains properties of the yellow ray, and the astral body contains the green ray. In the astral body we still have aspects of the personal self. The personal self seeks the greater spiritual dimensions. In astral projections we have these attributes. The individual is still in the personal self yet is also in the spiritual dimensions and psychic faculties. Then, within the spiritual body, we find the blue ray, or the forces of the altruistic self, for in the spiritual body we have the spiritual self, the dimensions of the personalized higher forces. In the personalized higher forces, we have the beginning of the personally realized being. The two higher dimensions and their alignment to the causal and soul bodies cannot be given at this time. Study past bodies of information concerning the forces of the subtle bodies to develop greater insights into these processes."

Q The spirit body is above the causal and soul bodies. One would think that the spirit body is associated with one of the higher rays.
    "The subtle bodies are not aligned with the seven rays in a graduating uniform order. It is also true that the causal body is as a linkage of various forms."

Q Is it true that the seven rays are attuned to the seven main chakras in a uniform manner? The first ray is aligned with the base chakra, the second ray with the second chakra, the third ray with the emotional chakra, the fourth ray with the heart chakra, the fifth ray with the throat chakra, the sixth ray with the brow chakra, and the seventh ray with the crown chakra?
    "This we find to be correct. These are also focal points where the rays enter the physical body."

Q Speak on the seven rays in relation to the seven main colors?
    "The rays actually have no color qualities in their own right. The colors identified with the rays are more so the perceptual reality relative to this plane. The rays travel beyond the speed of light; therefore, they do not exist with illumination aligned with color unless with electromagnetic colorations or color itself. At the same time, the seven rays can indeed be coordinated with the natural color spectrum. The first ray

could be considered red, extending to the level of the seventh ray as being violet, with the natural color spectrum falling in between the remaining numerological units.

"This pattern also has a natural alignment with the chakras and the meaning and purpose of each ray. As previously stated the activities of the rays focus on the main chakras. The chakric forces are the activities wherein the rays integrate to create the activities of the physical body. The rays are but the perceptual reality of the soul as an infinite force extending itself into all quadrants of the universe. When an individual seeks to perceive spatially the existence of the soul's force, the rays enable one to experience this energy.

"Each individual is a composite of all the rays and their represented forces. This is why there is often confusion as to the actual colors of the rays. There is often confusion that an individual is attuned to only one ray. It is more so that only that karmic quality is dominant within the individual. In presenting case histories, we have noted that individuals are aligned with several rays."

Q Discuss the seven rays in reference to their interacting with the influence of the natural color spectrum?

"The rays are isolated spectrums of the ether fields, the ether fields in their own right are carriers of light, and light stimulates activity. Thus there is a degree of sympathetic resonance of the individual rays and their points as a focus as they become an integrated force that stimulates physical reality. As noted even in thy sciences, colors at times stimulate specific psychological reactions. The rays create consciousness which in turn stabilizes itself in the human being as an expression of the physical, like the artist when he seeks to mold a mental concept into the sculptured object. Therefore, there can indeed be coordination between the final psychological realities that become the self and the personality and the forces of the mind, and the rays as pure strains of consciousness that extend themselves from the omnipresent existence of the soul and all quadrants in the spacial universe. There is sympathetic resonance in the observable spectrums of light and the psychological make-up interacting with the individual as a reflection of the principles of the rays. This is literally the principle of as above, so below."

Q Exactly why are the specific colors assigned to each different ray?

"There are seven levels of existence from which the rays extend themselves. These are the seven layers of consciousness with which the soul functions. Ye observe this as the four dimensions. It takes the fourth dimension to have any type of spacial existence in the time-space quadrant. The seven rays have the capacity to synchronize with such things as the color spectrum as reflected upon this plane. But the electromagnetic frequencies that perceptually become these colors are also a force independent of the natural color spectrum. The rays may be represented by, but are not those actual, angstroms or colorations. To go beyond this involves a complexity of physics that is not desired at this time."

For those interested in extensively studying the seven rays, the works of Steiner and Alice Bailey are suggested. Bailey did five texts which present a great deal of information on the seven rays.[6] Because the seven rays have such an important effect on our lives it is wise to understand their activities.

Q Describe the seven states of existence and how this relates to vibrational healing?

"Anyone who seeks to understand subtle energies must understand the higher levels and faculties of healing. First you must understand the subtle anatomies. They are dimensional states that project forward into the time flow and are actually connected with the seven dimensions that make up thy entire being. The subtle bodies are dimensional projections manifesting from the time flows of the universe and from the omnipresent level of the soul into the single crystallization that is the self on this plane. Everything is merely a crystallization of the time flow; everything has its own metabolism and rate in the time flow. The soul is outside the time flow. It can be either ahead or behind in time; it makes no difference. You are a hologram from the level of the soul. So your subtle bodies are clearing the time flow, before it reaches the physical body or potential disease state that has been recycled from the omnipresent past into the present. Using ethereal medicine to treat the subtle bodies educates and cleanses the subtle levels before an imbalance reaches the physical level, although imbalances may continue on the physical level even reaching death, depending on the existing conditions before treatment. The developing use of ethereal medicine today expresses the evolution of humanity and is a progression through the seven heavens. You are learning to treat man as a whole, united in mind, body, and spirit. Using vibrational remedies is a futurist treatment in that you are often treating imbalances before they have had time to crystallize or to crystallize fully into the physical body.

"The soul is infinite and omnipresent on all levels. The personality structure is localized on this plane like an ambassador for the soul. What you observe as the various subtle bodies are the projections of the soul on this localized level. Since the soul is omnipresent, it can make itself known on this plane merely by slowing down the time flow to be able to crystallize mass on this plane. By slowing down the velocity of the ethers, it drops down to the level of light and eventually, through the curvature called gravity, can transform itself into matter. Vibrational preparations can aid this process.

"There are three states of matter— the solid, liquid, and gaseous states. It is noted in traditional physics that a liquid expands to conform to its container while maintaining a constant volume. A gas, however, expands indefinitely. Matter is mass, but in a specific pattern or specific atomic structure. Mass has three levels to it similar to the three states of matter. Mass, when in a state of rest, is matter that is in a solid state. Then there is mass in its liquid state, which is light. Light is mass that has liberated itself from a state of rest and is attempting to return to the levels of the ethers. However, because the ethers are saturated at that point, there is no room in that dimension of time and space for light to expand its mass. Therefore, there is the illusion that it cannot expand beyond the speed of light. For instance, a package of photons are but particles of mass that are being squeezed between constant etheric pressures. The ethers are totally frictionless, so there is no resistance on these levels. Thus, light is motivated from constant undulations between trying to go to a state of rest and becoming matter and undulating in an attempt to achieve the state of the ethers. All this is an attempt to expand locally until it reaches the levels of the ethers where it cannot expand any further. This oscillation, or dynamic equilibrium, occurs at an incredible velocity. Finally, there is mass in its rarified or gaseous state which is referred to as the ethers. Everything is crystalized out of the ethers. The ethers are expanded mass, or the substance of matter rarified to such a degree that it is basically undetectable. The ethers are mass that has accelerated beyond the velocity of light. All you can do is observe its effects, which are gravity, electricity, electromagnetism, and the speed of light. In a similar fashion, you cannot observe the atmosphere, although thy scientists can now capture portions of it to reveal its different properties.

"There are seven dimensions. Within the laws of physics there is height, width, and depth. Within the fourth dimension is the source of time, space, and gravity. This source is not something that most people understand because few people can perceive in the fourth dimension. This source in the fourth dimension helps set up a pattern that you perceive as the lower three dimensions. Its elements consist of time, space, and gravity along with length, width, and height. In the transference of consciousness to the higher planes, many are becoming aware that these are illusions. Time is not real, while matter and things that appear solid fade away as your perception includes that which is available on the fourth dimension. It is not easy to express this because your languages have been created to explain three-dimensional concepts. The difficulty comes especially when you look at gravity because gravity as you perceive it is an effect, not a cause. What you perceive as gravity is caused by the vibrational pattern that is set up on a dimensional level higher than you are usually able to comprehend.

"Then there are electricity, electromagnetism, and consciousness to make up the other three dimensions. These are the levels ye must attain mastery over, for these levels and projections have direct correlation with the seven spiritual bodies. In these days ye are beginning to master the fourth dimension. In treating the subtle bodies, ye are beginning to reach the fulfillment of thyself as a four-dimensional being. You are moving beyond just the material, which occupies the three dimensions of height, width, and depth, into the content of mastering time and space.

"Gem elixirs and flower essences as vibrational therapies generally attune to man as a four-dimensional being. Some of these treatments extend into the fifth dimension. Homeopathy is primarily focalized as a fourth dimensional therapy. This is partly because these therapies affect the ethereal realms of people. The fifth dimension is associated with electricity and is synonymous with gravity. These ethereal preparations work and are seeking to work because ye are beginning to prepare individuals to become five dimensional. This brings people into synchronicity with the time-flow continuum. Many are beginning to understand that ye may occupy several positions in time and space relative to the observer. With the ability to move beyond the speed of light, you master the concepts of time and space.

"This is relevant to vibrational therapy in that it explains to the conscious mind some of the mechanics behind how vibrational remedies such as gem elixirs work. Gem elixirs and flower essences involve the transference of energy. You are transfering the vibration of the preparation to the organic level of the body physical. The intelligent pattern of the preparation is introduced to where it can be easily assimilated into the individual's molecular structure, where it eventually expands through the molecular to the cellular and then to the denser physical form for healing on the anatomical level. Vibrational preparations are a perfect energy pattern, or rather the transference of the energy from the ethereal to the level of orgone or prana to the physical form. Orgone energy is actually the process of translating the ethers into the physical universe. When there is a sympathetic bonding and it begins to act on the physical body, emotional tensions that get locked into the DNA even down to the molecular level cannot hold their presence and permeate the physical form. As the healing begins, the vibrational preparation puts the person into greater sympathetic bond with the pure energy that holds the whole pattern of the individual together.

"The ability to travel through the fourth dimension has already been accomplished on the level of the mind by the ability to dip into the future. There is mastery of the psychic abilities which function beyond the speed of light. Using the pendulum also expresses an ability to master the fourth dimension. You are bringing forth information from the higher levels and translating it to the level of the mind. There is an ability to obtain and apply information from the universal mind. This is mastery of the fourth dimension.

"Mastery of the fifth dimension is the ability to as bend and reshape the time flow. Study Geller and his ability to as project his mind into matter to reshape it. The simple bending of metals is but one step removed from the ability to use the molecular structure to reshape and create new elements. In mastering the molecular structure upon these levels there is mastery of the fifth dimension which is mastery of the physical reality from the level of the mind. Vibrational therapies are but one doorway to this mastery. They are educational tools to bring about such properties. Vibrational preparations are the next step in thy evolution. They are the mastery of the fourth dimension that lead as a portal into the fifth dimension. Many are now mastering the fourth dimension and are moving into the fifth. A few individuals such as Steiner have moved from the fifth dimension into the sixth state. Using the mind and gravity are sixth dimensional healing technologies."

Q It seems that these abilities and powers have no real meaning if there is no consciousness.

"Correct. This is why there must be mastery of the seventh dimension, which is consciousness. But one should ultimately ascend to the Godhead which lies beyond the seventh dimension."

Q Briefly define the higher dimensions beyond the seventh?

"As we understand it, what occurs in the higher dimensional levels is the point of creation. At the seventh to eighth dimensional shift, creativity seems to have more a mind of its own, i.e., its own path is self-directing to create its own natural laws. Because creativity on its grandest scale is an intrinsic part of this process, the shift from the seventh to the eighth dimensional level relates to the pure level of matter. Matter as you understand it is primarily three-dimensional, inert and devoid of all intelligence. In the shift into the eighth dimension, matter is created with degrees of consciousness for use by intelligent life everywhere. Then matter is also imbued with fourth dimensional characteristics. This is a beautiful and creative step. This form of creativity is unlimited in the three-dimensional world so that entire planets or mountains and oceans can be created. In the shift from the third to the fourth dimension, there are some limits on this form of creativity. These are the laws that are transmitted to what you perceive as the laws governing consciousness and man at the third and fourth dimensional levels. The way a being experiences a shift in consciousness in moving into these higher dimensions influences and creates the basic laws on the lower planes.

"There are other dimensional levels beyond the ninth dimension going to the twelfth dimension corresponding to the central part of all existence. This is what you might term the source of it all, the source of all sources. This is difficult to explain because you would think of a place in a three-dimensional context. The twelfth dimension is not a limit in itself. Indeed, there may be more dimensions beyond that level."

People interested in studying the various dimensional levels can read the monumental text, *The Principles of Nature* by Andrew Jackson Davis.[7] This book was trance channeled in 1847 by the man who was the most prominent channel in 19th century America. There is a detailed discussion of the higher dimensions. Unfortunately, the book is currently out of print so it can only be obtained from certain libraries.

Q Correlate the different dimensions to different religious states?

"Christ consciousness is mastery of all dimensions. Man may live in perfect harmony with the environment when he does as originally commanded—to be fruitful, to multiply, and to replenish the earth. In this you will become the ultimate gardener and will cause evolution within all things. But first there must be evolution within yourselves. These are the purposes of ethereal medicines. If you are to heal the self, there must be a reintegration to the level of the soul. The soul is master of all seven dimensions but you must patiently experience each in its own turn. By mastering patience and fasting and partaking less of the physical, you move closer to the higher ethereal vibrations.

"This is why nutritional qualities are offered in association with vibrational remedies. This is to integrate and educate the body physical to ultimately synthesize such properties from the ethereal levels. There is a need to reeducate and reorient the body physical and the mind to an understanding that ye are an ethereal being. The body physical is but a property for the containment of these ethereal energies. These ethereal energies are necessary to maintain the soul's focus upon this plane. Thy ethereal medicines are to cleanse the body physical and to educate the self and future generations that you are ethereal beings.

"The properties of the soul are always perfect. It is the flesh at times which seems to make war upon the spirit, not the spirit which makes war upon the flesh. There needs to be the clearing of the vessel and spiritualization of the flesh for clearer manifestation upon this plane. This is why the psychospiritual, as well as the psychological dimension, is provided. Through ethereal medicine the mind may be reeducated. These are but tools more in harmony with the divine state. Ye must always turn to the original source of the light, which is God who is within thee. These medicines shall not save any souls but they may allow for the clearer expression of God's law through example. God created nature so that you could wholly know him because these are reflections of his nature."

Q What is the relationship between the five primary forces and the seven ethers to this work?

"The five primary forces are the speed of light, ethers, gravity, electromagnetism, and the Godhead. Electricity, atomic energy, and the physical plane are subdivisions of electromagnetic forces. The seven main chakras are linked with the seven ethers which are but the seven levels and spectrums of dimensional existence. The chakras are the points where this energy integrates and becomes the physical form, stabilizing the conscious existence of man on the physical plane. This gives one awareness of one's existence on this plane. The seven ethers are the activities of the seven dimensions in that man moves through time and space almost as a hologram. The activities extend from the chakras in a holographic pattern from the level where man is integrated with all portions of the universe. Any misalignment with that holographic pattern creates an activity of nonalignment with the universe as a whole. When the four primary forces, the speed of light, gravity, electromagnetism, and the Godhead, become focalized, they become a single focus and give rise to the ethers. There is one energy that permeates all things. This divides itself into the four dimensions to give life on the physical plane."

Q Explain how the permanent or seed atom relates to this work? There is a belief that minerals, people, and animals have permanent atoms and that this is a special atom linked to the divine.

"The permanent atom is coordinated and linked with the ether fields. In the original construct of energy, the context was that energy could be neither created nor destroyed but only transferred from one form to another. The permanent atom relates totally and consistently to the three-dimensional form of existence. This atom is the very anchor upon which there is a focus for the perception of the ethers from this level of existence. Andrew Jackson Davis spoke of the geometric pattern of cells in the second volume of the *Great Harmonicum*.[8] That material has relevancy to the permanent atom. This atom or God spark dwells in people from the soul's original creation.[9] It is focalized in the heart and other parts of the body.

"Generally, these atoms are associated with the soul stream. So if a person is especially concentrated in the mental realms you may find a permanent atom residing in the brain. Frequently, it will be in the medulla oblongata, between the brows, or in the left or right brain. Sometimes, however, the permanent atom is transformed. It is etherealized. This change is necessary for the individual to remain on the earth. This is often the case for people who have had profound spiritual experiences. Such people will often contain an etherealized permanent atom in their subtle bodies, frequently in the astral and etheric bodies.

"Partly because of the relationship of the soul to the permanent atom, animals tend to have one continuous soul stream governing them, while humanity has begun to subdivide its soul stream. Thus, there are usually more permanent atoms in people than in animals. Ultimately, however, in the concept of the permanent atom there is seen to be but one permanent atom for each dimensional level. There is one atom that is the source point from all life streams."

Q Do all minerals and animals have a permanent atom?
"Yes. Generally minerals have one permanent atom, while animals usually have several."

Q Define the term soul stream, or life stream?
"The soul stream, or life stream, of humanity is a thread of consciousness that has gone on for a long time, even before there was humanity as you understand it today. The soul stream encompasses the overall purpose of a soul group. We refer to what the soul group is on the planet to learn and how that learning takes place here and later in nonphysical forms. Thus there is a uniting of individual souls to a single purpose. The ultimate purpose is, of course, to experience a full understanding of love. Generally, there are other life streams with different purposes that share the earth with humankind."

Q Is it true as Heindel said that there is a seed atom in the solar plexus?
"This will usually not be seen in Occidental people. The seed atom is often found in the solar plexus with people from the Orient. There the hara is often the center of one's

138

being. But there are many individuals who will fall into interesting patterns here. Even though one changes cultures, the permanent atom may not move."

Q Heindel also said that at death the permanent atom rises to the brain by way of the pneumogastic nerve, leaving the body through the sutures between the parietal and occipital bones. How accurate is this?

"This pattern does indeed take place with many people. Those who have claimed to measure the loss of weight as the supposed soul stuff leaves the body at death have partly observed this phenomena. But there are also many variations to this pattern."

Q In other words, different sources state different things about the permanent atoms because they reside in different parts of the body and can even undergo changes in the person?

"Yes."

Q Bailey said that there are three permanent atoms—physical, astral, and mental, and that there are six permanent atoms associated with human evolution. Please comment?

"The six atoms associated with human evolution are those which correspond to the overall soul stream. These are to unite humanity to a common vibration in the time yet ahead. During the interim time period, what are observed are those points of vibration that have a profound influence upon a human being. Therefore, observation will usually show these atoms as important points of vibration in all people. It is sometimes noted that one of these permanent atoms is more active than the others. The assumption is made that the others are there as well but do not play as important a role. There is some truth to this, of course, but because the other permanent atoms are usually found only in the subtle bodies and are not within a person's direct contact we would not generally recommend that they be the ones that one become more aware of."

Q Besides jasmine flower essence,[10] what other flower essences or gem elixirs activate the permanent atoms in people?

"Amber may activate the permanent atoms in people. Diamond sometimes activates the permanent atom to ease the passage from this plane at death. This can be a difficult matter because this activation provides a deeper understanding or memory of the inner soul stuff, and the person usually does not have a way to grapple with this change and understand it."

Q Do the new minerals now being discovered also activate the permanent atoms?

"Some of them do, but we are not permitted to say much about such substances."

Q That is more for the 1990's?

"Correct."

Heindel said the blood passing through the heart imprints fresh impressions of the current incarnation onto the seed atom in the heart. This atom contains all the details of one's present and past lives.[11] Several sources say that the seed atom is near the apex of the left ventricle in the heart.[12] All of our past life experiences are stored in the seed atom.[13] All atoms in the body physical vibrate in tune with the heart's seed atom. This atom is like a tuning fork giving the pitch to the rest of the body.[14] Numerous authors state that the seed atom responds to various spiritual vibrations and tones.[15] The seed atom enables us to master the physical environment and to be coordinated with the tones in the archetypal worlds.[16] Ann Ree Colton said that there are twenty-four corridors or chambers within the seed atom, and that this is related to the twenty-four elders spoken of in the Book of Revelations and the twenty-four divine chromosomes affecting our spiritual destiny.[17] White Eagle said that the seed atom aids in the creation of the physical vehicle that we will next inhabit.[18]

The silver cord is connected to the seed atom in the heart. The silver cord unites the physical and subtle vehicles with the higher dimensions.[19] At night while asleep we soul travel or astral project to various dimensions, with the silver-colored thread maintaining our link to the physical vehicle. At death this link is broken. The seed or permanent atom is an important part of our spiritual heritage which people should become more aware of. Meditation and creative visualization focusing on this atom can activate its qualities for enhanced spiritual awareness.

Q Explain how minerals get their properties?

"This involves a crystallization of the ethers.[20] First the student should understand the principles of the three states of mass, which are matter, light, and ethers. Crystalline structures allow for the ethers to penetrate into this plane in many ways that are detectable, such as with mild electromagnetic fields and piezoelectric effects. Movements in these fields are but the movement of the ethers, which allow the ethers to focus in a localized field of time and space. Since they are energies traversing beyond the speed of light, without these crystalline structures to focus on (not unlike the way a prism may as refract and focus ordinary light), you would not have the capacity to tap these fields except in your own meditations which activate the crystalline structures already existing in your physical form."

Q Speak on the relation of gemstones to intense heat and cold?

"This involves thermodynamic principles and crystalline structures. Heat and cold may have enhancing or atrophying properties upon crystals. In extreme cold the temperature in a crystalline structure can be gradually lowered to absolute zero and held suspended in a vacuum. This superconductive state allows electricity to flow unimpeded continuously.

"When electrical properties of gemstones in a superconducting state are attached to corresponding acupuncture points, there is an extreme activation of tissue regeneration in the associated organs. The capacity for tissue regeneration extends not only to promoting healing but even extends to the level of the central core of the nervous system. There is a direct tapping almost to the ethereal force itself because you are adding two dynamics to the crystalline structure. First, the crystalline structure becomes even more stabilized. Any time there is the complete removal of all outer resources and extensions of apparent energy, there is then only the exposure of solidified mass or matter to the ether fields which constantly shape its form. Therefore, by steadying the molecular structure of the crystal base that is found in all gemstones, the properties of the ethers are enhanced. Second, conductivity increases. Electrical fluidiums have always been but the carriers of ether fields rather than as a force in their own right. These then are the purer vehicles for the purer substance of ethers, holding its pattern and healing qualities. Therefore, it can be said that absolute zero in thermal forces acts as a crystallizing enhancer in its own right. Study the patterns of any fluidium when it reaches absolute zero.

"When gemstones are overheated, their properties are temporarily enhanced. The crystal slightly expands due to the increase of energy present from the heat source. This temporary point of expansion usually takes place at temperatures of 62 to 73 degrees up to 110 degrees. Above 110 degrees there begins to be a disinheritance of the gemstone's healing properties. This is because, at this point of expansion in the gemstone's molecular structure, expansion of the ether field as it passes through the gemstone is no longer stored in the gemstone but begins to move through the molecular crystalline structure of the gemstone. Thus the gemstone's resonancy and solidified pattern of ethereal energy begins to lose its construct."

Q Discuss the special electrical properties of gemstones?

"There are several different forces of electrical properties in gemstones. That of the simple accord is static electricity, which can come from the primary element of but the loosening of electrons. This has mild beneficial healing results when combined with other activities of the body physical. Static electricity is most effective or beneficial in promoting healing and stimulating consciousness by placing the gemstone upon the skin's surface at points where there are the most critical concentrations of nerve endings. These points include the hands, base of the feet, medulla oblongata, sacrum, and coccyx. This activity combines the mild static forces that exist upon the skin's surface with the forces that build up on the gemstone's surface. The gemstone is in a constant state of resonancy, if only from that which is known as Brownian movement which is the internal vibration of the molecular structure itself. This vibration is steady in its pulsation due to crystallization of the gemstone's properties slowly penetrating to its own surface. It becomes amplifiable to a measurable degree by the existence of the static electrical forces. These forces then create a stable static electrical force or mild field directly upon the gemstone's surface or crystalline structure. These patterns are continuously generated.

"It is possible with certain instruments to actually measure these mild fields around gemstones. This would have to be accomplished with electrical devices that seek to measure minute fields no bigger than one to three electrons, for this is approximately the depth of the field. This is actually part of what would be considered as electrical deterioration of the gemstone, not radioactive deterioration. This is a new principle of understanding the creation of matter, for you would find that mass that is lost through the process of rising to the surface from the core of the gemstone is replaced by the activities of the ethers. In this process there can be some minute measurable degree of the creation of mass within the gemstone. This is an etheric layering of the static electric field and should not be associated with the forces of radioactive decay. It is such a gradual process that, until specifically noted as a field, it is but the first layering and intertwining of normal static processes."

Q Why is it not related to radioactive decay?

"There is a unique distinction. Radioactive decay is as the throwing off of single protons and neutrons that is a portion of the decay of all matter. This is a consistent force and graduating pattern upon the surface of a gemstone. It is almost more so a portion of the physical resonancy, but it still is transferable to the electrical or static fields upon the surface of the skin.

"The key element is that these are the internal forces involved in the translation of ethereal energies into the earth plane. As these fields of an electrical or static nature integrate into neurological tissues, the process of steady pulsations of energy that is then translated into a neurological input increases the capacity for the body physical to have steady sources of information to correct itself. As previously stated, gemstones have internal forces of molecular resonancy with the chemical or biochemical makeup on the cellular, anatomical, and even nutritional levels of certain internal organs within the physical body. Placement of the gemstone's electrical properties close to neurologically concentrated impulses imprints into the body physical's own neurological functions, stimulating these processes throughout the physical form. The relaxation and reduction of stress within an individual that results aids in the healing process, and there is not an overtaxing of the physical system.

"There are also the activities found in quartz and other minerals with similar properties which are known as piezoelectric effects. This is energy or electricity that is reduced in the molecular structure when placed under direct electrical currents. When infrared or ultraviolet light is passed through crystals or crystalline structures such as ruby, emerald, and quartz and then reflected off the surface of lapis lazuli, pearl, and turquoise, there is the production of electrical effects. This effect generates mild electromagnetic fields that have healing properties."

Q Speak further on piezoelectric effects and how they relate to gemstones?

"The forces of piezoelectricity do not play a critical role in promoting healing or consciousness; they are most applicable for thought form amplification. Gemstones stimulate healing when there is the proper level of thought amplification. Thought is coordinated electromagnetic energy. Piezoelectric effects are basically inert energies or electrical forces stored within gemstones and crystalline structures that allow for the amplification of thought forms with the raising of consciousness. This is also the critical source of energy that can be used for thought form amplification as used in the mandalic patterns described in the astrological information. The thought forms filter through the quartz crystal sheet, totally enhancing these forms. This process of thought form amplification also aids in the removal of karma. As the light source passes through that which can stimulate thought form amplification, past life karma comes to the surface allowing the individual with a skilled therapist to confront and release various issues.

"The reflective surface properties of certain gemstones generate electrical forces upon their surfaces, particularly gemstones with healing properties such as pearl, turquoise, and lapis lazuli. Jet or opal could be made into a reflective surface of approximately four inches by four inches with a curvature of approximately three to nine degrees. The isolation of an ultraviolet or infrared frequency, or the merger of these frequencies, striking the gemstone's surface for three to eight minutes over the entire surface generates at a distance of about three to seven inches a measurable electromagnetic field. There is no difference in effect if only ultraviolet or only infrared is used. This field enhances the healing and conscious qualities associated with these gemstones. This field could then be applied to the body physical at the medulla oblongata, the base of the spine, or at a critical point where the gemstone corresponds with the neurological tissues connected to the spinal column that lead to the internal organ in need of healing. These naturally enhancing procedures induce themselves into the body physical through several processes. The neurological tissue and the meridians are stimulated, but only after their energy is translated through a measurable electrical field on the skin's surface, preferably when reflected by a gemstone into an associated pressure point. The reflective surface generates mild static and electromagnetic fields.

"The combination of piezoelectric and static electric forces can translate into healing through a laser process. It is possible to create a synthetic or merged gemstone by passing light through the gemstone to amplify light. You then have the optics necessary for healing because this greatly amplifies the properties of gemstones. And of course the laser points stimulate various neurological points. It is easier to do this with clear gemstones, but it can also be done with opaque minerals such as turquoise. For instance, if ruby and quartz were merged, perhaps with an opaque mineral, it could then be translated with proper optics to laser capacity. Researchers will need to experiment here and work out the details carefully."

Q Explain what is meant by the piezoelectric effects of gravity and the principles of thought form amplification?

"Gravity is a continuous pressure that is not pulling, but is due to the expansionary force that gravity truly is. All states of mass, due to a constant state of acceleration, are in a constant state of expansion. The piezoelectric effect is energy or electrons that are released when certain minerals are placed under pressure. Thus, gravity may be used as a source of pressure. Gravity is also the curvature in which mass travels. Therefore, thought forms are shaped by their curvature of remaining in the fourth dimension below the speed of light. In the same way that gravity may bend light, so in turn it gives curvature, shape, and dimension to thought forms, which are amplified by piezoelectic effects. There is an interlinking of gravity, piezoelectric influences, and the shaping of thought forms."

Q How can piezoelectricity be harnessed in the future as a new energy source?

"Crystalline structures hold the most promise for harnessing piezoelectric energy. This is connected with the activities of merging the principles of silicon and its photoelectrical effects and then transferring these subtle energies to the greater energy stored within quartz crystals. First, create a plate of pure silicon. Then expose this to the sun's rays, which generates a mild electrical voltage that could be transferred to a copper plate, then to a crystalline structure made of quartz that is placed within a pure vacuum. This quartz structure should be surrounded by copper, which is then connected back to the silicon plate, so that when there is a transfer of the photoelectric effect it would seek to merge and ground with the fields of the quartz structure. Then the quartz structure would begin to expand upon its own molecular level. This device would broadcast electromagnetic energy along those frequencies that ye have identified as microwave in nature. This energy could be greatly amplified and tapped for the generation of electricity on a practical level. The vacuum will reduce the conduction of heat from the crystalline structure, thus confining the energy to the structure's own molecular level.

"This device could also be used to tap the ethers. There could be the translation of energy directly from the ethers to almost the principle of free energy. These principles will, of course, have to be further studied to fully isolate the properties described. Researchers can explore this. Just as quartz crystals allowed for the necessary sensitivity in building thy broadcasting devices known as radios with electromagnetic energy, so in turn, as with the ancients, it is through these properties that you will eventually discover the fulfillment of broadcasting energies such as telepathy, astral projection, and healing at a distance, even to the foundations perhaps of levitation and mastery of psychokinetics."

The 'return' wire that connects back to the silicon photocell is called in typical electronics jargon a 'ground' wire, even though the wire may never touch the earth. It is necessary here to complete the electrical circuit.

"If there is any question how the small amounts of energy detectable within thy normal physics resonating from gemstones can have an impact on the body physical, the student need only look upon thy more primitive physics to the small amounts of energy necessary to bring forth the destruction of entire cities. More primitive studies of physics have been used to unleash greater quantities of energy from splitting atoms. Thy body physical is a complex system of delicately balanced, biochemical activity extending down to a complex dance upon the molecular level of energy resonancies. There is no such thing as matter, but only various states of liquidity of mass that are energy. Matter appears to be solid because we are moving relative to its position. Even a wall of electricity can appear to be solid because of its high velocity. By focusing and amplifying energy through crystalline structures, harmony can be achieved within isolated spectrums of the body physical. Indeed, people have always turned their eyes towards crystalline structures, for they have sensed that their activities are of an accord of having a natural resonancy."

Q Explain how infrared and ultraviolet can be used to activate the properties of gemstones?
"They stimulate the piezoelectric effect of gemstones. Even science would as confirm this. We do not suggest applying infrared, ultraviolet, or lasers directly to the body; they should be used to amplify gemstones. A suggested experiment would be to expose a gemstone whose properties have been isolated to ultraviolet for thirty minutes. A subject can then hold that mineral on the palm of the hand while being tested with biofeedback or brain-wave monitoring equipment. If lapis lazuli, for example, was used, a mild response would be noticed almost immediately in portions of the brain associated with speech. Lapis lazuli is associated with the vocal chords and the throat chakra. The person holding the mineral should not be told what mineral he is using to eliminate the power of suggestion. This method could be used to learn the clinical effect on the body physical of many different gemstones."

Q Would it be possible to do a laboratory test showing the relationship of infrared and ultraviolet to the thought form amplification effects and piezoelectric properties of minerals?
"There could be the outlining of such a program. There have already been certain studies by thy scientists using filtrations with different colors and lasers being passed through certain gemstones. In time it will be understood that this aids or hinders cell growth. Certain researches into DNA and concepts of cloning are touching on these areas. The evolution of thy material sciences are paralleling that which has already been as worked with as a technology on the ethereal levels."

Q Do you have anything further to offer on using infrared, ultraviolet, and piezoelectric effects, and the electrical qualities of minerals?

"Study the patterns of how infrared intermixed with silicon enhances direct solar electrical phenomena. Or study the pattern of how ultraviolet increases the fluorescence of certain minerals. The thought form amplification properties of minerals are activated under the effects of piezoelectric properties, which are forces within the accepted standards of physics, suggesting that gemstones do in fact have healing qualities and that they have fields unique unto themselves. It is the desire of the channel speaking to as point to these energy fields which the mystics have long spoken of as existing in gemstones and to note that this is gradually being confirmed by modern science.

"Most principles desired for the student have been presented at this time. These concepts are presented at an introductory level to stimulate thought. More information will be provided at a future time."

Those who understand the principles and concepts of new physics will perhaps most enjoy the material presented in this chapter. That developing science will in the coming years present much new information to increase our understanding of how and why vibrational remedies work.[21] In the future, combinations of gem elixirs and flower essences will be presented that enable the soul to enter the physical body to inspire our lives more directly. This is a very evolved form of therapy.[22] It is wise to develop an increased understanding of how the soul works in each individual and to reestablish a link with the higher spiritual dimensions.

1 Ernest Wood, *The Seven Rays* (Wheaton,IL: The Theosophical Publishing House, 1967).
2 Alice Bailey, *Telepathy and the Etheric Vehicle* (N.Y: Lucis Publishing Co.,1980), p.136.
3 James Sturzaker, *The Twelve Rays* (Wellingborough, Northamptonshire, England: The Aquarian Press, 1981).
4 Geoffrey Hodson, *The Seven Human Temperaments* (Madras, India: The Theosophical Publishing House, 1981), p. 50-61.
5 *The Harmonial Philosophy* (Mokelumne Hill,Ca: Health Research, 1974).
6 Alice Bailey, *Esoteric Astrology* (N.Y: Lucis Publishing Co., 1979).
_____, *Esoteric Healing* (N.Y: Lucis Publishing Co., 1980).
_____, *Esoteric Psychology, Vol. I* (N.Y: Lucis Publishing Co., 1979).
_____,*Esoteric Psychology, Vol. II* (N.Y: Lucis Publishing Co., 1975).
_____,*The Rays and the Initiations* (N.Y: Lucis Publishing Co.,1976).
7 Andrew Jackson Davis, *The Principles of Nature*, 1847.
8_____, *The Great Harmonia: The Teacher, Vol. II* (Mokelumne Hill,Ca: Health Research, 1973).
9 Annie Besant, *A Study of Consciousness* (Madras,India: The Theosophical Publishing House, 1975), p.66-88.
Max Heindel, *The Rosicrucian Cosmo-Conception* (Oceanside,Ca: The Rosicrucian Fellowship, 1977), p.97.
10 Gurudas, *Flower Essences and Vibrational Healing* (Albuquerque,N.M: Brotherhood of Life, 1983), p. 120.
11 Max Heindel,*The Rosicrucian Philosophy in Questions and Answers, Vol.I* (Oceanside,Ca: The Rosicrucian Fellowship, 1978), p.114.
_____,*The Rosicrucian Cosmo-Conception* (Oceanside,Ca: The Rosicrucian Fellowship, 1977), p.398.
12 ____,*The Rosicrucian Christianity Lectures* (Oceanside,Ca: The Rosicrucian Fellowship, 1972), p.79.
13 White Eagle, *Spiritual Unfoldment, Vol. I* (Hampshire,England: The White Eagle Publishing Trust,1982), p.99-100.
Mona Rolfe, *Man-Physical and Spiritual* (London: Neville Spearman,n.d.), p. 57.

14 Max Heindel, *The Rosicrucian Philosophy in Questions and Answers, Vol.I* (Oceanside,Ca:The Rosicrucian Fellowship,1978), p. 119.

15 Alice Bailey, A *Treatise on Cosmic Fire* (N.Y: Lucis Publishing Co., 1977), p. 507-536.

16 Ann Ree Colton, *Islands of Light* (Glendale,Ca: ARC Publishing Co., 1953),p. 104.

17_____,*The Lively Oracles* (Glendale,Ca: ARC Publishing Co., 1962),p. 7-8.

18 White Eagle, *Spiritual Unfoldment, Vol. I* (Hampshire, England: The White Eagle Publishing Trust, 1982), p.36.

19 Max Heindel, *The Rosicrucian Christian Lectures* (Oceanside,Ca: The Rosicrucian Fellowship, 1972), p. 80.

Mona Rolfe, *Man-Physical and Spiritual* (London: Neville Spearman,n.d.), p.56-57.

20 H.P. Blavatsky, *The Secret Doctrine*,Vol. II (Madras,India: The Theosophical Publishing House, 1979), p. 169.

21 Larry Dossey,M.D., *Space, Time and Medicine* (Boston: Shambhala Publications, 1982).

22 Alice Bailey, Esoteric Healing (N.Y: Lucis Publishing Co., 1980), p. 16-17.

CHAPTER X

GEMSTONES AND THE ENVIRONMENT

In many native folk religions and cultures it has long been understood that the earth is a living being.[1] This concept is increasingly influencing the developing science of new physics.[2] Metaphysical authorities such as Steiner[3] and Heindel[4] have also long had this understanding. This perception enables individuals to have greater attunement to nature and more sensitivity to use gemstones in healing and spiritual work.

Q Speak about the concept of the earth as a living being?

"What we are looking at here may be considered a whole new concept of life. In the past the description of life has basically been biochemical, or rather that the body was like a system of internal mechanistic pumps that assimilated various solid products. Since the body physical was thought of as being solid and a refined chemical system, life to many has been defined in a chemical and mechanistic manner.

"In the past when people spoke of the earth as a living being, it was noted that people contain water almost in equal proportion to the earth. There have been many philosophical insights and observations about the planet in relationship to man's own anatomy. The basic principle was that there was always an attempt to relate the planet to man as a biochemical or mechanical makeup.

"Today, many now look at man as a unit of energy that extends up from subtle levels of energy to more and more complex forms, until eventually you reach the tangible physical level. Thus, with the increased integration of new physics and molecular biology, an entirely new definition of life has developed which relates to the idea of man as energy. In this regard it will be found that gemstones are a constant source of various radiances of energy that penetrate and stimulates different forces in the environment, contributing to the life force of the planet.

"While some call the planet a living organism, the context is more that the planet is a living being. The concept of organism is based on the principle of individual cultures or cellular tissues that combine with various specialized functions to create a biochemical life form. This, in part, has been one of the classic definitions of life, when life has been defined within the principles of biochemical activity. The integration of various biochemical activities creates the patterns, philosophies, and harmonics of how these forces interact. It is wise to define many of these forces as products of life rather than life itself.

"The body physical is a state of being, or a state of energy, or more so an entity. The body physical is not a chemical process. The actual chemical processes within the body physical are but a by-product of superior forces upon the molecular level that coordinate the activities of the body. If the body physical may be considered an entity rather than an orthodox concept or organism, so in turn it is with the life of the planet itself. The planet should be considered as an entity, or as a being of energy. The body physical has within it subtle forces and energies that contribute to its state of well-being and health, and there are critical and measurable points for these energy patterns such as the meridians and acupuncture and acupressure points. Biological science has demonstrated that these energy patterns contribute to the life process. In a similar fashion the various mineral and crystalline deposits, the earth's electromagnetic fields, and all its other sources of energy integrate to create a matrix of various subtle forces. As these forces extend out from themselves and enter the earth's electromagnetic field to become part of the harmonics through which the body physical of man passes at all times, they become a lattice of subtle influences through the many generations of humanity. This process continues through all life forms and indeed is part of the evolutionary process. This exemplifies how the planet in its own right upon a simple level could be considered to exist as a single cell, in the sense that a single cell has continuous exchanges of energy on a biomolecular level but is not necessarily considered fully conscious of its ability to do programming of its own evolution and consciousness, as a self-aware being made up of many cells can do. However, the critical element regarding the planet as a living being is that it also possesses consciousness independent of the soul's force.

"Within the context of man's brain there are synapses between individual neurons, and synapses of energy exchange between the neurons, and their functions. Memory is stored here. These memories are as drawn up into a collective whole; they are a level of functioning consciousness that, when integrated with other stimuli from the five physical senses, becomes awareness. Organizationally, these forces then become intelligence.

"As the individual patterns of biochemical memory stored in the RNA shape the individual's electrical forces and exchanges, so in turn the functions of individual gemstones represent different seats of consciousness. Gemstones can be considered the neurological tissues of the planet. Just as you have a nervous system, so does the planet.[5] They are the refined seats of consciousness upon the planet. The different chemical makeup of various minerals records and represents the different seats of consciousness being actualized. Various minerals are still growing, although at a slightly less detectable rate than their original rate, as the earth has cooled. Therefore, the planet as a living organism should be thought of as a living being. The earth has become a living being by the outpouring over its surface of living tissue. This has come forth because the earth is in a state of consciousness, in a constant state of resonancy.

"These energies then extend out into the functions of the earth's electromagnetic field, creating a vast sea of potential consciousness. But it is the passing of the soul's force through this plane that creates awareness, for consciousness is the state of self-apparent existence. Awareness is a critical point of focused consciousness in a limited place in time and space. Therefore, the planet in its own right has consciousness independent of the soul's force and independent of man's observations on this plane. Many scientists have already agreed that there are demonstrations of consciousness even on the part of plant forms.[6] These activities are a focus, or more so, a residue of the original great spirit's passing through this plane, giving order and semblance."

Q How radically different is this from the orthodox perceptions of how matter and the earth were formed?

"These views are independent of thy current concepts of how the earth and matter were formed, for these constructs explain the dynamics by which consciousness has arisen upon the planet and has extended from inanimate mass or inanimate matter. It is not in contrast to orthodox origins, but is more an enhancement to those principles."

Q So a key distinction with the orthodox understanding in these areas is that they do not include consciousness?

"Correct."

Q Summarize how your views on the formation of matter and the earth can be fused with the orthodox view?

"Study physics, the three states of matter, and the seven rays, and you will find a progressive line and discourse upon the origins of inanimate mass and its translation into consciousness. Furthermore, study the information provided on tissue regeneration and how these forces integrate with the natural lines of evolution."

Several years ago I realized that the universe represented the body of God, and that the earth was associated with the heart of God. Various metaphysical sources state that this is a key planet because in many worlds people focus on developing the intellect. Here a key heritage and purpose of the human race is to master the emotions. While John would not comment on this understanding, it is interesting that Joseph Whitfield in *The Eternal Quest* has a similar perception.[7]

Q Discuss gemstones in relation to the four seasons?

"Here there can be a heightening of meditation, agriculture, certain psychological forces, healing of certain internal organs, and various other activities that are inclusive within the full spectrum of human needs. There shall be a discourse on how gemstones obtain their properties in relationship to the seasons and the influence and relevancy of gemstones to the seasons to understand these full forces and principles.

"First the individual should relate to the planet as a living entity mostly along the principles outlined by the individual known as Andrew Jackson Davis.[8] These principles are that the original foundation of the initial creative forces extended forth and began to set into motion those natural laws known as physics, and this is a graduating and self-actualizing process. Even as you are now redefining what life is, in the context of your own physical bodies, so in turn there is increased understanding of the principles as given through the individual known as Andrew Jackson Davis. The planet itself may indeed be considered a living being. It has even extended the self as a living being to having a biomolecular structure in all the various beings that it nurtures. Many now realize that there is great complexity within the internal workings upon the subatomic, atomic, and molecular levels. Indeed the biomagnetic fields that link up to the planet itself are still being discovered.

"In this more refined definition of life, it can be found that the planet is an actualized and living entity within the context of physical life and consciousness, moving perhaps in a different perspective of time and space. These activities are not immediately registered as though being a life unto self, but the principles contained within thy own molecular structure indeed are as found even within that which is considered as inanimate matter within the earth. Since the earth occupies slightly different frequencies in the time and space continuum, it moves at a slower pace. But all the activities that may be measured such as subatomic decay, the creation of crystalline structures, mineral deposits, and the transformation of minerals from one substance to another are the very source and root of biochemical life. These are also the processes of life in a state of energy and even in many biomolecular functions on the entire planet as an entity.

"Since you would find that the activities of the planet are indeed as living, then in turn its internalized forces which you find in the properties of gemstones may also be considered as a source and focus of a life force that is being actualized and has empathy with other sources. For even as ye assimilate properties upon the biomolecular level, these in turn are still more a process of energy rather than primitive chemical forces that ye observe closer to the anatomical function of the body physical and closer to the cellular level.

"It has been recently discovered in thy sciences that, in the twisting of the molecular structure from a righthand turn to a lefthand turn, molecular structure is not then integrated as an organic compound but merely passes through the physical system. These are principles of energy, not of chemistry. Ye are increasingly discovering that it is from sources of energy such as light that you receive physiological response such as in vitamin D, and these energy fields integrate to become mass within the physical body. So in turn is it with the subtler energies, with gemstones. But as these things apply, they are but more the foundation. Biochemical forces become active in the presence of initiative energy such as warmth and come to a standstill when there is a lack of the presence of the activiting energy of heat. This biochemical process is slow, and it is linked with the life form itself. So in turn would you find that the subtle energy of gemstones is as attuned to the four seasons, for even as life on the planet has adapted to the cycles of the four seasons in its biochemical or bioenergy makeup, so in turn is it with gemstones, only more so, as their subtler energies are linked to magnetic, electromagnetic, and gravitational forces in the earth's early formulations.

"But these were not haphazard forces as though created by chance; these are more so an actualizing force following along the natural flow of energy and substance that is the space-time continuum. These then find their activities and adapt and take in the energies cyclically by the positioning of their various embedded crystalline structures in their creation and re-creation, and with the expansion and contraction of the earth's outer crustlike structure according to that which creates diseases, i.e., the peculiar angle to the earth's axis in its inner relationship with the sun's gravitational and electromagnetic forces. But these are not so much forces as are exposure to heat and light as measured classically by the four seasons; these are more so an even distribution and linkage with the earth's electromagnetic field as then dictated by the seasons. These same forces in relationship to the angles of the earth also find their interlocking properties with interplanetary movements.

"The biomolecular rhythms find their resonancies with the planet itself. This is exemplified when man studies the physical body's needs during exposure to specific gravitational fields such as you would find when man is exposed to zero gravity. Then there is a slowing of certain metabolic processes, particularly within the skeletal structure which is designed and created to adapt man as a biochemical entity within the specific field and electromagnetic influence of the earth's gravitational pull. When this is changed, there is no longer the assimilation of phosphorus, magnesium, and calcium into the skeletal structure. Indeed, if anything, there is a reversal of this process. So in turn there is an empathy in the creation of gemstones under these self-same forces upon gravitational, electromagnetic, and piezoelectric forces contained within their own molecular structure. These then are the keys to understanding man's link with gemstones to the four seasons. This is not based on heat and temperature but more specifically upon the influence of the sun, the entire orbital pattern and influence of the earth in its elliptical path, and the exposure to these magnetic fields and fluxes as they are continuously exposed throughout the four seasons.

"Link this information to the discourse upon geometric structures or homes, gemstones, and the linkage to man's siddhis or powers and related forces. Then you will be able to understand this and expand on these principles. This then is the creation of these forces. The application of these forces is the specific isolation of gemstones in association with their seasons. These may be matched up with the seasons of the astrological accord. For instance, Capricorn find its heightened properties, of course, at the winter solstice. The forces in those stones associated with Leo find their potency in the summer. The continuing of these influences may be documented according to information given on astrological accords."

Q In other words, all twelve zodiac signs apply to the four seasons and this is how you can tell?
    "Correct."

Q Please comment on the belief that gemstones have greater value and use at different parts of the day and season?
    "This is a major issue that is more applicable during various seasons rather than during the twenty-four period. However, due to the complexity of seasons, planetary positions, and principles of harvest this information cannot be fully explored in this volume."

Q Explain the dynamics by which consciousness has arisen and has extended into matter?
    "The natural forces of the earth were set forth in motion since its foundation by one great spirit called God. Consciousness has always been present throughout all creation. Indeed, creation is but as the setting forth of certain natural laws of force which ye now observe and term physics. Physics and creation are not separate; they are one and the same. It is not unlike observing the anatomy of God. As individuals study and isolate these forces, they may recognize a pattern behind creation and understand that creation is not random chance as some theorize. This is not an instant understanding, but it is not beyond the comprehension of individuals.

    "In the philosophy of these things this is not to put man in awe but it is to realize that even on the most basic level, even in his most corporeal or material form, man is still part of and not separate from the incredible concept of the cosmos itself. Even if you were at one with these forces only upon the material level and even if one is only a child at this, then in turn how great is one's birthright that he is drawn off as the observer of these forces. Indeed what a great sacred trust that he would be the observer and the keeper of the truth of these forces as are found in physics. But of course man is more than just his material form, for he has sprung forth not from the bowels of the earth, but indeed from the mind of God, which is pure and divine. And in this ye would take and find that man is a consciousness and is a co-creator in the universe. He finds these reflections in his desire to create and to build. When man accepts this heritage, he will then be able to be as a co-creator upon the true higher levels. He will no longer be under the law, but he will be as the law, not to as rule over life and death, but to be the law itself. This is harmony and balance and a restoration of your natural birthright, which is to create and keep charge over the affairs that the one great spirit called God had originally set forth in motion.

"Therefore, in the philosophical issue that if man was but by his own design and his own statement only drawn up from the cosmos as a consciousness, but is material, there is but the smallest thread, the smallest hint of glory. How much more so is his glory when he comes to the full realization of himself as pure consciousness, as pure spirit. Man indeed rules not over the limited creation of his period of life on this plane before he passes away, but he is a continuous thread of consciousness throughout all creative acts. This allows the individual to come to the full understanding that indeed currently he is under the laws of physics in his very mortality. As he discovers this in his meditations and ponderances, eventually he will merge to become as the law and part again of that one great creation."

Q Explain how minerals are formed?

"To answer this we shall present an individual case study of the recently discovered mineral maghagendorfite,[9] from an esoteric point of view, and include some information based on its exact chemical makeup. General principles will be presented and the inquirer can seek to expand his understanding into further complexities. There will be a description of the normal molecular forces along with current geological explanations as to the creation of a crystalline structure. How these things then also have empathy as a living force shall parallel that description anchoring both the esoteric and currently known geological forces.

"First in calling the earth a living being it should be understood that there are several levels to defining life. There is life as created in the form of the spirit, in the sense of being independent of the corporeal form, but a spirit may indeed pass through a corporeal or physical form, animating it and giving it purpose, direction, will, mind, and other substances that may be defined as the spiritual dynamics of life. There is also the activity of biological life. Biological life is the drawing up of inanimate matter into consistent, self-repeating, and self-recurring biochemical patterns. It is the logistics or logistical pattern of chemical existence. The earth as a living being reflects both these activities, for you would find that in the biochemical pattern there is the activity of life forms or biochemical patterns taking into self inanimate matter and having it become organic and more intricate and complex. This principle of taking simple elements and creating more complex structures is a reversal of the procedure of the natural laws of thermodynamics. Thermodynamics affirms that all states of matter are in a state of decay, from whence they are as leaving complex forms and are through progressive decay upon the atomic levels becoming simpler in their forms.

"If maghagendorfite is carefully analyzed, it will be found that the earth as a living being has the capacity to readjust its makeup according to the reflection of the conscious beings that sprang forth from it. This particular mineral is a merger of several other base elements found in a peculiar and unique form, that enter more complex forms. Some of the experiments conducted on the surface of Mars have found that certain chemical forms imitate the self-perpetuating forms of life. If activated within periods of time and given opportunities to as reflect those patterns, this particular mineral would indeed perform similar functions."

Q How?

"It does this by performing the ability to reproduce itself upon the biological level. But until there is the presence of consciousness to as guide and uplift this presence, the totality of the life form is not activated. Therefore, this particular mineral makeup is an expression of a life form in a biological state that lays dormant until consciousness guides it. Its use in chemistry or in various experiments would be that the first stage of consciousness guiding it through these processes would indeed be the experimenters themselves seeking to activate a biochemical pattern of life. Until this was interwoven with other activities, this particular mineral would as lie dormant. This mineral will also be found to be a key element in cloning and genetic engineering. A minor injection of it into the process of mitosis during genetic engineering would allow for a triggering mechanism for the easy observation and isolation of various life forms, by increasing or diminishing its presence during their processes. It stimulates the cellular level promoting life-giving properties. This is an example of the earth as a living being in the sense that life as a biological process exists throughout many of its minerals' structures. But the key element here is that this particular structure has indeed become present and pulled itself up from simpler forms by the presence of the consciousness reflected upon this planet. It has synthesized itself to reflect that consciousness, and this is why it has been discovered during this particular time. This is but a demonstration of the planet bringing forth more complex mineral forms independent of any biological agent already present. It is reflective of the planet's consciousness in its most rudimentary state, since according to the laws of thermodynamics, these elements should be in a state of decay. Maghagendorfite can also be used in various combinations of vibrational preparations to enhance their effectiveness."

Q Is this a newly created mineral or is it an old mineral recently discovered?

"This depends upon the individual's concept. The origin of this particular substance dates back about three million years, but this is recent by geological standards."

Q What consciousness does this mineral represent?

"As a gem elixir this mineral is good for studying new physics. Science and its allied studies shall eventually be confronted with the concept that life is a process of consciousness entering matter, or with the concept of consciousness and matter being independent of each other yet creating each other on this plane. This will pose a philosophical question for people in these fields."

Q Speak on minerals as a form of life?

"This depends on the definition of life. In the concepts of biochemical form, there shall be as discovered in seabeds the beginning of mineral substances carrying out the functions of the forms of life. Certain chemical functions or reactions upon the surface of Mars reveal such chemical interactions of extraterrestrial life potentials. Indeed, the chemistry of minerals in their own form does seem to begin to enhance the prospective building blocks of biological life. This is the beginning of the rudimentary integration of spirit's movement through the physical vehicle and through the mineral kingdom."

Q Does this also refer to the fact that life did or does still exist on Mars or that it could?

"Life still exists on Mars, but it is more the content of minerals as indeed bearing life in the sense of spirit. However, they also bear life as the end to a transition into biologically more complex forms."

Q Give a practical example of the earth as a living being?

"This ties in with the fact that the planet is still producing life in its most rudimentary form upon the sea beds. There have already been discoveries by thy scientists of minerals performing lifelike properties on the ocean floor close to high thermal volcanic activity.[10] These are the most primitive forms of life producing the most primitive enzymal properties, but it is indeed the direct transference of the earths magma from its central core to the formation of life forms. This formation is continuing in abundance. Eventually these processes will be linked with the most rudimentary plankton feeding upon these particular life forms. Inanimate mineral structure upon the ocean's floor extends out into the most vital and active portion of the food chain upon which the planet is currently dependent. Thus magma from the center of the earth is still forming rudimentary minerals that ultimately are used to feed men and women, the most complex creations on this planet."

Q There are three places on the planet that have a greater variety of minerals than anywhere else. These areas include Crestmor, California; Franklin, New Jersey; and Langban, Sweden. Why is this, and is there anything special about these areas to examine?

"There are no particular properties to explore here. These are found to be natural formations of physical forces. These are not critical areas of planetary consciousness. These areas were originally close to volcanic activity. There is the peculiar notion that the rich mineral deposits were enhanced partly because these were also rift points during the sinking of Atlantis and Lemuria. These were specific stress points critical to the sinking of Atlantis. These may have also been points of contact during the original rubbing of the teutonic forces."

Q Do the three minerals named after these areas have any special value for future research?

"There is no special value here. But individuals living in these areas may have a tendency to formulate along homogenous lines of a collective consciousness, perhaps reflected in the political and cultural structure of these areas."

Q Do other areas of concentration such as Bisbee, Arizona and Idar-Oberstein, West Germany have any special value in this research?

"These areas are associated with the earth's ley lines. Further information would be too complex to review at this time. Each geographical area would have to be isolated with its specific history examined. There is no interconnectedness between these areas, and there are many such isolated areas."

Q Speak about diseases in minerals?

"Here there is disfunction, or the breaking, up of a mineral's own internal molecular structure, usually due to high exposure to radiation. Diseases stored in minerals activate allergic properties that could open the physical body to diseases, along the lines of homeopathic principles. Some of these minerals could be homeopathically prepared and used in the form of nosodes to treat certain imbalances."

Q Is this because of the imbalanced radiation?

"Yes, either that or the unstable functions in the elements."

Q Give an example of how one would get sick from such a mineral?

"Radiation sickness is the most common example. If someone wore a mineral that was very imbalanced in its molecular structure, they could get radiation sickness."

Q How would one recognize such a mineral?

"Perhaps by the mineral's radiation count or by unusual behavior displayed on the part of its own electromagnetic field. In native traditions there are certain spots that are considered sacred, where individuals display unusual or errative behavior. Minerals in such regions have generally been overexposed to radiation."

Q Certain minerals are naturally radioactive.[11] How can we best use such minerals? Include information here on background radiation, especially from the constellations that influence this planet.

"Background radiation upon the earth is always in a state of flux, especially from the sun's solar flareups. Solar flares account for a large part of background radiation. The earth's gravitational field is also sensitive to these activities. People often wonder how the influence of other planets affects the earth. Some wonder if gravitational influences are relevant. There is a resonancy so that after the earth has bathed in a specific radiation, that planet's gravitational influence remains imprinted in the earth's atmosphere as a trace influence. It is the planet's gravitational angle in position to the earth that constitutes the influence. The constellations are a milder influence, since their radiation constantly bathes the earth. It is more the earth's relative position to the constellations that constitutes the influence, rather than the stellar influences themselves.

"The central force here is the sun. The sun's energy integrates with the earth's forces, which are expansionary in their accord. As there is integration into the space-time continuum occupied by the earth's mass, it is the angular nature of the planets in relation to the position of the earth that leaves an indelible imprint upon the forces of the earth's electromagnetic field and background radiation. This is linked to the earth's electromagnetic field in that there is constant exposure to the earth's time-space continuum from various constellations. As the earth passes through relative points in the space-time continuum, sympathetic resonancies from specific constellations influence and integrate with background radiation.

"All energy is in a state of suspension and expansion through the etheric properties and energies of the ether fields. These energies also constantly penetrate the physical body. As the physical body moves though areas of resonancy, there are points when the resonancies penetrate into the physical form causing vibrations, which then work to the level of the physical. These resonancies integrate to become cumulative subtle influences within the body physical, which then influences the biological personality. These are not intimately linked with the soul's forces, although the soul's forces synchronize with these activities by surrendering portions of its consciousness to the biological personality.

"Crystalline structures and gemstones have, in part, been formulated under similar cumulative influences within the earth's internal workings and resonancies. Such stones are linked to these principles because they shape the etheric forces and resonancies and, with their association to astrological forces, they stabilize the ether fields that duplicate many of the principles of the planets' influence upon the earth plane. However, the stones, having been born of and bearing the imprint of this particular world, represent a stabilizing force in this local space-time continuum. Therefore, while exposure to gemstones carries some of the inherent properties of astrological vibrations and represents a portal for those vibrations, they are more so native to this planet. These stones expose and stabilize individual planetary influences and represent a sympathetic influence, activating only the positive qualities of that particular planet within the resonancies of the body physical.

"Background radiation from various constellations affects individuals' moods. These are the forces that make up astrology. Study the gemstones and metals that are associated with the twelve main zodiac signs to achieve balance here. A combination of twelve gem elixirs, each representing one of the twelve zodiac signs would help to remove the negative influences of background radiation from these constellations. Clear quartz gem elixir can be used to alleviate problems associated with background radiation from the sun and when people expose themselves to sun lamps for a deepening of the skin's pigmentation. These elixirs allow the physical body to develop a natural protection against background radiation. Moreover, gem elixirs that notably stimulate tissue regeneration are also quite effective in easing background radiation.

"Gemstones which are naturally radioactive may be used by some people to treat radiation sickness. They also can help people adjust to increased background radiation. For instance, people who have been exposed to high amounts of radiation from nuclear reactors, plutonium production, or high amounts of uranium would benefit by using certain gem elixirs such as quartz and malachite. Some may want to wear clear quartz or malachite. These elixirs, especially when used in baths, help the metabolism adjust to radiation. Clay baths and internal cleansing, especially of the circulatory system and to remove heavy metals from the body, are also very valuable for protection against radiation. It would be wise to drink three cups a day from a several-gallon container of pure water that contains up to seven drops of clear quartz elixir, if one lives near an area of concentrated radiation. If fasting partly to remove radiation toxicity from the body, one should drink one-fifth of a gallon of quartz-amplified water each day for five days.

"These particular gemstones also promote the evolutionary development of future generations. Natural background radiation contributes to the natural evolutionary force. Mild increases in background radiation have often been critical in the creation of new life forms. Study the patterns of new bacterial life forms identified after the eruption of Mt. St. Helens. This was not based on thermodynamics, but on the released radiation. A mild increase in background radiation stimulates resiliency in the DNA, not mutations. These preparations can also ease male and female sterility. They enhance but do not totally stimulate tissue regeneration. Cell tissues are made more sensitive."

Q Since radioactive gemstones are very valuable, why have you not included any in this current system? Are they too advanced for this time period?

"Today, only a few people would have the capacity to assimilate these energy patterns. Too much toxicity would be generated and properties of the radiation and stellar miasms could be activated.[12] Not only would the regulatory agencies interfere with the use of radioactive minerals in healing systems, but there is still an extremely negative thought form associated with using radiation in healing, despite the fact that orthodox medicine has been using radiation treatments for some years. There is a great fear of radiation in humanity particularly amongst those who experienced difficulties with radiation during past lives in Atlantis. Such people tend to attune to the powerful negative thought form of fear that is associated with all radioactive substances. If humanity had decided that radiation and radioactive substances such as used in nuclear reactors were a positive step, then there would not be such a powerful negative thought form associated with radiation today. Those who understand and strive towards higher states of consciousness will be the first to find it easy to work with radioactive vibrational remedies in future healing systems. Individuals who do not understand or experience higher states of consciousness and who are strongly resistant to the possibility that vibrational or energy medicine can manifest healing also have strong blockages at the transformational level. Such individuals would be especially harmed by radioactive substances, not so much because these substances would affect the radiation and stellar miasms or cause radiation sickness, but because of the individual's resistance to transformational changes which can be stimulated by radioactive substances.

"Just as resistance at any level causes blockages to form at that level, resistance to conscious change would be amplified by the use of radioactive gem elixirs. If the individual was unable to move through this resistance, the added vibrational energy of the elixir would likely help the person to create an etheric blockage to stop the action of the elixir. On an etheric level, to halt the action of a radioactive gem elixir, etheric lead would likely be created. This can, of course, create other difficulties, due to the toxic nature of lead on any level."

Q If people could properly use these gemstones, it would be of major benefit, but it is not too feasible now?

"Correct. Then there could be more conscious direction of the evolutionary process with control over mutations. It is possible to present a healing system not only of radioactive minerals but also of radioactive isotopes prepared as gem elixirs and homeopathic remedies. Many of these substances are radioactive even at the homeopathic level. For instance, homeopathic plutonium would present some danger until homeopathically potentized above 200c. Aside from overcoming the fear and negative thought forms associated with radiation, there is no intrinsic reason why mankind cannot use a system of vibrational preparations prepared from radioactive substances. Given the current progress of the human race regarding radiation, it may be possible that many will be able to use such a healing system in about ten or fifteen years. In the future we may present some material in this area."

Q Is it true that a system using radioactive minerals and isotopes would be especially valuable to treat serious mental illness?

"Certainly. Indeed, there are many ways in which radiation sickness parallels certain kinds of mental illness."

The issue of radiation is a topic of great importance that I am very interested in. Later there will be a text presented just on this problem. The various radioactive isotopes play a key role in many diseases and emotional imbalances. This is a far greater problem than is yet understood by scientists, although there is increased recognition of the issue.[13] Over the years the level of exposure to radiation that has been considered safe has continued to be lessened.[14] Unfortunately, many have died from being exposed to levels of radiation that were supposed to be safe. As many increasingly realize, there are powerful vested interests within the nuclear power industry. In the anthroposophical teachings of Rudolf Steiner there have been some interesting insights into the nuclear problem from both a spiritual and metaphysical perspective.[15] Hilarion in *Seasons of the Spirit* discusses some of the problems the Atlanteans had with nuclear weapons.[16] Some may want to examine these works.

During a discussion about the potential dangers of radiation, I once heard a physician state that background radiation has existed in the environment for many ages and that this suggests that many are unnecessarily concerned about present day levels of radiation. This is a most unfortunate and dangerous misunderstanding. While background radiation has indeed existed for millions of years and is a positive part of the natural evolutionary process, such mild exposure is something the physical body has had ages to adjust to. This is radically different from the sudden and massive amounts of exposure to radiation that have occurred in recent years since World War II.[17] Orthodox medicine has increasingly shown that exposure to even low levels of radiation is directly related to an increase in various diseases such as in many types of cancer.

While the dangers from radiation toxicity are far greater than most understand, they are rather easy to treat. Certain baths, gem elixirs, and flower essences discussed in my previous books can greatly alleviate radiation toxicity. Physically wearing certain stones such as quartz and malachite can also be essential, if the level of constant exposure is high. It is also wise to keep these stones in your home. Traditionally, pitchblende was placed in a leather bag and applied to the head for the effective relief of severe headaches.[18] Pitchblende is the principle ore of uranium and radium. The American Indians and other native folk cultures have traditionally used certain hot springs with high concentrations of radiation as curative centers. One such spot in the U.S. is the radium hot springs in New Mexico. In anthroposophical medicine there is available a dilution of uraninit or uranous oxide.

Q What benefits do people derive by bathing at radium hot springs in New Mexico?

"These baths speed up the process of self-healing. The heat generated by radium as it transforms into lead stimulates healing. This is a heat that involves transformation and letting go of what is not needed."

Q Describe the uses of uraninit or uranous oxide that is available in anthroposophical medicine?

"Some of the claims made concerning this substance are not valid. It is very effective to release and to understand the source of the radiation miasm. However, it does not have a similar relationship to the stellar miasm. Second, it is useful because of its relation to the radioactive isotopes of uranium 235 and 238. Uranium was transformed in Atlantis and then buried by the Atlanteans in the Black Hills of South Dakota in a coordinated effort to help people experience a deeper attunement with the earth so that substances of radioactive origin would no longer harm the body. This was also done partly to help foster a culture that the Atlanteans knew would later develop in that region. We refer to the American Indians and their reverence for the mother earth. Thus, uraninit enables one to experience a deeper attunement with the earth. It also has validity for those unwilling to change and for those who have not fully blossomed from their childhood. The key focus is change or transformation."

Q Is it true that all radioactive minerals enable people to have a deeper attunement with the earth?

"No, some radioactive minerals are of extraterrestrial origin. For instance, certain transuranic elements especially the larger ones often are from extraterrestrial places. The uranium-based minerals usually do stimulate a closer attunement with the earth."

Q Give a full talk on unisolated and undiscovered elements?

"There shall be a presentation of the general principles involving unknown elements and the implications this has on these elements and unknown minerals because minerals, of course, consist of combinations of various elements. There are five key unisolated elements in this age. When there is the activity of the elements of those atomic structures yet to be discovered, they, in part, are difficult to maintain in three dimensions due to their instability as well as the heaviness of their forces in the center of gravity. Thus, they remain close to the molten core or center of the earth. These particular elements were used by the Lemurians to ground the aspects of their content and nature for both balance of consciousness and to draw upon the higher forces. The very outer limits that they occupy upon the physical spectrum in their instability is symbolic of their ability to ground consciousness yet remain within consciousness. That they are just now coming into physical reality is symbolic of their ability to stabilize consciousness. When they are as molded and combined into various mineral structures, they aid in the advancement and promotion of consciousness for entire nations, rather than but as for the single individual. These elements are for the entire planet.

"As these elements slowly come into focus, they shall be significantly linked with the planetary consciousness for the final stabilization and establishment of that which is considered the New Age. These elements shall indeed find their focus and balance in the activities of the totality of the crystallization of thought and be as totally applied by individuals who seek to work only with transformational forms of consciousness. They will initially have as little or no implication in the general healing arts; they are more so for the creation of consciousness within individuals truly desiring initiation into the higher planes. These physical forces coming into full advent shall be of a totality and a balance of system and structure to wherein there shall also begin to be initiated the full arising of Atlantis. Some of these elements are as yet preserved within the hall of records in Egypt. Indeed, some of these elements have been temporarily isolated in thy nations of great science including the U.S., Russia, China, and France. While some of the five as yet unisolated elements have been spotted in these nations, their physical plane existence is so brief that the results are not yet certain![9]

"The combination of these various elements would approach a rudimentary factor of the missing catalysts for the creation of the alchemical philosopher's stone and all the implications therein. These elements are at times detectable within the magma flows of Hawaii, Mt. Shasta, Mt. Etna, and Krakatoa in Java."

Q Why? Because the lava is coming from close to the center of the earth?

"That is part of the reason. It is more accurate to refer to magma structure rather than lava flows because the flow of lava implies activity more upon the earth's surface. The magma comes from closer to the earth's center where this activity actually takes place. That is where these elements and minerals are formulated."

Q So would it be possible to measure these unisolated elements with extremely sophisticated equipment during an eruption by one of these volcanos such as in Hawaii or Washington?

"It is possible, but it would be very difficult because these elements disintegrate extremely fast.

"When these elements are merged they will have application in the medicinal and nutritional needs of the body physical to fully allow for the etherealization of the body physical. These merged elements will allow the body physical to exist in full consciousness, and they will become part of the normal dietary makeup of the individual, perhaps during the coming thousand years of brotherhood. When these substances are merged they become stable and not toxic to the body physical. This is not unlike the fact that salt is a merger of two toxic substances, yet they become inert when combined. The merger of these substances will likely yield many interesting and intriguing results.

"The merging of these elements will only be possible once there is a deep understanding of their properties on all levels. This understanding will only be available to those who have both the proper understanding of the laws of nature, as they can perceive them, and the awakening of consciousness. Such people are likely to understand the laws under which these elements operate. When there exists this understanding and actual merging of these elements, they will then affect the physical body to improve health as well as to expand consciousness. There will be some exceptions and accidents, but generally, at least two of these elements will need to be merged for the physical body to be affected, while their greatest effect on health and consciousness will take place when all five elements are merged."

Q Is the effect of these elements on consciousness and on the physical body directly related to when they become more directly stabilized on the physical plane?

"Yes, once people realize the importance of these new elements and the new minerals containing them many will become interested in their use."

Q Speak on the future discovery of as yet unisolated elements and gemstones?

"It is only now that man is beginning to develop the technologies and also the consciousness to begin to fully appreciate the ethereal and even measureable electromagnetic properties, such as piezoelectricity, that gemstones possess. It is only now that sufficiently sensitive instruments and systems of study beyond the capacity of simple faith have been developed. Documentation of clinical cases enables open-minded individuals to appreciate increasingly the subtle qualities of gemstones in both healing and in the promotion of consciousness, as well as in other technologies yet to be as developed.

"As has previously been stated, there has only recently been the discovery of certain gemstones and mineral substances. Even thy own system of mathematical calculus upon the atomic scale, elicits to as yet undiscovered elements. These are to bring forth knowledge not only to promote the scientific consciousness of man, but indeed his spiritual or psychospiritual consciousness, which eventually will as become integrated into his capacity to live in society in his own right."

Q Discuss the principles involved in new minerals appearing on the planet and old ones disappearing?

"In the context of this review, there will be a general examination of those things which are known in physics, as well as some esoteric applications. Quartz is the deterioration of all mineral substances as though entering from a complex form into a simpler form, or that which is known as radioactive decay. There are temporary conditions which exist in time and space which may be comparable to quartz, as well as those things which only exist temporarily in the space-time continuum. There are also forces associated with the planet so that when there is a shift in its axis and a realignment of the resonancies of the various molecular structures according to the angles and harmonics of the planet, in balance with the sun's own molecular magnetic fields, this may cause the rapid deterioration of certain minerals. This is not from greater exposure to rays and heat, but is more from greater exposure of a varying angular nature of imbedded crystalline structures within the crust of the earth to a different gravitational and electromagnetic pull. Thus, the angular changes destabilize the mineral makeup on the molecular levels that had stabilized and crystallized along those molecular planes. These unstable elements then would gradually deteriorate over a geologically brief period of time of 1,000 to 3,000 years, perhaps lying undiscovered. Some of these unstable elements may still be discovered, but only in certain locations.

"These unstable elements then are not so much radioactive in their decay, but are unstable in other ways. They act more as a corrosive substance, rather than merely as an element of the slow process of oxidation. There is an unwinding at the very core of the molecular structure. But the unhinging of these unstable elements causes a gradual deterioration of the original lines of force in the earth's electromagnetic field along which they had stability. These create temporary pockets of anti-gravity, which could be as measured by high concentrations of mild electromagnetic fields. Some points upon the planet have already been discovered manifesting these forces."

Q Will this process cause new minerals to appear and others to disappear?
"Correct."

Q Can you explain in a clearer fashion why quartz is a deterioration of all mineral substances from complex to simpler forms and that this is associated with radioactive decay?
"This statement shall remain intact for those who are students of physics.

"The appearance of these substances would merely at times be the restabilizing of formerly deteriorated beds of many of these crystalline and mineral-like structures. The shift of the earth's axis will bring about a point of return of exposure to the gravitational fields and lines of force along which they had originally crystallized. So it is not so much as though there is the appearance of mass, it is more a resetting in line with the crystalline structures and a realignment with those original forces. This will enable new minerals to appear gradually and old minerals to be rediscovered. This will come about after the year 2000, but closer to the year 2025. However, the process has already begun."

Q Previously, you said that sports or naturally occurring new species of plant forms in nature express new states of consciousness on the planet. Does this general principle also usually apply to new minerals?
"Yes."

Q Do each of these five unisolated elements have a special relationship with the five key chakras above the head—the first element relating to the eighth chakra and the fifth element relating to the fifth chakra above the head?

"Correct. It is quite possible that one of the first effects of working with substances containing these five unisolated elements will be to alert humanity to the consciousness contained within these higher chakras. The awakening of the five upper chakras will also help stabilize the five unisolated elements on this plane."

Q How will substances containing these unisolated elements affect people in the coming years?

"There will be an expansion of consciousness. For instance, certain individuals who have a life-long set of motivating factors that do not work may be quite affected. There are certain people who always have felt that they could move an object or switch out a light or radio by using their mind even though they are sitting ten feet away. While they have never succeeded at this, they always instinctively understood that it should work. Such individuals when working with these substances will find that missing link so that they will be able to do these things."

Q There is a very deep cave about ten miles below Tucson, Arizona that has never been fully explored in its lowest regions. Does this cave reach inner regions of the earth where there are as yet undiscovered minerals?

"That cave does not reach the very center of the earth, but it does penetrate to levels where new minerals may be discovered."

Q Does it reach regions where people live in the center of the earth?

"That information will not now be provided."

Q Do most of the as yet undiscovered minerals contain some or all of these five unisolated elements?

"This is correct. They all contain some base factor of these elements."

Q A supplement to the 1980 *Glossary of Mineral Species* [20] listed thirty-eight new minerals that have been discovered in the 1980-1981 period. Do some of these new minerals contain some or all of these five unisolated elements?

"Some of them formerly contained the pattern of these elements, but they have since removed themselves from interlocking in the molecular structure. Sophisticated scientific apparatus could possibly detect the former presence of these elements in the mineral makeup."

Q Why did this removal occur?

"This is part of their natural properties. These elements, as they appear and disappear, are part of the key factor that was elsewhere spoken of when there is the bringing forth of new and more complicated systems of minerals involving these thirty-eight new minerals."

Q Do any more common minerals have traces of these five unisolated elements?

"No, traces of these elements are only found in the minerals now being discovered, or recently discovered, by thy scientists. A number of these new minerals were commonly used in Lemuria."

Q Why do some minerals contain these five unisolated minerals and others do not?

"This cannot be given at this time. In the future, the atomic scale and exact chemical structure may be provided for these five unisolated elements."

Q When was the first year that the vibration of these five unisolated elements began to appear in recently discovered minerals?

"This began around 1977. In that year, many of the seeds were sown for radical social change and new ways in which individuals will appreciate human consciousness."

Q When is the first year that these five unisolated elements will actually appear on the physical plane in newly discovered minerals?

"This will probably start in 1988, although some of the new minerals discovered since 1977 contain enough of an echo of these elements to be used by those who have the eyes to see. However, many will not recognize these new minerals for what they are, and it may take five or ten years for many people to recognize what has been presented."

Q Where will these new minerals be discovered in the coming years?

"They will be found in Australia, China, Egypt, Russia, the southwest U.S., and in some of the Peruvian mountains. These are interesting power centers, and sometimes the places where the stones surface will not always be geographically related to the place in which they may be found buried. Indeed, some will manifest in new and unusual ways to individuals in these places. Thus, the person residing in such a power center is far more important than the actual gem being created there by natural means."

Here Hilarion is also referring to the fact that these new minerals may even materialize before some people living in these regions. In fact, I have already learned of this happening to a channel in Southern California. A friend recently saw this ususual stone.

Q Beyond 1977 and 1988, is there a third key time period when these five unisolated elements will become far more common on the planet, especially in newly discovered minerals?

"Yes, by the end of the 1990's or so, it is highly likely that these substances will be required by mankind, especially by those who are beginning to understand consciousness. At such a time, if it is necessary, more of them will be allowed into the earth plane.

"These elements may actually begin to make their final isolated appearances between the years 2025 and 2075. They will begin to make their appearance after there has been a shift of the earth's axis triggering yet untapped magma flows. The shift in the earth's axis will be synonymous with the change of consciousness on the planet. There is already documentation by thy scientists as to the properties and nature of at least two or three of these unisolated elements on the atomic scale, although these elements have not yet been discovered.

"It would be wise to examine the studies now going on regarding geological formulations near Mt. St. Helens. Some scientists have already discovered new life forms of bacteria connected to the intense release of radiation and thermal activity in this area. A number of these minerals are found towards the center of the earth, while others are found on the earth's surface. Some of them are contained within identified minerals, but they have not yet been isolated."

Q Will the increased presence of these unisolated elements occur partly because there will then be so many active volcanoes?

"Yes, but it is also because there will then be so many repositories of consciousness. You might call such people human volcanoes. These people will require some of these substances as they begin to understand themselves. These substances will, of course, be one more way to higher consciousness. There are many ways to enlightenment. However, these substances as they are understood will be adjuncts of great utility towards the end of the century, or soon after. The exact years when these things will unfold still depends on developing planetary conditions."

Q Will new minerals be found around the end of this century that will have a much higher concentration of these five unisolated elements?

"There is a high possibility of this."

Q Will some of these new minerals be especially valuable because they will contain all five unisolated elements, while other minerals will have only a few of these elements?

"Correct."

Q Would it be wise for me to start now making gem elixirs of these newly discovered minerals and the ones found from 1988 on?

"We would like to make an analogy here. Many of the discoveries that Madame Curie made were quite useful for humanity. But because she did not always understand what she was working with, she and others around her were exposed to more radiation than they were able to transmute on their own. Thus, to work with these substances too soon would be playing with fire. There can be great benefit, but we suggest waiting at least several years before working with these new minerals.

"Some researchers who felt ready could begin working with these minerals now, but they should not be released to the general public before 1989 or 1990. People working with these minerals now would not necessarily suffer serious health problems. What would probably happen is that there would be a deep effect on one's consciousness, and the impact of this might not be felt or understood for many years. This is similar to what happened to Madame Curie in that the difficulty with radiation did not, in many respects, become obvious for many years. It is important to meditate with these new minerals to understand and respect their properties so that they can be properly used in a balanced fashion."

Q Is it safer to work initially with some new minerals found since 1977 to become used to the vibration of these five unisolated elements?

"Correct, but remember not all the minerals discovered since 1977 have the vibration of these unisolated elements."

Q Does the recently discovered Russian minerial charoite contain the vibration of some of these five unisolated elements?

"Yes, and this gem is safe for the vast majority of people to use. The potential danger occurs when gemstones are used that have the actual physical presence of these five unisolated elements, as will occur in the next few years. Already, the echoes of these unisolated elements are being felt throughout the entire mineral kingdom."

Q Is it true that after 1989 or 1990 these new elements will become sufficiently stabilized on the physical plane so that people will be able to work with them with no danger?

"As the consciousness on this planet expands, this will gradually occur. This time period does seem likely from this vantage point, but it also depends on the course of humanity in the immediate years ahead."

Q There was a suggestion that these five unisolated elements will become part of our diet. Is it that magma flows containing these elements will become much more common and ways will be found to naturally synthesize these elements?

"Yes, both these factors will develop. A process of biological synthesis will be discovered. And it is possible that certain ways of crystal growing will be applied with some of the new minerals. Another key factor is that it is not necessary to obtain large quantities of these elements. Individuals need only to experience the vibrations of these elements. Moreover, in the coming years in many regions of the world, plants will be grown that contain concentrations of these unisolated elements. The countries that we have already listed as being likely locations for minerals containing the unisolated elements are also slightly more likely to produce plants containing these unisolated elements, but these plants will be found throughout the world. To some extent researchers will accidentally develop and discover these new plant forms."

Q What types of plants are most likely to contain the five unisolated elements?

"These plants will be discovered and created in many different ways. To some extent, there will be a merging of new strains of algae. Other plants that have not been used before will be taken from deep within the oceans. These plants will be associated with very cold streams that move through the oceans. Other plants will only grow under very unusual conditions relating to high air pressure. There are many possibilities here. But a general underlying theme is that these plants will each be seen by those involved in bringing new foods to mankind as a new food with unusual capacities. They will often have an extra high amount of protein or of various minerals and vitamins. These foods will be considered to be valuable new sources of vitamins, minerals, and proteins.

"Ultimately, these elements will be recognized on a microscopic level all over the world. They will become so common partly because environmental pollutants will carry them all over the planet. This is partly associated with the complex procedure involved in creating pollutants in the upper atmosphere that lead to acid rains. Some people who study such environmental pollutants will ultimately discover the presence of these minute elements as part of various pollutants."

Q Speak on the feasibility of using these new minerals as homeopathic remedies?

166

"It is unlikely that most people in the homeopathic profession will understand or use these new minerals for some time. The homeopathic potentization of these substances can be quite potent, so care should be exercised in that research or there could be more harm than good."

Q Is it true that certain of these new minerals such as maghendorfite will create new life forms and will help in the organic growing of substances that have these five elements in them?
"To a large extent this is correct, partly because the substances themselves impart a certain consciousness to their immediate environment."

Q Has it been common for certain minerals to disappear from the earth in past ages?
"Yes, some minerals have been withdrawn due to the activity of the space brothers in the U.F.O's."

The Boji stone, a mineral that I discussed in *Gem Elixirs and Vibrational Healing, Vol. 1* exemplifies the pattern of a mineral now disappearing from this planet, at least in central Kansas. A woman in Denver who visits central Kansas to obtain this stone in certain fields has mentioned that a number of them now lie disintegrated into powder. John mentioned that the change in planetary forces has caused this.

Q Has diamond so reached a state of perfection that it will ultimately disappear?
"This is linked with the theories of Andrew Jackson Davis and of the planet as a living being."

Presently approximately 2,900 different minerals have been identified on this planet.[21] Upon first learning this I was amazed. It is fairly common for about ten or twenty new minerals to be discovered each year. In fact, the International Mineralogical Association has a Commission on New Minerals and Mineral Names. More new minerals are now being discovered partly because more sophisticated equipment is now available. One can often identify these new minerals because they have long unpronounceable names, often Russian or East European in origin. James Dana completed the first systematic catalogue of minerals over 100 years ago. Today, there are several good reference texts listing many minerals.[22]

Ann Ree Colton said that new minerals will be discovered by the north and south magnetic poles, and that they will be far more energizing than any minerals now used on earth.[23] In the *Spiral of Life*, Mona Rolfe stated that every planet has an intimate connection with a metal. Whenever a new planet is discovered, a new metal will also be found.[24]

Cathie, in *The Pulse of the Universe*, has numerous interesting observations about the undiscovered elements on the atomic scale. He understands that they have an extremely short life span due to radioactive decay and that some of these new elements will probably be found towards the center of the earth. He also understands that the number of elements in the atomic scale is 144.[25] John stated the same things, although he noted that, except for the five unisolated elements, the other elements will not be found in this universe, at least for many years. They are of too high a frequency for this region. Georg Blattmann, in *Radiant Matter: Decay and Consecration*, also offers some interesting insights into the elements and the periodic table.[26]

In discussing the new elements and the spectacular effect they will have on consciousness in the immediate years ahead, I will also take this opportunity to discuss briefly the potential work of the Teacher of Righteousness, (henceforth referred to as

T.R.). In previous talks, John has mentioned that he is again living on the earth and that he may play a major role in transforming the consciousness of this planet by helping to expand the Christ consciousness on this plane. John also said that T.R. is the first of the 144,000 spoken of in the Book of Revelations.

Some may be aware that certain Bible scholars feel that T.R. lived before Christ and that he appears to have been an important religious leader. There is a fascinating discussion of T. R., or the true teacher, in *The Essene Odyssey* by Hugh Schonfield.[27] There is also some discussion of T.R. in the dead sea scrolls.[28] I even found one book on the dead sea scrolls in the Boulder public library in which it states that there is a historical belief that T.R. will return to earth shortly before Armageddon to help save the world from destruction. John mentioned that T.R. lived about 100 years before Christ and that he came to the earth to help prepare the way for Jesus to incarnate and to develop the innermost sect of the Essenes, one of the Jewish religious orders of that time.

John also has mentioned that other scrolls will be found discussing in great detail the work of T.R. and the deep understanding that the ancient Israelis had of what we today call holistic health. The ancient Israelis, as a direct carryover of the ancient teachings of Atlantis and even of Lemuria, had an understanding of health and illness far beyond what we today perceive. When those teachings are released, they will provide an important impetus in the continuing shift from the current orthodox medical approach back to a more natural and spiritual perception of health care. In 1981, I spoke of T.R. to someone who the previous night had dined with a person who worked in one of the Bible centers that specialized in translating ancient manuscripts. That center was just quietly bringing over newly discovered manuscripts found in the Middle East. Hilarion said this center will soon translate ancient documents which will specifically reveal the location of other buried documents. These other documents will contain detailed information on T.R. and the heritage of the Essenes in treating people with natural medicine.

John has noted that, in the last few thousand years, there has been a polarity in the West of a few key people manifesting the Christ consciousness and the anti-Christ consciousness for the world. While a certain number of people have experienced such a consciousness, only a handful have reached that state to a degree that it affects the entire planet. I refer to Melchizedek, Jesus, and St. Germain, along with Julius Caesar, Napoleon, and Hitler. In the immediate years ahead, it is likely that there will again be such a polarity on the planet, with T.R. probably coming forward as will the person who is to manifest the anti-Christ consciousness. Both will come from the Middle East. The anti-Christ has been clearly identified by John on several occasions. I will just say that he will come out of Persia and that when the Shah's family is again in place, he will be in position. T.R. was born in Lebanon in the 1962-1963 period. In fact the anti-Christ was also born in that same period. Some misguided people will confuse the identity of these two people. This is part of the test. Another spiritual leader born in this period will probably come forward after the year 2025.

Part of the plan from above was that Krishnamurti was to take on the mantle of Christ consciousness for the entire planet back in the 1920's. Some may remember that the theosophists identified him as a world religious leader and set up a religious order with Krishnamurti as the leader. Numerous personality conflicts developed, and in 1929 Krishnamurti disbanded that organization and renounced such a leadership role. A few months later, as a direct result of Krishnamurti's action, the world depression began and the power of radical politicans such as Hitler increased. If the Christ consciousness had been properly stabilized on this plane, these things would probably not have taken place. This is why certain metaphysical teachers have said that the conflicts leading up to World War II were originally expected to have been worked out on the higher planes.

I realize that this discussion does not put Krishnamurti in the kindest light. I had the pleasure of seeing Krishnamurti several times and have always had much respect for his work. I am not trying to attack or place any value judgment on him but feel the need to state these facts because we speak of a powerful truth that has deeply affected the lives of countless millions of people. When Krishnamurti rejected the role of Christ consciousness for this planet, the divine plan for the earth was radically disrupted. The result was a sharp drop in consciousness, as expressed by the world depression and wars that have since occurred. As a direct result of this situation, millions of people volunteered in a spirit of service to reincarnate back to this plane anywhere from a few years to many thousands of years sooner than their souls had planned. As numerous metaphysical teachers have stated, the soul almost always plans an incarnation years in advance, usually having a strong past life connection with one or both parents. Because of the radical disruption of the divine plan for this planet, such careful planning rarely took place with these souls. This is the key reason why various New Age teachers sometimes mention that we live in an age when an unusually high number of people are living who feel very uncomfortable being in a physical body. This is also the reason why many people with New Age consciousness feel so alienated from their families. There was not the proper grounding of soul roots, and individuals in these families have radically different outlooks on life from a conscious perspective. Again, there was not time for the soul to establish a close family alignment. It should be understood that the parents also made a sacrifice in agreeing to be the vehicle for a soul to incarnate when they had no close past ties with that individual.

There is a trilogy here. If Krishnamurti had provided the spark of Christ consciousness, then, as John noted in a public lecture, the teachings of Steiner would have by now replaced or been in direct competition with most of the current materialistic perceptions in the sciences and arts. Indeed, John said this planet would today have been several hundred years advanced in consciousness. Steiner, with his thousands of speeches and hundreds of books, would have provided the mental part of the transition, while Krishnamurti would have provided the spirit. In this eternal trilogy, the body aspect was to have come onto this plane in the 1930's through a particular healing system that would have a profound effect on uplifting and healing the body so that there could be a shift into the higher planes. In many respects this healing system represents the culmination of Steiner's medical teachings. Steiner was well aware of this medical technology but only hinted at it while he lived.

I have been working on this advanced healing system since 1980 and hope to release it some time in the 1990's as planetary conditions allow. My early books are now being done so that there will be a body of work and collective consciousness that is ready and open to these new teachings. With this healing technology, there will be the capacity to generate complete tissue regeneration within the body to the degree, for instance, of restoring sight with the blind and complete mobility for those with severed spines. While such results will not initially occur that often, gradually, as the consciousness shifts on this planet, many remarkable healings will take place with this ancient technology. John said that approximately one percent of the general populace taking these elixirs would achieve enough assistance in their spiritual work to possibly experience total knowledge of the self, or God realization, as that term is generally defined and understood in the Eastern religions. These would be individuals who have been dedicated to spiritual growth for many life times.

When I first learned of T.R. and the connection with Krishnamurti, I understood that Krishnamurti would pass away in the 1985-1986 period. This just happened in early 1986. This is connected with the passing of the mantle of Christ consciousness from Krishnamurti to T.R. as he prepares for his work. In addition, the work of Steiner remains in place, although far fewer people have been influenced by that body of work than had been previously expected. Once again the eternal mind, body, and spirit trilogy is in place to perhaps play a key role in manifesting the New Age consciousness.

The information on T.R. is not only channeled guidance. In 1980 I was inspired to visit the Middle East. Before that trip, I was introduced to T.R. by Ram Das in a visionary dream. Hilda Charleton, a respected spiritual leader in New York City, was also in the room when I met T.R. A few weeks later, during a visit to one of the holy places in the Middle East, I spotted someone who immediately stood out as a very evolved soul. I went to a quiet corner in that center to meditate and soon realized that I had just seen T.R. I went back to meet him but he was gone. John later said this was similar to Mary Magdalene again searching for the body of Jesus after he had risen.

When I saw T.R. I also noted that he had an average build, but in the visionary dream he was quite fat. John said this is symbolic of the fact that T.R. is now taking on the karma of this planet. John has also mentioned that some of the guides of T.R. include the four archangels of the Order of Melchizedek. We refer to Raphael, Gabriel, Michael, and Uriel. Elsewhere, John said that if someone has the direct guidance of at least two archangels, it creates a polarity that manifests world change. In the last few years, I have mentioned the potential work of T.R. to a certain number of people. In several instances, individuals have directly attuned to T.R. on the higher planes. Anyone who is ready has the capacity to attune to his love. He is already offering direct guidance to many people.

While it is difficult to be exact as to when T.R. may begin appearing before the public, there is the possibility that the public phase of his work will begin in the 1990's, especially in 1993 or soon after. In discussing these things, I must also add that there is no guarantee that T.R. will come forward with his teachings. Little in life can be stated with a 100 percent guarantee. Indeed, John said that even on the higher planes it is not yet known how T.R. and his teaching will be received, but that if he is rejected the coming cleansing of this planet will be much more severe than need be. We are born with free will. In fact, one reason why I am allowed to discuss this is so that those who are ready will attune to T.R. now and in the immediate years ahead to assist in the manifestation of his work.

With the potential work of T.R. and the effect that the five unisolated elements will soon have on the mineral kingdom and on people's consciousness, it is possible that there will be many changes in the coming years. Indeed, the mineral kingdom will play an increasingly important role in the shift into the New Age.

It is also wise to use minerals to enhance and live in greater attunement with the environment. This is an especially relevant issue in an age when so many people live in congested cities. Even in cities, minerals can be used to improve living conditions.

Q Speak on using minerals to bring greater harmony and balance to live in the environment?

"One of the key elements to the developing consciousness in these days is that individuals must develop greater sensitivity and integration with the environment, whether it be in metropolitan or rural areas. People should merge with the natural elements, rather than seek to enslave them.[29] This can be accomplished by using the properties inherent in gemstones. For instance, if quartz crystals were used with radionics in agriculture, there would be a closer merging with the natural principles of nature to repel and balance invading insects that from time to time threaten man's crops.

"Gemstones can also be used to balance the chakras to bring the physical body into alignment. Often this is where healing stops because seeking to only heal through the chakras is in itself an imbalance, in the sense that the chakras also have their own function, independent of the body physical. Indeed, it is through the chakras and the various meridian flows that man extends himself into the environment and creates the very depths of his reality, particularly his ability to harmonize with the environment. Since man is a being of energy even to the physical level, he subjugates the environment by his very exposure to it. The soul's forces, as emitted through the various chakric and meridian points, are the consciousness of nature itself and are the focus of conscious activity that brings about balance. Using gemstones to align the chakras automatically brings an individual to a point of focus, unlocking the accumulated information within the physical form. Gemstones can also be used to activate the cellular memory. In the future, this will be a key point for unlocking languages stored within the cellular memory of individuals.

"In the days of Atlantis, the primary focus was to balance the chakras with physical healing being a byproduct of that. Today, you work more from the material plane to balance the chakras so as to bring forth physical healing because that is what ye observe and identify with. But the true purpose should be to balance the chakras because they are critical to the element of the entire anatomy of the self, even as they use the physical instrument to find their focus, to have activity on this plane. Thus, the body physical was thought of but as the ability to have a focus on this plane, and the chakras were aligned for activities on this plane. Through aligning each chakra, man's consciousness extends into the environment. When there is imbalance within the chakras, there is imbalance in man's behavior and his very ability to integrate with the environment.

"When the chakras are aligned, certain accords develop. For instance, there is an increase in the appetite for food in a natural state as well as greater sensitivity and allergic reactions to the chemical environment that man has created for himself to inhabit. These imbalances initially cause increased sensitivity in the auric fields that may first register as imbalance, paranoia, or radical hypertensive behavior. However, as individuals become more knowledgable, they realize that these are behavioral patterns or healing crises stimulated in both the physiological and ethereal accords that guide individuals back into the natural accords of environmental balance. For instance, even as the individual gets nauseous in reaction to certain foods which weaken or are toxic to the physical form, so in turn does the pattern of improper magnetics in the ethereal pattern cause misalignment in the chakras. These may become confused clairvoyant experiences leading the individual to imbalances within the physical form as a whole.

"When there is the cutting off from the natural accords of man as a being of energy through the dynamics of the human aura and other personal accords, man comes into a critical state of imbalance within the environment as a whole. Because of this, in certain nature cultures there were specific rituals of dance and the use of quartz, jade, turquoise, and other forms of stabilized mineral substances to create the necessary ornaments for amplifying the natural properties within the collective culture. This then, of course, extended into various behavioral patterns within the culture, which was then reflected in nature's activity. This stimulated balance within the environment. The true environment which man inhabits on the planet is not the artificial environment that he creates, unless that environment also enhances the properties that are built upon the natural accord."

Q Speak further on how gemstones were used in Lemuria and Atlantis to bring balance with the environment?

"Then quartz, amethyst, diamond, jade, and other alchemical stones were used. Balance was maintained in the chakras to increase the capacities of thought form amplification. Gemstones and crystals were used to generate natural sources of electrical flows. These flows were broadcast along certain natural magnetic lines so as not to upset the natural environment. This was independent of the ley lines and was more in accord with the magnetic flows of the earth."

Q Speak on the principles involved in using gemstones in architectural structures to keep in tune with the environment?

"There are certain gemstones that, when coordinated with specific shapes and forms, amplify those properties. For instance, as already given, quartz when shaped in a pyramidal form creates certain capacities for enhancing the natural form. There are many shapes that relate to specific gemstones that enhance their properties. This is part of the tradition of talismans. This is not magic but is a means to enhance the natural properties inherent with the natural order of things.

"When gemstones are arranged into certain patterns, especially in the home environment, they can stimulate cellular memories stored within individual tissues. Meditation was usually the key to activating these properties. Therefore, it was more that gemstones were used and integrated with the architectural structures of geometric forms so that individuals could obtain advancements in consciousness and health benefits. Entire floors consisted of emerald, diamond, or preferably quartz. This was not so relevant to the economic status within the community, but was more a force contributing to the health and benefit of the individual."

Q Why were emeralds and diamonds so common then, when they are not today?

"This is because of earth changes. They are very common on the sea beds, especially in the Pacific Ocean, which was once Lemuria."

In recent years there have been little publicized reports that huge new deposits of diamonds have been discovered in Australia. The price of diamonds has not changed because the businesses that control the diamond industry have bought these fields to control the supply. Australia was, of course, connected to Lemuria.

Q What would be the best minerals to use today to create these mandala patterns?

"This varies widely according to various economic patterns and individual needs. This should be pursued within each individual form. A general suggestion by the channel speaking, in their order of priority, includes quartz, granite which contains quartzlike properties, turquoise, malachite, and lapis lazuli. These are universally applicable, although some individuals will be more drawn to other stones."

Q Give further information on how gemstones were used in these homes?

"Most of these homes were dome-like structures. Some were complete spheres. Gemstones were not only placed on the floor in mandalic patterns, they were also placed in a circular pattern going upwards to the top of a sphere or dome. Sometimes entire walls were mandalas. Pyramidal forms were usually preserved as chambers for meditation. Only a few were able to handle and live directly under such a radical energy. Houses were built with these different shapes so that different energies could be assimilated at various times.

"In addition, dome-like structures were used to create a natural environment in which all the stones could reach their full capacity. But mostly, these were used for creating an environment of luminosity that allowed the individual dwelling in that environment to obtain a naturally heightened state of health both physically and in the subtle anatomies. We have previously stated that the cubical form that ye today often use in thy homes causes a degeneration in the body physical. To expand beyond this is not wise because the patterns and structures desired would vary with each individual. People should seek inspiration perhaps from the Lemurian context."

Q Speak on the effect of living under a pyramid versus living under a structure with six sides and a sloping roof?

"Pyramidal structures generate and focus all energy present, whether it is positive or negative. If any negative energy is present, that is gradually overcome. The six-sided structure with a sloping roof creates a more neutral, rather than an enhancing, environment. Rectangular structures common in most western structures are degenerative.

"A wise pattern to persue would be to study the mummified remains in the Mayan, Egyptian, Syrian, Chinese, and Japanese cultures. The gemstones found in those sarcophagi correspond exactly with various disease states that would be detectable through pathological examination of the mummified forms. These were usually gemstones that those individuals favored throughout their lives. If the particular palace or housing structure of the mummified form or individual were examined, it could be discovered that there were specific mandalas placed upon those forms. For instance, there has already been the discovery of certain Mayan mummified forms and the location of their household structures or palaces. A pathological study of the physical condition of these mummies would show that upon the floor of their palaces there had been certain gemstones worked into mandalic patterns. These gemstones corresponded with the anatomical needs that the individuals displayed throughout their life form. These concepts were used in Mayan, Egyptian, Toltec, and Minoan kingdoms. These principles were also carried out, to a lesser degree, in Greece and Babylon.

"The rebuilding of some of the social forces and structures as found in Lemuria are found today in the use of gemstones and meditations in Findhorn. These principles are still integrated into the society of India. Designs to build a new city at Pondichery express many of these accords. It is also wise to study the works of Steiner and Andrew Jackson Davis."[30]

Today, many people increasingly understand the need to live in tune with the environment and that buildings should be built to express a balance with nature.[31] In ancient China, it was the custom to have someone dowse the land to see if it was appropriate to build a structure on that site.[32] In recent years, I have heard of various individuals doing this. If one lives directly over certain mineral deposits or where some underground streams cross, it can be quite deleterious to one's health.

When I first moved to Colorado, I placed a number of minerals about my home, especially several birthstones. I also planted certain minerals in some key areas about Colorado. This helps to stabilize my energy with my new home. Others would benefit by doing this.

1 John G. Neihardt, *Black Elk Speaks* (N.Y: Pocket Books, 1975).
2 Jose Arguelles, *Earth Ascending* (Boston: Shambhala Publications, 1984).
Rodney Collin, *The Theory of Celestial Influence* (Boston: Shambhala Publications, 1984).
3 Rudolf Steiner, "The Cycle of the Year As A Breathing Process of the Earth," (March 31,April 1,2,7,8, 1923, Dornach).
_____, "The Earth As A Being With Life, Soul, and Spirit," (March 30-April 1, 1918, Berlin).

173

_____, "The Requirement of Our Time Is to Give An Earth-Soul to the Earth Body," (April 30, 1918, Ulm-Donau).
Guenther Wachsmuth, *The Etheric Formative Forces In Cosmos, Earth, and Man* (Spring Valley, N.Y: Anthroposophical Press, 1932).
4 Max Heindel, *The Rosicrucian Christianity Lectures* (Oceanside,Ca: The Rosicrucian Fellowship, 1972), p. 260.
5 Joseph Whitfield, *The Treasure of El Dorado* (Washington,D.C: Occidental Press, 1977), p. 57.
6 Peter Tompkins and Chris Bird, *The Secret Life of Plants* (N.Y: Harper and Row, 1984).
7 Joseph Whitfield, *The Eternal Quest* (Roanoke,Va: Treasure Publications, 1983), p. 86, 109-110.
8 Andrew Jackson Davis, *Great Harmonia, The Teacher, Vol. II* (Mokelumne Hill,Ca: Health Research, 1973).
9 *The American Mineralogist,* LXV (July-August,1980), 810-811.
10 John M. Edmond and Karen Von Damm, "Hot Springs On the Ocean Floor," *Scientific American,* CCXLVIII (April, 1983), 78-93.
Richard Lutz, "Deep-Sea Hydrotheramal Vents: Oasis On the Ocean," *Yearbook of Science and the Future* 1985, 226-242.
11 Sterling Gleason, *Ultraviolet Guide to Minerals* (San Gabriel,Ca: Ultra-Violet Products,Inc., 1972).
12 Gurudas, *Flower Essences and Vibrational Healing* (Albuquerque,N.M: Brotherhood of Life, 1983).
13 Linda Clark, *Are You Radioactive?* (N.Y: Pyramid Books, 1974).
Martin D. Ecker,M.D. and Norton J. Bramesco, *Radiation* (N.Y: Random House, 1981).
14 House Subcommitte on Energy and Environment, *Radiation Standards and Public Health,* Hearings, 94th Cong., (Washington,D.C: Government Printing Office, 1978).
15 Michael Jones, *Nuclear Energy: A Spiritual Perspective* (Edinburgh: Floris Books, 1983).
George Unger, *On Nuclear Energy* (Spring Valley,N.Y: Anthroposophical Press, 1982).
16 Hilarion, *Seasons of the Spirit* (Toronto: Marcus Books, 1982), p. 6-9.
17_____,*Answers* (Toronto: Marcus Books, 1983), p. 3-5.
18 George F. Kunz, *The Magic of Jewels and Charms* (Philadelphia: J.B. Lippincott Co., 1915), p. 128-129.
19 B.L. Cathie, *The Pulse of the Universe: Harmonic 288* (Sydney: A.H. & A. W. Reed, 1977), p. 65, 198.
20 Michael Fleischer, *Glossary of Mineral Species* (Tucson: The Mineralogical Record, 1983).
21 Ibid.
Brian Skinner and Catherine Skinner, "Is There A Limit to the Number of Minerals," *The Mineraolgical Record,* XI (September- October,1980), 333-335.
22 Michael O'Donoghue, *The Encyclopedia of Minerals and Gemstones* (N.Y: G.P. Putnam's Sons, 1983).
Willard Roberts, George Rapp, Jr., and Julius Weber, *Encyclopedia of Minerals* (N.Y: Van Nostrand Reinhold Co., 1974).
23 Ann Ree Colton, *Watch Your Dreams* (Glendale,Ca: ARC Publishing Co., 1983), p. 130.
24 Mona Rolfe, *The Spiral of Life* (Sudbury, Suffolk, England: Neville Spearman,Ltd., 1981), p. 87-88.
25 B.L. Cathie, *The Pulse of the Universe: Harmonic 288* (Sydney:˙A.H. & A. W. Reed, 1977), p. 53-65, 198.
26 Georg Blattman, *Radiant Matter: Decay and Consecration* (Edinburgh: Floris Books, 1983).
27 Hugh Schonfield, *The Essene Odyssey* (Shaftesbury, Dorset: Element Books, 1984).

28 A. Powell Davies, *The Meaning of the Dead Sea Scrolls* (N.Y:New American Library, 1956).

29 David Dunlap, "Future Metropolis," *Omni,* VII No. 1 (October, 1984), 116-129.

Paolo Soleri, *Omega Seed: An Eschatological Hypothesis* (N.Y: Anchor Press/Doubleday).

30 Rudolf Steiner, *Ways To A New Style In Architecture* (N.Y: Anthroposophical Press, 1927).

31 Claude Bragdon, *The Beautiful Necessity* (Wheaton,IL: The Theosophical Publishing House, 1978).

George Adams, *Physical and Ethereal Spaces* (London: Rudolf Steiner Press, 1978).

Gyorgy Doczi, *The Power of Limits* (Boston: Shambhala Publications, 1981).

32 Ernest Ertel, *The Science of Sacred Landscape In Old China* (London: Synergetic Press, 1984).

CHAPTER XI

FUTURE TRENDS IN USING GEMSTONES
AND GEM ELIXIRS

A key reason why gemstone therapy will become much more popular in the coming years is the fact that the human race is now becoming much more sensitive and spiritualized. Thus, there is an increased need for natural and vibrational preparations for treating these individuals, as treatments using chemotherapy and radiation are becoming increasingly outdated. This is one reason why people have increasingly negative or allergic reactions to drugs. Clinical experience in orthodox medicine continues to reflect this pattern. Moreover, it is becoming increasingly obvious that bacteria and viruses are becoming immune to a growing number of orthodox treatments, so new and potentially more harmful chemicals are needed. This pattern never occurs with natural, vibrational preparations because they are an organic energy pattern with a harmonic life force.

Many will find that quartz crystals are also a doorway to the entire mineral kingdom. Numerous holistic practitioners, especially those using flower essences, herbs, radionics, and homeopathy, will gradually be drawn to the use of gem elixirs and related therapies using gemstones.

Q Please give a full discourse on the future of using gemstones in healing and spiritual growth?

"The immediate priority for using gemstones with any degree of acceptance among the orthodox structures of thy society is to isolate the active chemical makeup of certain gemstones that have traditionally been used in healing. It will gradually come to be understood that because of the chemical makeup of certain gemstones, they as physical supplements actually do have healing properties. Studies are now taking place with crushed ruby and malachite. Research will indicate that ruby promotes healing of bone lacerations, while malachite is indicated for some forms of leukemia and fibrous tumors. These studies, which are now taking place in the U.S. and Europe, will probably be openly announced within a six-year time period.

"There will also be increased studies of gemstones and other mineral properties and their healing effects from many highly intuitive and sophisticated native cultures. Over a five to seven year period, there will be an advancement and confirmation of the healing properties attributed to various stones, or there will at least be an acknowledgement of some of the beneficial physiological responses to these healing stones. However, this will unfortunately be considered simply physiological in response, rather than be attributed to spiritual or energy levels.

"There will also be the examination and isolation of electrical properties attributed to gemstones that shall be found to have peculiar effects upon tissue regeneration. This, however, will remain in a rudimentary phase over a ten-year time period. The actual application of gemstones with any degree of acceptability among the orthodox community, and even at times among segments of the holistic movement, will not even begin for a fifteen year time period. However, gem therapy will be increasingly practiced by many individuals already steeped in holistic and vibrational traditions. A key element regarding the acceptance of gemstones' healing properties will be their impact when they are prepared as elixirs with the homeopathic method. These, in part, are as a blueprint or construct for the evolution of gemstones within thy current society and its framework for a fifteen year time period.

"Other forces to consider are that gemstones shall continue to be practiced and elaborated upon by various lay practitioners who eventually will extend their studies into the more esoteric aspects of gem therapy, particularly the capacity of stones to generate consciousness. These studies will gradually merge with the mainstream of society within twenty to twenty-five years. For it will be in those days that consciousness shall be emphasized as the source of balance and the critical element in the makeup of man and his nature.

"There is already taking place an alignment of the necessary political forces to allow freedom of choice. These shall come along the lines of political freedom in the choice of governing one's own physical form. Political forces are now aligning partly because individuals no longer seem to have control over their own physical form when it comes to the various choices and levels of treating the disease state. In addition, there will be political pressure to release studies showing that certain laser lights, certain filtrations of colors, and certain gemstones, which act as screens for specific colorations, have physiological impacts upon the cellular tissue causing an increase or decrease in cell growth. While these studies are currently known in some scientific circles, when they are released to the public, it will increase the general awareness of the value of holistic health. Much of thy current biological and biochemical research, especially that on DNA and concepts of cloning, touch on these areas. Thy material sciences are gradually evolving along a course paralleling that which has already been as worked with as a technology on the ethereal levels. Thus there shall once again come into practice the general acceptance of the entire homeopathic principle and its reapplication through the ability to have freedom of choice. Gem elixirs shall achieve full acceptance in a pattern now evolving with the Bach flowers.

"Further forces affecting the use of gemstones include the fact that individuals should examine where gemstones have already been accepted within thy society. Ruby is already used in certain laser technologies and watches, while quartz is often placed within certain machines of calculus and computation. The piezoelectric effects of quartz have been extensively researched. Various minerals such as salt are used in the generation of solar heat. The fact that these minerals and gemstones are already being as used, either in their pure or synthetic state, gives us hints as to the direction of society in its futuristic trends. These properties have always been intuitively, or indeed clearly, understood by the ancients. Therefore, to fully understand the purpose of the future use of gemstones, individuals need only to look to the ancients. Indeed, this would be as where the past is also the future. Gemstones shall be as used in advancing consciousness, promoting healing on the physical level, and even be incorporated into thy technologies of machines and electronics.

"The most advanced stone that shall be used and that will find its most multipurpose use is quartz. This shall be the first stone, in combination with magnetics, which shall be accepted as having general healing practices and purposes. Eventually thin sheets of this particular stone shall be as placed over the physical body, and it shall be as discovered that by amplifying the patterns passing through it, there can indeed be internal readings of the body physical's organs. The first rudimentary experiments with this technique shall take place over the next six years. Other properties that will be discovered will be that tempered quartz will eventually be used to replace bone tissues and promote healing of neurological tissue. Quartz and crystalline structures will be used first in healing, then in the generation of energy, and finally for spiritualization of the self. As a byproduct of spiritualizing the self, the intellect will be spiritualized. These things will gradually be seen within a ten to fifteen year time period.

"Too radical a projection upon these elements would as diffuse the vision of the healer, lessening the ability to as focus upon his or her studies and seek to manifest these things into the flow of society, for it is found that the future begins with the present by interweaving and working towards it. In many respects, ye are the future in the application of gemstones. Each thing has its own season and its own time."

Western medicine is already using quartz and silica in many areas. One need only examine the Index Medicus in any reference library to appreciate this. For example, liquid quartz or silica commonly called Durofil, is now often used in dentistry as filling material to replace decayed tissue.

Q Why has gem therapy so remained in the public consciousness over the last few thousand years in comparison to flower essence usage, which has been lost until recent years?

"Flower essences have never been fully lost to the human race. It is only now that they are arising as a current, more popularized form of healing within Western consciousness. And there is now a general rise in consciousness and a return to nature as a source of alignment and consciousness. As more people meditate, this will allow flower essences to become more compatible with individuals. Therefore, it is more so that flower essences receded from the popular context within the race as a whole but not from the race altogether.

"Gem therapy is more self-apparent and closer to the physical dynamic. Gem elixirs were as used not only for their vibrational properties, but also for their mineral content and makeup. And traditionally some flower essences were prepared with the belief that the medical dynamics of the physical flower were also being activated."

Q Briefly list important areas on the planet where certain minerals will be discovered in the coming years, and discuss the type of consciousness that these minerals will promote.

"The oceans in particular have not yet been recognized as sources for the minerals that they contain, nor for the vibrations contained therein for those with the ability to understand. This will emerge in the future as various deep sea technologies are developed. There are certain deep ocean trenches in the Indian Ocean that are associated with diamond, emerald, ruby, and new minerals. Because of their lack of contact with society for many thousands of years, these minerals retain a Lemurian energy which will assist people working towards an internal transformation. This is a difficult matter to contemplate, for some of these minerals have not yet been discovered and their exact effect on humankind cannot yet be predicted.

"Certain islands in the South Pacific have not been entirely understood. Here the gemstones such as coral are not particularly rare or unusual, but what is not understood is that the energy of certain ley lines that pass through some of this region create a peacefulness in the people of that area. In a sense, this has allowed the people living in this area to be removed from the stream of consciousness of humanity. This was aided by World War II. The fighting in the Pacific Ocean caused those people to draw inward to preserve their culture. After that war, those islands were generally left along by the rest of the world for many years. This stimulated a sense of peacefulness in the minerals and people found in that region. Many of these islands have not really been discovered by the public. The energy contained within many of the minerals found in this region are excellent for meditation. For instance, it would be better to use coral from this region than from other areas.

"Next, the Southwest U.S. will come into prominence regarding gemstones that have traditionally been revered by the Indians living in that region. Some of these traditions have been held in secrecy, passed on only by word of mouth. Gradually, these traditions will be revealed. This concerns many of the gems commonly found in this area, such as the entire quartz family of minerals, especially when they are found in a geode structure. Some of these revelations will be considered quite magical as they are found in the Indian tradition. These minerals will promote a sense of unity in understanding the ways of the earth. This will be symbolized by the joining together of the different American tribes that will become more important in the future. These tribes will increasingly explore other religious ideas such as is found in Tibetan Buddhism. There will always be the focus of honoring the earth and a deeper understanding of how to bring people together to work in a spirit of conscious respect for the earth in a frame or structure that makes sense for all of humanity.

"Interesting minerals will be discovered near the Amazon River, especially in the northern area where the Amazon River is quite deep. This region has not yet been fully explored or understood. Many interesting minerals such as ulexite will be found here. Many of these minerals have a deep significance regarding mankind's understanding and willingness to aid in choosing the pathway by which children will be brought into the world. These minerals will aid the birthing process and will involve the evolution of humanity.

"The last area to mention is the Soviet Union. Individuals there have only begun to recognize the full power and depth of gemstones. The Russians are beginning to recognize the power and potential within every living thing and are beginning to discover the wisdom of bringing latent talents to the surface. It will soon be recognized in Russia that gems and flowers have much value to release such latent talents. They will work with many native stones, especially certain ones that have had little contact with humanity. Emerald will also become quite popular. Even certain mineral heirlooms will be rediscovered. To a degree, the Russians will be rediscovering part of their heritage. The power of these objects is also great because the Russians will be rediscovering their connection to the internal ley lines of the earth. These ley lines connect minerals deposits all over the world. Thus, through an expanded use of minerals many in Russia will rediscover their connection with people all over the earth. This can only benefit humanity."

Q Some claim that increased environmental pollution has resulted in the partial destruction of xenon gas in the atmosphere and that this has increased negativity on the planet. Is this true?

"Yes, this imbalance has resulted in a mild increase in negativity."

Q Are some UFO's now seeding the atmosphere with xenon gas to restore the balance?

"They are neutralizing the problem. This problem was first discovered by the space brothers in 1969. The space brothers are not fully correcting the problem because that would be too much of an interference with the affairs of this planet. This imbalance has limited mankind's ability to evolve in consciousness during recent years when there has been no large global conflict."

Q Does this have some relationship to the five as yet unisolated elements which you previously referred to?

"Yes."

Q Have other elements become imbalanced due to environmental pollutants?

"This has occurred with many other elements. This information may be discussed in the future."

Q Are the higher forces working to neutralize these problems?

"Yes."

Q Explain the relationship between gemstones and the inert gases?

"This is a good supplement to include because there is already a well-developed body of knowledge that would be wise to pursue. To review the individual inert gases at this time is not the intention of the channel speaking, but it is wise to explore this topic and expand this body of information. We find the Hilarion material to be sufficient to date.[2]

"As to a brief discourse on gemstones and the inert gases, we find inert gases are in a stabilized or crystallized gaseous state. By exploring the natural spectrum that the inert gases occupy along the atomic scale, it is possible to align them to specific chakric points. When the inert gases are attuned to specific chakric points, we find their natural attunement to gemstones also aligned to these chakras. Argon is associated with the base chakra, helium with the fifth, sixth, and seventh chakras, krypton with the heart and throat chakras, neon with the base, second, third, and fourth chakras, and xenon with the third and seventh chakras. The inert gases, as they climb the atomic scale, break down into systems of three, seven, and nine. The major linkage here is that the inert gases have an inherent property when breathed into the body physical in that they stimulate and stabilize the positive and negative ions and their influence on the body physical. These ions also integrate with and amplify the electrical and ionic properties contained within gemstones.

"It is also wise to place specific gemstones, linked to the inert gases by their attunement to certain chakras, within an enclosed chamber containing one or more inert gases. Gemstones placed in such chambers have greatly enhanced properties. This should be done for thirty minutes to twenty-four hours. These effects are especially amplified during meditation. Furthermore, when gemstones are put in these inert chambers, sufficiently sensitive instruments could measure an electrical charge or the stimulation of certain inert gases within the gemstone. There is, in the atmosphere of a gemstone, the breaking down of the original atmosphere and the generation of inert

180

gases within the presence of charging such gemstones. This is indicative of the link of the gemstones with the properties of the inert gases. This concludes the brief discourse on the inert gases to stimulate the student to further study and expand the Hilarion material."

While there will be future research on the use of gems with inert gases, my main reason for mentioning the inert gases now is to alert readers to the value of this technology, which, in a rudimentary form, is already extensively used in orthodox medicine.[3] From free energy devices to various modalities in holistic health, the inert gases in Atlantis were used in many areas. Hopefully, in the coming years, many will be inspired to explore this work.

In the coming years many people will use gem elixirs, flower essences, and homeopathic remedies as nutritional supplements. Many individuals now using vitamins and minerals will also use these vibrational preparations as a more conscious way of absorbing nutrients. With millions of people now using nutrient supplements, many will not be surprised to see this trend as it develops. Doctor Cousens, who wrote the foreword to *Flower Essences and Vibrational Healing*, is now doing a text on spiritual nutrition, which will contain more information on this subject. Here John explains how gem elixirs help the body assimilate different nutrients.

Q Please explain how gem elixirs help the body assimilate various nutrients?

"In the translation of minerals through the gem elixir procedure, and even inclusive of certain flower essence and homeopathic principles, the accord is that they are as bound by the patterns of the life force. Minerals are in a life-bound field, which makes them palatable to digestion within the physical system. Inanimate minerals, or those that have not been bound organically by the process of preparation into a gem elixir, become palatable for stimulating the assimilation of nutrient values into the physical body by having or maintaining the presence of the organically bound mineral pattern. This then enters the physical body and stimulates upon the cellular level the necessary enzymes. The body physical, upon the subtle level within the etheric anatomy, associates the presence of such energy patterns as a signal for the body's need to obtain and assimilate specific nutrients that are associated or closely bound with that mineral. For instance, if someone took gem elixirs that contained calcium, phosphorus, and magnesium, there would then be the assimilation of the ethereal pattern of these nutrients from the gem elixirs. The body physical would be alerted to the possible need for these nutrient properties which it would then obtain, if needed, from various foods. Gem elixirs also restimulate the body's ability to assimilate these nutrient factors. If someone had arthritis and an inability to assimilate calcium, certain minerals, not organically bound but ingested in the elixir state, would restimulate the body physical's ability to assimilate the necessary nutrient properties for rebinding calcium correctly to the bone's tissue."

So much material was channeled on gemstones that there was not sufficient time to include certain related topics. Originally, there was to be a chapter on fossils as a subsystem. Instead, there will later be a text just on fossil elixirs. However, some of this material is included in this text in that abalone, amber, coal, coral, jet, limestone, and petrified wood tend to contain fossils.

"Fossil elixirs amplify the life force, especially activating one or more chakras. There is greater attunement between these elixirs and people because both come from organic tissue. Having previously been living matter, these elixirs also often stimulate the spiritual body, which few vibrational remedies do. Fossils radiate orgone naturally because the orgonic pattern exists, but they are made out of inanimate substance."

What has come to be called Willard's water is an interesting expression of the tremendous life force stored in fossils. Using water extracted from a specific fossil, this liquid has been demonstrated to have great healing properties for treating people and animals. Yet no one currently understands how or why it works![4]

Another important topic to be reviewed in the future concerns how we are affected by various underground mineral and water deposits, especially when they exist under where people live. This topic has been well researched for many years in Europe, especially in Germany. Literally hundreds of articles and books have been written on this topic. Ultimately, someone will translate some of this material into English and health-conscious Americans will better understand the importance of this subject. Occasionally, interesting articles on this topic appear in the journals of the American Society of Dowsing and the British Society of Dowsing.

Using certain gemstones to treat radiation-related problems, including background radiation, is another subject of great importance. The ultraviolet, fluorescent, and radioactive minerals have great value here.[5] Various stars and constellations play a much greater role with our health than most people understand.[6]

The use of other gemstones as gem elixirs will later be discussed. The many violet-purple minerals in the mineral kingdom[7] usually have great spiritual properties. Some fascinating new minerals that I have obtained at gem trade shows for future research include charoite, erythrite, kaemmerite, and lepidolite. Numerous other gemstones have also been obtained. Future quartz gem elixirs to be examined include dendritic quartz, lepidocrocite hematite quartz, rutilated smoky quartz, and quartz from Cairgorm, Scotland. Star quartz is especially valuable. Many other interesting minerals will be studied.

"Dendritic quartz stimulates healers, the dream state, and astral projection, and it removes negative thought forms. It has traditionally been used in agriculture and for deeper attunement to nature. Lepidocrocite hematite quartz stimulates the removal of anxiety, while quartz from Cairgorm, Scotland stimulates psychic sight and removes baser thought forms.

"Cacoxenite aligns the three lowest chakras, restores balance in base chakra problems, and activates intuition, creativity, and sensitivity. Charoite stimulates the crown and sixth chakras, balances the analytical and intuitive nature, and alleviates fear of higher plane experiences. Cinnabar, which has traditionally been used in alchemy to stimulate longevity, is a specific for alleviating candida albicans. The flower essence silversword can also be quite effective for this problem. Electrum balances the intellect, opens the heart, removes blockages in the meridians and nadis, and is good for healers to use to overcome personal blockages, especially when there may be oversensitivity regarding issues of the third and fourth chakras. Electrum also stimulates the electrical properties of the body. Erythrite, which was used in Lemuria, stimulates visions. It also activates the brow chakra and stimulates the ability to interpret dreams. Garnet hessonite opens the heart and stimulates the base chakras in the feet for greater attunement to the energy of the earth's magnetic flow. Hiddenite is a specific for tissue regeneration. Jadeite can be used in agriculture. Red jasper eases throat problems, balances the throat chakra, and cools fevers and intense mental states such as anger. It also develops yang energy and stimulates insights into various issues. Kaemmererite links the throat and brow chakras for enhanced expression of spiritual and personal experiences. Kermesite is a traditional alchemical stone that stimulates alchemy in the esoteric anatomy. It stimulates the psychic centers in the medulla oblongata for increasing the life force in the body. Labradorite helps remove long held grudges, especially from childhood. Use it for treating child abuse. It also is good to use in Reichian therapy to remove emotional tension stored in the body. Labradorite-spectrolite activates the feet and hand chakras, so it stimulates the meridians and attunement to the earth's energy and is good for healers. Lava aids in nutrient absorption. Lepidolite reduces anger, hostility, unreasonable fears, and other negative emotions, transforming these negative emotions to a more positive state. It also balances the third chakra. Mother of pearl (oyster shell) activates dreams and creativity and is excellent for color consultants. Nealite stimulates the second and fourth chakras. It can be used in tantric activities, although it is not an aphrodisiac. It also stimulates intuition and can be used by artists to overcome lethargy. Neptunite activates the kundalini. Phenakite enables people to function better in group dynamics. Quartzite stimulates higher ideals to alleviate possessiveness. Staurolite aligns people with the major and minor planetary chakras. This activates the chakras in individuals; gives one a sense of planetary purpose; and lifts people beyond local, national, and geographical prejudices. Tiger's Eye aligns the base chakra with the brow chakra, linking understanding to a higher purpose."

An interesting development in future years will be the use of natural methods to grow minerals. For some years minerals have been synthetically grown,[8] but there are organic techniques to grow minerals in a more holistic fashion.[9] Several years ago, I met someone who was using loadstone, copper wire, barley, alcohol, and meditation to grow a mineral in a more harmonious fashion. In future years, we may even witness a debate on the value of synthetically or organically growing minerals as has gone on for many years with plants. John has discussed this subject.

Q Is there any significant difference between natural and artificially produced minerals?
"Synthetically made gemstones carry only the weakest portion of the ability of thought form amplification. Thy scientists have already discovered that artificially produced crystals do not have sufficient stability for long-term use in certain industries. There needs to be greater attunement to the earth's natural forces. Science is not yet able to duplicate the forces of life in the laboratory, even though there has been the isolation of many of the necessary elements of life. However, if artifically created crystalline structures were combined with natural silicates, there would be some transference of properties."

Q Is there a way to amplify the properties of artifically produced minerals?
"The placement of a natural crystal near a synthetically made crystal for a while would have a positive effect on the synthetic crystal. One suggested technique is to place natural and synthetic crystals under a cone surrounded with copper wire using twelve volts and DC current. The resulting electromagnetic field stabilizes the synthetic crystal. A spiritually evolved person with strong mental discipline could enhance the process by focusing on the synthetic crystal. People meditating around a natural and synthetic crystal would also activate properties in the synthetically made mineral. Then the crystal could be place under a pyramid for a while."

Q What gem elixirs and flower essences can be used to grow minerals more organically?

"This is interesting because there are many that are of benefit here. The various minerals that may be formed into crystalline shapes have interesting vibrations associated with them. The general principle to use is that of the colors of various gems and flowers. Note that the growth of a mineral is an acceleration upwards of consciousness. Note the colors that are attuned to the seven main chakras. For instance, if you try to grow ruby, use orange colored gems or flower essences to enhance the process. Orange is associated with the second chakra, and red is associated with the base chakra. Much information on this technology can be provided in the future."

New information on many of the minerals discussed in Volume One of this series will be presented in the future. Topics to be discussed with each gem include the treatment of genetic diseases, their use in modern industrial technology, and their etheric properties. There will later be an advanced text on gemstones, which will delve more into the technical areas of gemmology. For instance, the size, volume, purity, weight, and geometric shapes of gems will be examined. There are better ways to cut, polish, measure the gravity of, and identify gems. How gems age, how they obtain their properties, and how they can be used to construct various musical instruments will also be discussed. The developing concepts of new physics have much relevance to better understand how minerals can be used in their full potential. Minerals have special electrical properties that need to be further explored. Intense heat and cold, as well as infrared and ultraviolet light, activate certain properties in minerals. The subdivision within each of the seven rays as well as other important rays is another fruitful topic to be explored.

The homeopathic preparation of various minerals is another significant area of research. The Steiner-oriented pharmacies have already conducted some research in this area. There is also further information to be explored in the relationship of minerals to agriculture, ethers, nature spirits,[10] sound,[11] talismans, and the future evolution of the human race and the mineral kingdom.[12] Techniques will be presented to use specifically shaped gemstones in meditation to release information, such as long forgotten languages from past lives stored on the cellular level in the genetic code. Ways to learn what information is stored in minerals from ancient civilizations and how to release that information will also be studied.

Further principles will be offered to amplify gems, to use them in baths, and to use them during spiritual practices that can be enhanced with minerals. The minor chakras and obscure trace minerals also need to be examined in relationship to minerals. Later, new combinations will be presented to bring the forces of the soul and higher self more into one's daily life. This is a major issue. Gemstones were commonly used for surgery in Atlantis. Much fascinating material needs to be examined here, especially as surgery in Western medicine is transformed. Certain minerals have a fascinating and complex karmic pattern from Atlantis. There also needs to be a detailed understanding of the interlocking nature of the devic forces and the principles that bind the mineral and plant kingdoms together.

"It is necessary to prepare thy public consciousness in the use of gemstones and flower essences to prepare for more radical technologies. The first few volumes are not only to enhance principles, but to develop more complex forms of gemstone uses and their medical properties. The first two volumes stress the use of gemstones as elixirs, while the advanced volume will examine the properties of gemstones and expand the knowledge of how the elixirs can be applied. These first two volumes on gemstones are a forerunner for others. Thus, simplicity is the key."

There must be a gathering of a collective consciousness about this work. Otherwise, it would remain too radical and be rejected by many people. One need only examine the Urantia Book[13] to understand that during the course of evolution whenever radical new information is released too soon people tend to reject it.

Sometimes information on the tapes of the channelings cannot be retrieved when they are played back because of static. John recently had an interesting comment on this when asked about coral.

"Those static fields were generated by higher forces to eliminate it. Even though information is given it must coordinate with the expanding body of consciousness of the general populace. Otherwise it is eradicated."

Q Is there any indication when the consciousness of society will sufficiently expand and what the nature of that consciousness is, so that more advanced material can be released?

"There is a three-year cycle requiring a spiritualization or respiritualization of society. Society is currently standing as though in a period of time stagnation. This is the period of time spoken of in the Book of Revelations where the four angels stand at the four corners of the earth holding the winds in abeyance. There must be further spiritual and mental development of individuals to assimilate that which has been gathered unto them to date."

John is of course partly referring to the current attack on holistic health by the organized medical profession with its allies in business and government. These reactionary forces will have their day for a while, but it is inevitable that natural healing and the principles of holistic health will gradually become the dominant form of medicine practiced in the U.S. and other Western countries. Another issue is the fact that a number of people in the New Age have trouble accepting channeled material, especially when it is trance channeled and is of a more scientific or technically organized mode, as is this work. This problem exists partly because we as a people are still too left-brained, requiring reasoning and scientific methodology to prove the validity of everything we choose to accept. Right-brain activity, with increased sensitivity and intuition, is still looked down upon by many, although recent developments such as the growth of the women's movement and the respiritualization of society certainly show that this pattern is changing.

An interesting pattern in this transitional period is that, traditionally, for many years, channeled material has presented the eternal spiritual truths with an attunement to the second ray. Now, with more people ready and open, channeled teachings will increasingly be presented which is technical and scientific with an attunement to the fifth ray.[14] Some of this material will be trance channeled with the sources openly acknowledged, while in other instances it will be consciously channeled information with the author perhaps not even being aware of the real source of his or her intuitive perceptions. My books will generally vibrate with the fifth ray, as have two interesting titles by Hilarion: *Body Signs* and *Einstein Doesn't Work Here Anymore*,[15] and two fascinating trance channeled texts through Richard Zenor: *The English Cabalah, Volumes I and II,* edited by Eisen.[16]

It is interesting that Western medicine has for many years spent millions of dollars investigating the folk medicines of many native cultures throughout the world. Yet where were the double-blind studies among these native cultures? Their knowledge of how various herbs, flowers, and minerals can be used for health and spiritual growth came through meditation, channeling, intuition, and many years of trial and error. Yet when individuals in the U.S. present similar remedies, from herbs to flower essences or gem therapies, they tend to be labeled as unproven or even dangerous treatments. And, of course, the medical-political establishment in this country has almost all of the medical research money locked into chemotherapy and radiation-related treatments.

While my initial books have been very well received by thousands of people, this has not been the case with certain more traditional individuals, especially in the homeopathic establishment. Ultimately, this body of work will be fully accepted even in the most orthodox and conservative scientific circles, with many then forgetting the original source of this material. History has shown this to happen in countless instances. Such is the nature of the human condition.

Below John discusses one other interesting phenomenon that was not mentioned in my previous books. People should understand this principle.

Q Is it true, that with gem elixirs and flower essences, their more spiritual effects will become more common in future years as consciousness expands?
"Correct."

Q Is this a key reason why people now rarely experience the keen spiritual effects you quote and why such preparations should be amplified with various quartz crystal and pyramid technologies?
"Yes, as has often been stated, it is the consciousness of the individual that is the final phenomenon. Spiritual qualities grow in the pattern of each individual. If individual psychological or behavioral studies were done, people would find their consciousness enhanced by gem elixirs and flower essences with a radical spiritualization of behavioral patterns taking place, more than would be the case with others not taking these preparations. It would also be found that these effects would be independent of any placebo-like influences."

When it is noted, for example, that star sapphire can manifest a state approaching samadhi, or that passion flower enables one to attune to Christ consciousness, very few people today will experience such exalted states. Yet as the respiritualization of society takes place, gradually a small but growing number of individuals will experience these states. Ultimately, we will again experience a state approaching the consciousness of Lemuria so that almost all people using vibrational preparations will innately understand and experience the total effects of these preparations in mind, body, and spirit. We all look forward to that day.

In addition, well over one hundred individuals have told me that they could tell that vibrational preparations amplified with quartz crystals and pyramids work faster and stronger in them and their clients than has been their experience with other vibrational preparations not receiving this amplification. These individuals happen to have the sensitivity to understand the effect that such techniques have on vibrational preparations. Yet most people today do not have the sensitivity to detect this in vibrational preparations. In the coming years, more and more people will have the sensitivity to tell almost immediately if a gem elixir, flower essence, or homeopathic remedy has been amplified and if it has been done properly. It is inevitable that all manufacturers of such preparations will use quartz crystals and pyramids to amplify such products.

"Previously there was as the prognostication that eventually all men and all women would become as worthy of entering into the temple to place upon themselves the breastplate of not only the Judaic tradition. It was also accepted throughout most ancient cultures that those things formerly held sacred to the priesthood would eventually be revealed to all people. There were prognostications that eventually all these things, as a

186

model, would become thoroughly integrated and applied to society as a general principle, rather than as necessitating the limitations of these knowledges. So even as thy scientific consciousness has promoted the recent discovery of many minerals, and these further advance thy scientific technologies, so in turn shall the future discoveries of various gemstones promote thy spiritual consciousness. Indeed, they promote that which men and women are and are becoming, which was and will always be. Ye are as spirit. These faculties and these forces that ye work with indeed are as ethereal in their content and makeup. These faculties integrate thee more fully back into the element of treating thyselves as ethereal or spiritual beings to spiritualize society as a whole.

"There has been the growth of many individuals in this process as each person becomes a student to this work. Vibrational remedies advance and enhance the concept of thyself as energy. Energy is unified with spirit and consciousness so ye enlighten thyself to the great accord to wherein you merge the total concept of mind, body, and spirit; even though you have divided these things into various sciences and art forms. Indeed, these begin to approach the level of that integration known as the Christ principle, for the Christ principle is the manifestation of God's nature on this plane and the merger of mind, body, and spirit.

"God is love and love is harmony and harmony begets peace. It is harmony that ye seek in thy own personal endeavors through interrelationships with each other. For indeed, life is interactivity with thy fellow beings and fellow souls, be they incarnate or discarnate, or in the various accords that ye seek to bring them to harmony with. This accord is consciousness.

"Take all this information and know that there are many techniques and many concepts, but none must supplement the content and nature or even be as given as the higher priority, than to know that God is within you. These things that are given forth are teachings, then as applied teachings, then as to stimulate more that each and every one of thee may as make progressions and evolve towards that which ye already are, which is God's love, which is within thee, which begets harmony and peace."

1 Scott Holmberg,M.D., "Drug Resistance Salmonella From Animals Fed Anti-Microbials," *The New England Journal of Medicine*, CCCXI No. 10 (Sept.,6,1984),1.
2 Hilarion, *Einstein Doesn't Work Here Anymore* (Toronto:Marcus Books,1983).
_____, *Answers* (Toronto:Marcus Books,1983),p.37-38.
_____, *The Nature of Reality* (Toronto:Marcus Books,1980),p.12.
_____, *Seasons of the Spirit* (Toronto:Marcus Books,1982),p.6,24-25.
_____,*Symbols* (Toronto:Marcus Books,1982),p.70-72.
_____, *Threshold* (Toronto:Marcus Books,1980),p.19-22.
3 William Grant, *Medical Gases: Their Properties and Uses* (Buckinghamshire,England: HM+M Publishers Ltd.,1978).
4 U.S. House of Representatives, *Catalyst Altered Water A Briefing by the Subcommittee on Health and Long-term Care of the Select Committee On Aging* July 7,1980, Publ no. 96-240 (Washington,D.C: Government Printing office, 1980).
5 Sterling Gleason, *Ultraviolet Guide to Minerals* (Turland,Vt: Charles E. Tuttle Co.,1972). Robert Jones,Jr., *Natures Hidden Rainbow* (San Gabriel,Ca: Ultra-Violet Products,Inc.,1970).
6 Rudolf Steiner, *Man and the World of Stars* (Spring Valley,N.Y: The Anthroposophic Press, 1982).
7 Walter D. Yoder,Ph.D, "A Royal Suite: The World of Purple- Violet Minerals," *Lapidary Journal*, (January,1980), 2126-2140.

8 J.J. Gilman, ed., *The Art and Science of Growing Crystals* (N.Y: Wiley,1963).

Alan Holden and Phylis Singer, *Crystals and Crystal Growing* (Cambridge,Ma: M.I.T.,1982).

Michael O'Donoghue, *A Guide to Man-Made Gemstones* (Florence,Ky:Van Nostrand Reinhold,1983).

9 Charles W. Littlefield,M.D.,*Man, Minerals, and Masters* (Albuquerque,N.M: Sun Books,1980).

10 Alice Bailey, *A Treatise On Cosmic Fire* (N.Y: Lucis Publishing Co.,1977),p.640.

11 Ibid,p.495.

12 Alice Bailey, *Esoteric Psychology,* II (N.Y:Lucis Publishing Co.,1975),p.238-239.

13 *The Urantia Book* (Chicago: Urantia Foundation, 1978).

14 Hilarion, *Symbols* (Toronto:Marcus Books, 1982),p.25-26.

15_____, *Body Signs* (Toronto: Marcus Books, 1982).

_____, *Einstein Doesn't Work Here Anymore* (Toronto:Marcus Books,1983).

16 William Eisen, *The English Cabalah,* Volume I (Marina Del Rey,Ca: DeVorss and Co.,1980.

William Eisen, *The English Cabalah* Volume, II (Marina Del Rey,Ca: DeVorss and Co.,1982).

APPENDIX I

THE HARDNESS OF GEMSTONES

As a general principle, it is usually true that gemstones harder than seven on the Mohs' scale of hardness give off more energy, and the softer gemstones under seven on this scale take in more energy. Because of this, there is some benefit to understanding the exact hardness of gemstones on the Mohs' scale. Harder stones are better able to resonate with vibrations. Gemstones, such as those in the quartz family, are number seven on this hardness scale, so they are a in perfect balance between broadcasting and retaining energy.

The Mohs' scale of hardness is a scale of resistance. The resistance a mineral offers when it is scratched on its surface indicates its hardness. Originally, this scale was defined by ten selected minerals, with talc at number one, the softest mineral, and diamond at number ten, the hardest mineral. Each mineral will scratch those below it on the hardness scale. While the Mohs' scale is not perfectly accurate, it is widely used as a simple, readily available scale that is fairly reliable. Different sources list a slightly different hardness for individual minerals.

Q With numerous gemstones the hardness varies. For instance, aquamarine, varies from seven to eight on the Mohs' scale. What does this mean?

"There is a slight variance in the ability of the gem to give forth and retain energy.

"All gemstones have the property of thought form amplification, mostly because of their crystalline structure. Some stones such as herkimer diamond are better able to bind thought forms and to store information than is the case with other stones, such as quartz crystal, even though both have a hardness of seven. There are many complex factors."

Q Explain how gemstones give off and pull in energy?

"Merely study the patterns of the yin yang properties in gemstones. The yin stones generally attract energy, and the yang stones usually give off energy."

MOHS' SCALE OF HARDNESS FOR GEMSTONES

Abalone	2.5	Eilat Stone	N.A.
Agate (Botswana)	6.5-7	Emerald	7.5-8
Agate (Carnelian)	6.5-7	Enstatite	5-6
Agate (Fire)	6.5-7	Flint	7.0
Agate (Moss)	6.5-7	Fluorite	4.0
Agate (Picture)	6.5-7	Galena	2.5-2.75
Albite	6-6.5	Gallium	1.5
Alexandrite	8-8.5	Garnet(Rhodolite)	6.5-7.5
Amazonite	6-6.5	Garnet(Spessartine)	6.5-7.5
Amber	2-3	Glass (Fulganite)	5-6
Anhydrite	3.5	Gold	2.5-3
Apatite	5.0	Granite	5.5-6
Aquamarine	7-8	Graphite	1-2
Asphalt	1-2	Gypsum	1.5-2.5
Atacamite	3-3.5	Halite (Salt)	2-2.5
Aventurine	5.5-6	Hematite	5-7
Azurite	3.5-4	Herderite	5-5.5
Azurite-Malachite	3.5-4	Herkimer Diamond	7.0
Benitoite	6-6.5	Ivory	2-3
Beryl	7-8	Jade	6-7
Beryllonite	5.5-6	Jamesonite (Feather Rock)	2.5
Bloodstone (Heliotrope)	7.0	Jasper (Green)	7.0
Bog (Peat)	N.A.	Jasper (From Idar-Oberstein)	7.0
Boji Stone	N.A.	Jasper (Picture-Brown)	7.0
Brass	3-4	Jasper (Yellow)	7.0
Bronze	N.A.	Jet	4-5
Calamine (Hemimorphite)	4.5-5	Kunzite	6.5-7.5
Calcite	3-3.5	Lapis Lazuli	5-5.5
Carbon Steel	4-5	Lazulite	5-6
Chalcedony	6.5-7	Lazurite	5-5.5
Chrysocolla	2-4	Limestone	3.5
Chrysolite	N.A.	Loadstone(Negative and Positive)	5.5-6.5
Chrysoprase	7.0	Magnesium	2.0
Clay	N.A.	Magnetite(Negative and Positive)	5.5-6.5
Coal	1-2.5	Malachite	3-4
Copper	2.5-3	Marble	3.0
Coral (Pink, Red, Red-White		Meteorite	4-5
and White)	3.5	Moonstone (Adularia)	6-6.5
Cream of Tartar	N.A.	Morganite	7-8
Creedite	4.0	Natrolite	5-6
Cuprite	3-4	Nephrite	6.5-7
Diamond	10	Obsidian	5-5.5
Diopside	5-6.5	Onyx	7.0
Durangite	5.0	Opal (Cherry)	5-6.5

Opal (Dark)	5-6.5	Tourmaline (Green)	7-7.5
Opal (Jelly)	5-6.5	Tourmaline (Quartz)	7-7.5
Opal(Light)	5-6.5	Tourmaline (Rubellite)	7-7.5
Pearl (Dark,Light)	2.5-5	Tourmaline (Watermelon)	7-7.5
Peridot	6.5-7	Tourmaline (White or Uvite)	7-7.5
Petrified Wood	7.0	Turquoise	4.5-6
Platinum	4-4.5	Variscite	3.5-5
Porphyry	N.A.	Zircon (Hyacinth)	6.5-7.5
Portlandite (Quick Lime)	2.0	Zoisite	6-7
Pyrite	6-6.5		
Pyrolusite	6-6.5		
Quartz (Amethyst)	7.0	N.A.-Information not available	
Quartz (Black or Smoky)	7.0		
Quartz (Blue)	7.0		
Quartz (Citrine)	7.0		
Quartz (Lepidocrocite-Geothite)	7.0		
Quartz (Rose)	7.0		
Quartz (Rutilated)	7.0		
Quartz (Solution)	7.0		
Quartz (White or Colorless)	7.0		
Rhodochrosite	3-4		
Rhodonite	5.5-6.5		
Rhyolite (Wonderstone)	6-6.5		
Royal Azel (Sugilite)	4.5-6		
Ruby	9.0		
Rutile	6-6.5		
Sand	N.A.		
Sandstone	N.A.		
Sapphire	9.0		
Sard	7.0		
Sardonyx	7.0		
Scarab	N.A.		
Sepiolite (Meerschaum)	2-2.5		
Serpentine	2.5-5		
Shattuckite (Plancheite)	3.5		
Silver	2.5-3		
Smithsonite	4-5		
Soapstone	1.0		
Sodalite	5.5-6		
Sphene	5-6		
Spinel	5-8.5		
Star Sapphire	9.0		
Sulfur	1.5-2.5		
Talc	1.0		
Topaz	8-8.5		
Tourmaline (Black or Schorl)	7-7.5		
Tourmaline (Blue or Indicolite)	7-7.5		
Tourmaline (Cat's Eye)	7-7.5		

GLOSSARY

Acicular: Needle like.

Akashic records: Cosmic records of all human deeds, thoughts, and events from the past, present, and future. They may be consulted by those with a proper spiritual evolution.

Alchemy: The art of transmuting metals and other substances into silver or gold, generally to produce a healing elixir called the Philosopher's Stone. In its highest form, alchemy involves transforming the self.

Allopathy: A term used especially in homeopathy to describe orthodox medical practice.

Amulet: An object worn to protect someone and ward off negative vibrations. Traditionally, it is believed to enhance health and consciousness.

Androgyny: The actual physical state of being joined together into one sex-male and female.

Apportation: The movement of an object through the ethers from one location to another. This is usually accomplished by stabilizing the interior molecular dynamics of the object to be moved within the ethers.

Astral body: One of the subtle bodies surrounding the physical body.

Astral projection: Also known as an out-of-body experience. The astral body temporarily separates from the physical body. This usually occurs when asleep, but can also occur when awake.

Atlantis: An ancient civilization covering what is now the Atlantis Ocean.

Aura: An invisible, luminous radiation or halo that surrounds the physical body. It varies widely in size, density, and color depending on the evolution of each person, and it exists around all life forms. Some psychic or sensitive individuals see it.

Biofeedback: The ability of the mind to control involuntary body functions.

Biomagnetic: The patterns of magnetic energy that are generated as a by-product of molecular activity. The released energy becomes part of the aura.

Biomolecular: Refers to the chemical activity in the subatomic level within each cell.

Birthstone: The belief in astrology that the vibrations of certain stones positively affect someone born under one sign more than another.

Cat's eye: An optical effect in gemstones in which a single band of light traverses the stone.

Causal body: An ethereal body that exists around the physical body.

Cellular level: At the level of each individual cell.

Chakra: A spiritual energy center just outside, but connected to, the physical body.

Channel (Medium): An individual who serves as a vehicle or instrument for one's higher self and soul or for guides on higher planes to speak through. The person may be awake or in trance when this process takes place.

Clairaudience: The ability to hear sounds from other dimensions.

Clairvoyance: A general term signifying many psychic gifts such as the ability to see things miles away.

Collective consciousness: The combined thoughts or feelings of large groups of people.

Creative visualization: The use of the mind to create a mental image.

Doctrine of signature: The principles that there is a relationship between the anatomy of people and the color, odor, shape, taste and texture of gemstones and plants. In this relationship lie many clues as to how gemstones and plants can be used in healing and conscious growth.

Emotional body: A subtle body that exists around the physical body.

Endorphins: Recently isolated cells in the brain that release a sense of pleasure when activated. They are activated through physical exercise and various vibrational preparations.

Ethereal fluidium: Part of the etheric body that is connected to each cell.

Etheric: Refers to the formative forces that exist vibrationally in relation to all life on earth.

Etheric body: A subtle body that exists just outside and around the physical body.

Ethers: Seven or more dimensional states that vibrate faster than the speed of light.

Gem elixir: The placement of a mineral specimen in pure water for several hours under the sun to transfer the mineral's vibration into the water. The diluted liquid is ingested for healing and conscious growth.

Hara: An energy center in the human body located near the navel.

Higher self: The location where all higher principles and experiences from past lives are stored in the person.

Integrated spiritual body: This, and the term spiritual body, signify the combination of the spiritual properties of the subtle and physical bodies.

Karma: A Sanskrit word meaning the sum total of a person's actions in their many lives. These past life traits are carried over into each new life with continuing opportunities for growth.

Kinesiology: A system of muscle testing to see if a remedy should be prescribed to someone.

Kundalini: A powerful spiritual energy normally lying dormant in the physical body at the base of the spine. Once carefully awakened, spiritual growth ensues.

Lemuria: An ancient civilization covering what is now the Pacific Ocean.

Levitation: The ability to lighten the body so that it naturally lifts into the air defying gravity.

Mantra: A word or phrase continuously repeated which produces a positive or negative effect. The term is often considered sacred. OM is the best known mantra.

Matrix: The rock in which a mineral specimen is embedded.

Mental body: A subtle body existing around the physical body.

Meridians: Ethereal patterns of energy that carry the life force into the physical body.

Miasms: Various subtle imbalances residing in the cells and subtle bodies that are activated to cause numerous diseases when karmic patterns prevail.

Mohs' scale: A hardness scale of minerals established by the German Mohr in 1820. The softest minerals such as talc have a one value, while the hardest minerals such as diamond have a value of ten. The scale goes from one to ten.

Molecular: Refers to the chemical activity in the subatomic level within each cell.

Nadis: An extensive ethereal nervous system just outside the physical body, but directly connected to the nervous system.

Nature spirits: Souls living on a higher frequency than the physical plane that are intimately associated with the various forms of nature.

Nosodes: Biological toxins that are prepared into homeopathic remedies.

Pendulum: A small item attached to a thread and used to analyze or diagnose.

Philosopher's stone: An alchemical term traditionally meaning a powerful elixir that will transmute base metals into gold or silver. It can also be used to treat ill people and to stimulate spiritual illumination.

Prana: A Hindu or yogic term used to describe the life force.

Psychokinesis: The ability to move an object with mental power.

Psychometry: The ability to divine from direct contact or proximity with an object the attributes of that object or of a person who has been in contact with that object.

Radionics: The use of an instrument and operator for sending to, and receiving vibrations from, a person miles away. It has been used as a modality in healing and in agriculture for many years.

Soul body: A very ethereal subtle body that exists around the physical body.

Spirit guides: Individual souls existing in other dimensions who assist people on the earth plane. They may speak through someone in trance.

Subtle bodies: A general term referring to all the bodies that exist just outside and around the physical body.

Talisman: An object worn to protect someone and to ward off negative vibrations. Traditionally, it is believed to enhance health and consciousness.

Telepathy: The transmission of thoughts between two people from any distance. This communication takes place without the normally understood senses being used.

Thermal body: A heat field existing just outside the physical body near the etheric body.

Thought forms: Semi-materialized ethereal forms or shapes that the mind builds.

Tissue regeneration: The complete rebuilding of parts of the body to full health.

Trance: A state of intense concentration and sleep-like condition in which the mind and body are overshadowed by the higher self or spirit guides from other dimensions.

BIBLIOGRAPHY

BATH THERAPIES
Barber, Bernard. *Sensual Water: A Celebration of Bathing*. Chicago: Contemporary Books, Inc.,1978.
Buchman, Dian D. *The Complete Book of Water Therapy, 500 Ways to Use Our Oldest and Safest Medicine*. New York: E.P. Dutton,1979.
Cerney, J. *Modern Magic of Natural Healing With Water Therapy*. San Diego: Reward Books,1977.
Finnerty,Gertrude, and Theodore Corbitt. *Hypnotherapy*. New York: Frederick Ungar Publishing Co.,1960.
Fleder,Helen. *Shower Power: Wet, Warm and Wonderful Exercises for the Shower and Bath*. New York: M. Evans and Co.,Inc.,1978.
Frazier, Gregory, and Beverly Frazier. *The Bath Book*. San Francisco:Troubador Press,1973.
Lust,John. *Kneipp's My Water Cure*. Greenwich,Ct: Benedict Lust Publishing,1978.
Ramachakara, Yogi. *Hindu-Yogi Practical Water Cure*. Jacksonville,Fl: Yogi Publication Society, n.d.
Szekely, Edmond Bordeaux. *Healing Waters*. San Diego: Academy Books,1973.

COLOR AND CONSCIOUSNESS
R.B. Amber, *Color Therapy*. Calcutta: *Firma KLM Ltd., 1976*.
Birren, Faber. *Color and Human Response*. N.Y: Van Nostrand Reinhold Co., 1978.
_____.*Color In Your World*. N.Y: Collier Books, 1967.
Burroughs, Stanley. *Healing For the Age of Enlightenment*. Kailua,Hi: Stanley Burroughs, 1976.
Clark, Linda, and Yvonne Martine. *Health, Youth and Beauty Through Color Breathing*. Millbrae,Ca: Celestial Arts, 1976.
Gimbel, Theo. *Healing Through Colour*. Saffron Walden Essex: C.W. Daniel Co., 1983.
Graham, F. *The Rainbow Book*. N.Y: Random House, 1979.
Hall, Manly. *The Symbolism of Light and Color*. L.A: The Philosophical Research Society, 1976.
Heline, Corinne. *Healing and Regeneration Through Color*. L.A: New Age Press, 1976.
Hill, Norah, ed. *You Are A Rainbow*. Boulder Creek,Ca: Univ. of the Trees Press, 1979.
Hunt, Roland. *Color: Key to the Nu Clear Age*. Lakemont,Ga: CSA Press, 1968.
_____.*The Eighth Key to Colour*. Romford,Essex,England: L.N. Fowler and Co.,1978.
_____.*Man Made Clear For the Nu Clear Age*. Lakemont,Ga: CSA Press, 1969.
_____.*The Seven Keys to Colour Healing*. Saffron Walden, Essex, England: The C.W. Daniel Co. Ltd., 1977.
Hylton, Dr. *Colour In Health and Disease*. London: Greater World Association, 1979.
Jones, Alex. *Seven Mansions of Color*. Marina del Rey,Ca: DeVorss and Co., 1982.
Kargere, Audrey. *Color and Personality*. York Beach,Me: Samuel Weiser,Inc., 1979.
Latimer, Robert. *Cosmic Color Rhythms of the Universal Mind*. N.Y: Vantage Press, 1984.
Lewis, Roger, *Color and the Edgar Cayce Readings*. Virginia Beach,Va: A.R.E. Press, 1973.
Ott, John. *Health and Light*. N.Y: Pocket Books, 1976.
_____. *Light Radiation, and You*. Old Greenwich, Ct: Devin-Adair Books, 1982.
Ouseley, S.G.J. *The Power of the Rays*. London: L.N. Fowler and Co., Ltd., 1975.
_____.*Colour Meditations*. London: L.N. Fowler and Co., Ltd., 1976.
Steiner, Rudolf. *Colour*. London: Rudolf Steiner Press, 1979.

_____."Colour and the Human Race." (March 3, 1923).

_____."Colour and Tone." (Jan. 1, 1915).

_____."The Nature of Colour." (Feb., 21,1923).

Stevens, M.D., Ernest. *Lights, Colors, Tones and Nature's Finer Forces*. Mokelumne Hill,Ca: Health Research, 1974.

Tibbs, Hardwin. *The Future of Light*. London: Watkins, 1981.

GEMSTONES AND GEM ELIXIRS IN HEALING

Abehsera, Michel. *The Healing Clay*. Brooklyn,NY: Swan House Publishing Co.,1979.

Alexander, A.E., and Louis Zara. "Garnet: Legend, Lore and Facts." *Mineral Digest*, VIII (Winter,1976), 6-16.

Anthony, R. *The Healing Gems*. Ottawa: Bhakti Press, 1983.

Ballard, Juliet B. *Treasures From Earth's Storehouse*. Virginia Beach,Va: A.R.E. Press, 1980.

Battacharya, A.K. *Gem Therapy*. Calcutta: Firma KLM Private, Ltd.,1976.

_____.*The Science of Cosmic Ray Therapy or Teletherapy*. Calcutta: Firma KLM Private, Ltd., 1976.

_____.*Teletherapy*. Calcutta: Firma KLM Private, Ltd., 1977.

Beard, Alice, and Frances Rogers. *5000 Years of Gems and Jewelry*. New York: J.B. Lippincott Co., 1947.

Benesch, Friedrich. *"Apokalypse" Die Verwandlung Der Erde, Eine Okkulte Mineralogie*. Stuttgart: Verlag Urachaus,1981.

Budge, E.A. Wallis. *Amulets and Superstitions*. New York: Dover Publications,Inc.,1978.

Cayce, Edgar. *Gems and Stones* Virginia Beach,Va: A.R.E. Press, 1979.

Chadbourne, Robert, and Ruth Wright. *Gems and Minerals of the Bible*. New Canaan,Ct: Keats Publishing,Inc., 1970.

Clough,Nigel. *How To Make and Use Magic Mirrors*. Wellingborough, Northamptonshire,England: The Aquarian Press, n.d.

Colton, Ann Ree. *Watch Your Dreams*. Glendale,Ca: ARC Publishing Co.,1983.

Crow, W.B. *Precious Stones*. York Beach,Me: Samuel Weiser, Inc.,1980.

Dertreit, Raymond. *Our Earth Our Cure*. Brooklyn,NY: Swan House Publishing Co.,1974.

Dorothee, Mella. *Stone Power: Legendary and Practical Use of Gems and Stones*. Albuquerque,NM: Domel, Inc., 1979.

Evans, Joan. *Magical Jewels of the Middle Ages and the Rennaissance*. New York: Dover Publications, Inc., 1976.

Fernie, Dr. William T. *The Occult and Curative Powers of Precious Stones*. New York: Harper & Row, 1981.

Gems, Stones, and Metals For Healing and Attunement: A Survey of Psychic Readings. Virginia Beach,Va: Heritage Publications, 1977.

Glick, Joel, and Julia Lorusso. *"Healing Stoned," The Therapeutic Use of Gems and Minerals*. Albuquerque: Brotherhood of Life,1979.

_____.*Stratagems A Mineral Perspective*. Albuquerque,NM: Brotherhood of Life, 1985.

Goethe. "An Essay On Granite." *Mineral Digest*, VIII (Winter,1976), 56-63.

Gurudas. *Gem Elixirs and Vibrational Healing, Vol. I* Boulder,Co: Cassandra Press, 1985.

Hall, Manly. *The Inner Lives of Minerals, Plants, and Animals*. Los Angeles: Philosophical Research Society, Inc.,1973.

Hindmarsh,Robert. *Account of the Stones*, London: James S. Hodson,1851.

Hodges, Doris M. *Healing Stones*. Perry,Ia: Hiawatha Publishing Co., 1961.

Huett, Lenora, and Wally Richardson. *Spiritual Value of gem Stones*. Marina del Rey,Ca: DeVorss and Co.,1981.

Isaacs, Thelma. *Gemstones, Crystals and Healing*. Black Mt.,NC: Lorien House, 1982.

Kozminsky, Isidore. *The Magic and Science of Jewels and Stones.* New York: G.P. Putnam's Sons,1922.

Kunz,George. *The Curious Lore of Precious Stones.* New York: Dover Publications,Inc.,1971.

_____.*The Magic of Jewels and Charms.* Philadelphia: J.B. Lippincott Co.,1915.

_____.*Natal Stones.* New York: Tiffany and Co.,1909.

_____.*Shakespeare and Precious Stones.* Philadelphia,Pa: J.B. Lippincott Co.,1916.

Littlefield,M.D., Charles W. *Man, Minerals, and Masters.* Albuquerque,NM: Sun Publishing Co., 1980.

Mills, Meredith W. "Kunzite." *Lapidary Journal,* (July,1984),p.546-552.

Pavitt, Kate, and William Thomas. *The Book of Talismans, Amulets and Zodiacal Gems.* North Hollywood,Ca: Wilshire Book Co., 1974.

Perkins, Jr., Percy H. *Gemstones of the Bible.* Atlanta: n.p.,1980.

Peterson, Serenity. *Crystal Visioning.* Nashville,Tn: Interdimensional Publishing, 1984.

Raphaell, Katrina. *Crystal Enlightenment.* N.Y: Aurora Press, 1985.

Read, Bernard E. *Chinese Materia Medica Turtle and Shellfish Drugs Avian Drugs A Compendium of Minerals and Stones.* Taipei: Southern Materials Center,Inc., 1982.

Regardie, Israel. *How To Make and Use Talismans.* Wellingborough, Northamptonshire, England: The Aquarian Press, 1982.

Sing, Lama. *Benefits and Detriments of Talismans, Stones, Gems and Minerals.* Orange park,Fl: E.T.A. Foundation, 1977.

Stewart, C. Nelson. *Gem-Stones of the Seven Rays.* Mokelumne Hill,Ca: Health Research, 1975.

Sturzaker, Doreen. *Gemstones and Kabalah.* International Order of Kabbalists, n.d.

_____. *Gemstones and Their Occult Powers.* London: Metatron Publications, 1983.

Stutley, Margaret. *Ancient Indian Magic and Folklore,* Boulder,Co: Great Eastern, 1980.

Uyldert, Mellie. *The Magic of Precious Stones.* Wellingborough, England:Turnstone Press, Ltd., 1981.

_____.*Metal Magic.* Wellingborough,England: Turnstone Press, Ltd.,1982.

Vogt, B.W., and W.P. Vogt. *Gem & Mineral Kingdom Digest.* n.p.,1979.

HEALTH AND VIBRATIONAL HEALING

Aero, Rita. *The Complete Book of Longevity.* East Rutherford,NJ: G.P. Putnam's Sons,1980.

Badgley, M.D., Laurence. *Energy Medicine.* San Bruno,Ca: Human Energy Press, 1986.

Ballard, Juliet B. *The Hidden Laws of Earth.* Virginia Beach,Va: A.R.E. Press, 1979.

Brooks, Wiley. *Breatharianism.* Arvada,Co: Breatharianism International, Inc., 1982.

Burne, Jerome. "The Intimate Frontier." *Science Digest,* LXXXIX (March,1981), 82-85.

Burr, Harold. *Blueprint For Immortality.* Subdury, Suffolk, England: Neville Spearman, Ltd., 1972.

Butler, Francine. *Biofeedback: A Survey of the Literature.* New York: Plenum Publishers, 1978.

Chia, Mantak. *Awaken Healing Energy Through the Tao.* New York: Aurora Press, 1983.

Clark, Linda. *Are You Radioactive.* New York: Pyramid Books,1974.

Cooke, Ivan. *Healing by the Spirit.* Liss,England: The White Eagle Publishing Trust, 1980.

David, William. *The Harmonics of Sound, Color, and Vibration.* Marina del Rey,Ca: DeVorss and Co., 1980.

Davis, Albert R. *The Anatomy of Biomagnetism.* New York: Vantage Press, Inc.,1982.

_____, and Walter Rawls. *Magnetism and Its Effects on the Living System.* Hicksville,NY: Exposition Press, 1974.

_____.*The Rainbow in Your Hands.* Hicksville,NY: Exposition Press, 1976.

Diamond, John. *Behavioral Kinesiology.* Los Angeles: Regent House,1981.

200

Eagle, White. *Heal Thyself*. Liss,England: The White Eagle Publishing Trust, 1982.

Edmunds and Associates, and H. Tudor, *Some Unrecognized Factors in Medicine*. London: The Theosophical Publishing House, 1976.

Gallert, Mark. *New Light on Therapeutic Energy*. London: James Clarke & Co., Ltd.,1966.

Golvin, V. "The Kirlian Effect in Medicine." *Soviet Journal of Medicine,* (August 11, 1976).

Guirdham, M.D., Arthur. *A Theory of Disease*. Sudbury, Suffolk, England: Neville Spearman, Ltd., 1957.

_____. *The Psyche in Medicine*. Sudbury, Suffolk, England: Neville Spearman, Ltd., 1978.

_____.*The Psychic Dimensions of Mental Health*. Wellingborough, England: Turnstone Press, Ltd.,1982.

Gurudas. *Flower Essences and Vibrational Healing*. Albuquerque,N.M: Brotherhood of Life, 1983.

Hall, Manly. *Healing: Divine Art*. Los Angeles: Philosophical Research Society,Inc., 1971.

_____.*The Secret Teachings of All Ages*. Los Angeles: The Philosophical Research Society, Inc.,1977.

Hartmann,M.D., Franz. *Occult Science in Medicine*. York Beach, Me: Samuel Weiser,Inc., 1975.

Heindel,Max. *Occult Principles of Health and Healing*. Oceanside,Ca: The Rosicrucian Fellowship,1938.

Hilarion. *Body Signs*. Toronto: Marcus Books, 1982.

Holland, John. "Slow Inapparent and Recurrent Viruses." *Scientific American,* CCXXX (February, 1974), 32-40.

Hunte-Cooper, Le. *The Danger of Food Contamination by Aluminum*. London: John Bale Sons and Danielson, Ltd., 1932.

Irion, J. Everett. *Vibrations*. Virginia Beach, Va: A.R.E. Press,1979.

Joy, Brough. *Joy's Way*. Los Angeles: J.P. Tarcher, 1979.

Lad, Dr. Vascant. *Ayurveda: The Science of Self Healing: A Practical Guide*. Santa Fe: Lotus Press, 1984.

LaForest, Sandra, and Virginia MacIvor. *Vibrations: Healing Through Color, Homeopathy, and Radionics*. York Beach,Ca: Samuei Weiser,Inc.,1979.

Lakkovsky, George. *The Secret of Life*. Mokelumne Hill,Ca: Health Research, 1970.

Mann, John A. *Secrets of Life Extension: How to Halt the Aging Process and Live a Long and Healthy Life*. San Francisco: And/Or Press, 1980.

Medical Group. *The Mystery of Healing*. London: The Theosophical Publishing House, 1958.

Medicines For the New Age. Virginia Beach, Va: Heritage Publications, 1977.

Mendelsohn, M.D., Robert. *Confessions of a Medical Heretic*. New York: Warner Books, 1980.

The Mystery of the Ductless Glands. Oceanside,Ca: The Roscrucian Fellowship, 1983.

Null, Gary. "Aluminum: Friend or Foe." *Bestways,* X (October, 1982),60-65.

Oberg, Alcestis, and Daniel Woodward. "Anti-Matter Mind Probes and Other Medical Miracles." *Science Digest,* XC (April,1982), 54- 62.

Oster, Gerald. "Muscle Sounds." *Scientific American,* (March,1984),p.108-114.

Pfeiffer, M.D., Carl. *Mental and Elemental Nutrients*. New Canaan,Ct: Keats Publishing Inc.,1976.

Pykett, Ian L. "NMR Imaging in Medicine." *Scientific American,* CCXLVI (May,1982), 78-88.

Reichenbach, Baron Karl Von. *The Mysterious Odic Force*. Wellingborough, England: Thorsons Publishers, Ltd., 1977.

Rolfe, Mona. *Man-Physical and Spiritual*. Sudbury, Suffolk, England: Neville Spearman, Ltd., n.d.

_____.*The Sacred Vessel*. Sudbury, Suffolk, England: Neville Spearman, Ltd.,1978.

Russell, Edward. *Report On Radionics*. Sudbury, Suffolk,England: Neville Spearman, Ltd., 1973.

Scheer, James F. "Electroacupuncture: New Pathway to Total Health." *Bestways*, X (June,1982), 40-47,119.

Schmich,Mary T. "Debate on Health Effects of VDT Use Continues Unabated." *The Denver Post*, August 16,1985, sec. B, p.3.

Sutphen, Dick. *Past-Life Therapy In Action*. Malibu,Ca: Valley of the Sun Publishing,1983.

_____.*Unseen Influences*. New York: Pocket Books, 1982.

Tansley,D.C., David. *Dimensions of Radionics*. Saffron, Walden, Essex, England: Health Science Press, 1977.

Tomlinson,H. *Aluminum Utensils and Disease*. Romfort,England: L.N. Fowler & Co.,1967.

Ulmer, M.D., David. "Toxicity From Aluminum Antacids." *The New England Journal of Medicine*, CCLXXXXIV, (January,1976), 218-219.

Waite, Arthur F. ed. *The Hermetic and Alchemical Writings of Paracelsus*. Boulder,Co:Shambhala Publications,1976.

Westlake, M.D., Aubrey. *The Patterns of Health*. Boulder,Co: Shambhala Publications, 1974.

Wickland,M.D., Carl. *Thirty Years Among the Dead*. Hollywood,Ca: Newcastle Publishing Co., 1974.

Wingerson, Lois. "Training To Heal the Mind." *Discovery*, III (May,1982), 80-85.

HOMEOPATHY

Blackie,M.D., Margery. *The Patient Not the Cure*. London:Macdonald and Jane's, 1976.

Boericke, M.D., William. *A Compend of the Principles of Homeopathy*. Mokelumne Hill,Ca: Health Research,1971.

_____.*Materia Medica With Repertory*. New Delhi: B. Jain Publishers, 1976.

_____,and Willis Dewey,M.D. *The Twelve Tissue Remedies of Schussler*. New Delhi: B. Jain Publishers, 1977.

Choudhuri,M.D., N.M. *A Study on Materia Medica*. New Delhi: B. Jain Publishers,1978.

Clark,M.D.,J.H. *A Clinical Repertory to the Dictionary of Materia Medica* Saffron, Walden,Essex, England: Health Science Press,1971.

_____.*Constitional Medicine*. New Delhi: B. Jain Publishers,1974.

_____.*Dictionary of Materia Medica*. Saffron, Walden,Essex,England: Health Science Press, 1977.

Coulter,Ph.D., Harris. *Divided Legacy: A History of the Schism in Medical Thought*. Vol.III, Washington,D.C.: Wehawken Book Co.,1973.

Farrington, M.D., E.A. *Clinical Materia Medica*. New Delhi: B. Jain Publishers,1975.

Hahnemann,M.D., Samuel. *The Chronic Diseases-Theoretical Part*. New Delhi: B. Jain Publishers,1976.

_____.*Organon of Medicine*. New Delhi: B. Jain Publishers,1977.

Hubbard-Wright,M.D.,Elizabeth. *A Brief Study Course in Homeopathy*. St. Louis,Mo: Formur,Inc.,1977.

Kalm, Hans. *Organotropia As A Basis of Therapy*. Finland: n.p.,1977.

Kent,M.D.,James T. *Lectures on Homeopathic Philosophy*. Calcutta: Sett Dey & Co., 1967.

_____.*Repertory Materia Medica*. Chicago: Ehrhart and Karl,1957.

Muzumda,M.D.,K.P.*Pharmaceutical Science in Homeopathy and Pharmacodynamics*. New Delhi: B. Jain Publishers,1974.

Nash,M.D. E.B. *Leaders in Homeopathic Therapeutics*. Calcutta:Sett Dey & Co.,1959.

202

Ortega, Dr. Proceso S. *Notes On the Miasms or Hahnemann's Chronic Diseases.* New Delhi: National Homeopathic Pharmacy, 1983.
Roberts,M.D.,Herbert. *The Principles and Art of Cure by Homeopathy.* Saffron, Walden Essex,England: Health Science Press,1976.
Tomlinson,M.D., H. *Aluminum Utensils and Disease.* London: L.N. Fowler & Co.,1967.
Tyler,Dr., M.L. *Homeopathic Drug Pictures.* Saffron, Walden, Essex, England: Health Science Press, 1975.
Vithoulkas, George. *The Science of Homeopathy.* New York: Grove Press,Inc.,1980.
Weiner, Michael, and Kathleen Goss. *The Complete Book of Homeopathy.* New York: Bantam Books,1982.
Whitmont,M.D., Edward. *Psyche and Substance.* Richmond,Ca: North Atlantic Books,1980.

MUSIC AND CONSCIOUSNESS
Abrahamsen, Aron and Doris. *Attunement of Body, Soul and Spirit Through Music and Color.* Everett, Wa: Aron and Doris Abrahamsen,1978.
Bonny, Helen, and Louis Savary. *Music and Your Mind.* London: Harper and Row, 1973.
Bonny, Helen. *The Role of Taped Music Programs in the GIM Process.* Baltimore: ICM Books, 1978.
_____. *GIM Therapy Past, Present and Future Implications.* Baltimore: ICM Books, 1980.
Carter, Mary. *Creative Man: A View of the Arts from the Edgar Cayce Readings.* Virginia Beach,Va: A.R.E. Press, 1968.
Colton, Ann Ree. *The Third Music.* Glendale,Ca: ARC Publishing Co.,1982.
Danielou, Alain. *Introduction to the Study of Musical Scales.* London: Oriental Books,n.d.
David, William. *The Harmonics of Sound Color and Vibration.* Marine del Rey,Ca: DeVorss and Co., 1980.
Diamond,M.D., John. *The Life Energy In Music.* Valley Cottage,N.Y: Archaeus Press, 1981.
Fry, D.B. *Some Effects of Music.* Tumbridge Wells, Kent,England: The Institute for Cultural Research, 1983.
Godwin, Jocelyn. "The Crisis of Hinduism." *Studies In Comparative Religion,* (Spring,1971), p.110-126.
Gutheil,M.D., Emil. *Music and Your Emotions.* N.Y: Liveright, 1970.
Hall, Manly. *The Therapeutic Value of Music Including the Philosophy of Music.* L.A: Philosophical Research Society, Inc., 1982.
Halpern,Ph.D., Steven, and Louis Savary, Ph.D. *Sound Health.* N.Y: Harper and Row, 1985.
Halpern, Ph.D. *Tuning the Human Instrument.* Belmont,Ca: Spectrum Research Institute, 1978.
Hamel, Peter. *Through Music to the Self.* (Boulder, Shambhala Publications, 1979.
Heindel, Max. *Mysteries of the Great Operas.* Oceanside,Ca: The Rosicrucian Fellowship, 1975.
Heline, Corinne. *Beethoven's Nine Symphonies.* L.A: New Age Press, 1971.
_____.*Color and Music in the New Age.* Marina del Rey,Ca: DeVorss and Co., 1982.
_____.*The Cosmic Harp.* L.A: New Age Press, n.d.
_____.*Esoteric Music Based on the Musical Seership of Richard Wagner.* L.A: New Age Press, 1953.
_____.*Healing and Regeneration Through Music.* L.A: New Age Press, 1970.
_____.*Music: The Keynote of Human Evolution.* L.A: New Age Press, 1965.
Heline, Theodore. *The Archetype Unveiled.* L.A: New Age Press, n.d.
Hodson, Geoffrey. *Clairvoyant Investigations.* Wheaton,IL: The Theosophical Publishing House, 1984.

_____. *Music Forms*. Adya,Madras,India: The Theosophical Publishing House, 1976.

Hunt, Roland. *Fragrant and Radiant Healing Symphany*. 1949.

Illiana. *Harmonious Well Being Through Music*. Brookfield,Ma: New Age Teachings, n.d.

Katsh, Shelley, and Carol Merle-Fishman. *The Music Within You*. N.Y: Simon and Schuster, 1985.

Keyes, Laurel. *Toning:The Creative Power of the Voice*. Marina del Rey,Ca: DeVorss and Co., 1982.

Khan, Inayat. *Music*. York Beach, Me: Samuel Weiser, Inc., 1977.

_____.*The Music of Life*. Santa Fe,N.M: Omega Press, 1983.

_____.*The Mysticism of Sound*. Mokelumne Hill, Ca: Health Research, 1972.

Lhalungpa, Lobsang. "Tibetan Music: Sacred and Secular." *Studies In Comparative Religion*, (Spring,1969), p.97-106.

Lingerman, Hal. *The Healing Energies of Music*. Wheaton,IL: The Theosophical Publishing House, 1983.

Manners, Peter. *The Sound of Healing*. England, n.d.

The Musical Scale and the Scheme of Evolution. Oceanside,Ca: The Rosicrucian Fellowship,1982.

Rudhyar, Dane. *The Magic of Tone and the Art of Music*. Boulder: Shambhala Publications, 1982.

_____. *The Rebirth of Hindu Music*. York Beach, Me: Samuel Weiser, 1979

_____. York Beach,Me: Samuel Weiser, 1979.

Schafer, R. Murray. *The Tuning of the World*. Philadelphia: Univ. of Pennsylvania Press, 1980.

Schenker, Heinrich. *Harmony*. Chicago: The Univ. of Chicago Press, 1980.

Scott, Cyril. *Music Its Secret Influence Throughout the Ages*. York Beach,Me: Samuel Weiser, 1969.

Stebbing, Lionel. *Music and Healing*. London: New Knowledge Books, 1963.

_____.*Music Its Occult Basis and Healing Value*. London: New Knowledge Books, n.d.

Steiner, Rudolf. *The Arts and Their Mission*. Spring Valley,N.Y: Anthroposophic Press, 1964.

_____."Concerning Music." (Nov., 12,26, 1906).

_____. *Eurythmy As Visible Music*. London: Rudolf Steiner Press, 1977.

_____.*The Inner Nature of Music and the Experience of Tone*. Spring Valley,N.Y: Anthroposophic Press, 1983.

_____."The Occult Basis of Music". *Golden Blade*, 1956.

_____."Parsifal." (July, 29,1907). *Anthroposophy Quarterly*, n.d.

_____."Richard Wagner In the Light of Anthroposophy." *Anthroposophical News Sheet*, n.d.

_____."Wagner's Development of the Ideas of Goethe On Art and Schopenhauer On Music." (Oct., 11,1906).

Szekely, Edmond. *Ludwig Van Beethoven*. Tecate,Ca: Essene School of Life, 1947.

Tame, David. *The Secret Power of Music*. Northamptonshire,England: Turnstone Press, Ltd., 1984.

Wescott, Juanita. *Magic and Music*. Tucson: Abbetira Publications, 1982.

Winston, Shirley. *Music As A Bridge*. Virginia Beach,Va: A.R.E. Press, 1972.

Zuckerkandl, Victor. *Sound and Symbol*. Princeton: Princeton Univ. Press, 1973.

PREGNANCY AND BIRTHING

Glas,M.D., Norbert. *Conception Birth and Early Childhood*. Spring Valley,N.Y: Anthroposophic Press, 1973.

Hall, Manly. *The Mystery of Human Birth*. L.A: Philosophical Research Society, Inc., 1956.

Hodson, Geoffrey. *The Miracle of Birth: A Clairvoyant Study of A Human Embryo.* Wheaton, IL: The Theosophical Publishing House, 1981.
"Mother and Child." *Weleda News, 1982.*
Zur Linden, Wilhelm. *A Child Is Born: Pregnancy, Birth, Early Childhood.* London: Rudolf Steiner Press, 1980.

QUARTZ CRYSTALS
Achad, Frater. *Crystal Vision Through Crystal Gazing.* Chicago: Yogi Publication Society, 1923.
Alper, Rev., Dr. Frank. *Exploring Atlantis.* 3 Vols., Phoenix: Arizonia Metaphysical Society, 1982-1985.
Atkinson, William W. *Practical Psychomancy and Crystal Gazing.* DesPlaines,Il: Yoga Publication Society, 1908.
Baer, Randall, and Vicki Baer. *Windows of Light.* New York: Harper and Row, 1984.
Besterman, Theodore. *Crystal-Gazing.* New Hyde Park,NY: University Books, 1965.
Bonewitz, Ra. *Cosmic Crystals.* Wellingborough, Northamptonshire, England: Turnstone Press, Ltd., 1983.
Bryant, Page. *Crystals and Their Use.* Albuquerque,NM: Sun Publishing Co., 1984.
Burbutis, Philip. *Quartz Crystals For Healing and Meditation.* Tucson: The Universariun Foundation, Inc., 1983.
Burka, Christa Faye. *Clear Crystal Consciousness.* Albuquerque,N.M: Brotherhood of Life,1986).
Deaver, Korra. *Rock Crystal: The Magic Stone.* York Beach, Me: Samuel Weiser, Inc., 1985.
Delmonico, Damyan. *I Was Curious-A Crystal Ball Gazer.* Philadelphia: Dorrance & Co., 1972.
Dolfyn and Bluejay. *Crystal Wisdom.* Atlanta: Blue Dolfyn Press, 1984.
Eerenbeemt, Noud van den. *The Pendulum, Crystal Ball and Magic Mirror.* Wellingborough, Northamptonshire, England: The Aquarian Press, 1982.
Ferguson, Sibyl. *The Crystal Ball.* York Beach,Me: Samuel Weiser, Inc., 1979.
Garvin, Richard. *The Crystal Skull.* New York: Pocket Books, 1974.
Holden, A., and P. Sanger. *Crystals and Crystal Growing.* Cambridge: The MIT Press, 1985.
Lavander. *Quartz: Crystals A Celestial Point of View.* Reserve,NM: Lavandar Lines Corp., 1982.
Melville, John. *Crystal-Gazing and the Wonders of Clairvoyance.* Mokelumne Hill,Ca: Health Research, 1968.
Petschek, Joyce. *The Silver Bird: A Tale For Those Who Dream.* Millbrae,Ca: Celestial Arts, 1981.
Smith, Michael G. *Crystal Power.* St. Paul: Llewellyn Publications, 1985.
Thomas, Northcote W. *Crystal Gazing.* Mokelumne Hill,Ca: Health Research, 1968.
Walker, Dale. *The Crystal Book.* Sunol,Ca: The Crystal Co., 1983.
Wilson, Frank. *Crystal and Cosmos.* London: Coventure,Ltd.,1977.
Wood, Elizabeth. *Crystals and Light.* New York: Dover Publications, Inc., 1977.
Zimmer, David. *Crystal Power.* Minneapolis: Good Vibes, 1983.

Index

For information on this continuing research, please contact:

Gurudas
P.O. Box 2044
Boulder, Co. 80306

For Purchasing quality quartz crystals, please contact:

High Peak Crystal Co.
1272 Bear Mt. Court
Boulder, CO. 80303